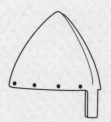

"NORMAN"-STYLE
CONICAL HELMET,
10TH-13TH CENTURY

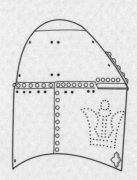

THE BLACK PRINCE'S
GREAT HELM,
ENGLISH, C. 1370

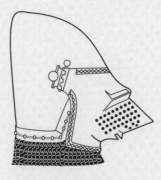

VISORED BASINET
WITH AVENTAIL,
NORTH ITALIAN,
C. 1390

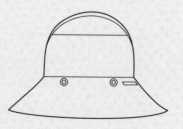

KETTLE HAT WITH
SIGHTS, GERMAN,
C. 1460

EARLY BASINET,
GERMAN, C. 1330

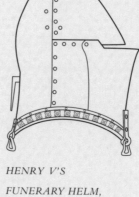

HENRY V'S
FUNERARY HELM,
ENGLISH, C. 1400

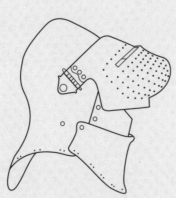

GREAT BASINET
FROM PAMPLONA
CATHEDRAL,
SPANISH, C. 1425

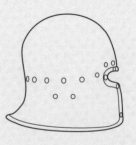

BARBUTE WITH
T-SHAPED OPENING,
C. 1450

VISORED BASINET,
GERMAN OR
NORTH ITALIAN,
C. 1370

KETTLE HAT,
ITALIAN, C. 1475

SALLET, NORTH
ITALIAN, C. 1450

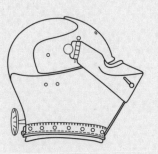

ARMET À RONDEL,
MILAN, C. 1450

*SALLET WITH
BELLOWS VISOR,*
MILAN, C. 1490

*"PEAR-STALK"
CABASSET,* NORTH
ITALIAN, C. 1600

GOTHIC SALLET,
GERMAN, C. 1470-80

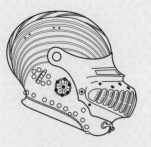

*ARMET IN
MAXIMILIAN STYLE,*
INNSBRUCK,
C. 1510

*SALLET WITH
REINFORCED BROW,*
MILAN, C. 1500

COMB MORION,
NORTH ITALIAN,
LATE 16TH
CENTURY

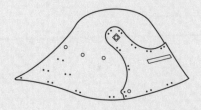

"BLACK" SALLET,
GERMAN, C. 1490

*BURGONET
("CASQUETELE"
TYPE),* MILAN,
C. 1510

ARMS AND ARMOR

Arms and Armor

THE CLEVELAND MUSEUM OF ART

Stephen N. Fliegel

Published by the Cleveland Museum of Art

This publication was made possible by a generous grant from The Reinberger Foundation

Editing: Kathleen Mills
Design: Laurence Channing
Production: Charles Szabla, assisted by Carolyn K. Lewis
Illustration: Carolyn K. Lewis
Museum photography: Gary Kirchenbauer
Printing: Snoeck, Ducaju & Zoon, Ghent, Belgium
Composed in Monotype Bembo

Front cover: Pompeo della Cesa (Italian, Milan, active 1572–93), *Half-Armor for the Foot Tournament*, c. 1590 (detail). The John L. Severance Fund CMA 1996.299

Back cover: *Rapier,* Germany, c. 1630–50 (detail). Gift of Mr. and Mrs. John L. Severance CMA 1916.1498

Library of Congress Cataloguing-in-Publication Data
Fliegel, Stephen N., 1950–
    Arms and armor : the Cleveland Museum of Art / Stephen N. Fliegel.
        p.   cm.
    Includes bibliographical references and index.
    ISBN 0–940717–47–6 (hc.) — ISBN 0–940717–46–8 (pbk.)
        1. Armor—Themes, motives—Catalogs.
2. Weapons—Themes, motives—Catalogs.
3. Severance, John L. (Long), 1863–1936—Art collections—Catalogs. 4. Severance, John L., Mrs.—Art collections—Catalogs. 5. Armor—Private collections—Ohio—Cleveland—Catalogs.
6. Weapons—Private collections—Ohio—Cleveland—Catalogs. 7. Armor—Ohio—Cleveland—Catalogs. 8. Weapons—Ohio—Cleveland—Catalogs. 9. Cleveland Museum of Art—Catalogs. I. Cleveland Museum of Art. II. Title.
NK6602.C6C645   1998
739.7'074771'32—dc21   98–25093
                                                    CIP

Note to the reader
In captions, bracketed numbers refer to the Checklist of the Severance Collection, page 162.

Contents

Foreword

At the time of its opening to the public in 1916, the elaborate display of arms and armor in its Armor Court was the Cleveland Museum of Art's centerpiece presentation. Indeed, for subsequent generations experiencing the Armor Court was a signature aspect of a visit to the museum. It truly became one of the most cherished and revered spaces in Cleveland, and in the minds and imaginations of Clevelanders and other visitors. Its construction was inspired by John L. Severance's gift of the funds to purchase an extensive collection of arms and armor. Although in recent years various pieces from the original Severance bequest have not met the standards of modern scholarship and connoisseurship—some ensembles were revealed as pastiches, some pieces as outright forgeries—the armor collection today consists in large part of works from Mr. Severance's gift. Taken as a whole, the Severance Collection remains one of the finest groups of armor ever assembled by an American museum.

For a variety of reasons, the Armor Court lost much of its original luster over the decades, and the panache and drama of its original installation became only memories. The publication of *Arms and Armor* coincides with the September 1998 reopening of a thoroughly renovated, reinstalled, and, I hope, re-enlivened Armor Court, designed to evoke once again the excitement of the original. While our work has been inspired by the character of the 1916 installation, we have incorporated many advantages afforded by modern design techniques and technology into the new installation. Moreover, both in this book and the installation, the newest scholarly findings inform the presentation. Several person-years of work have been devoted to conservation of the objects now on view. Indeed, it took a sizable team of specialists working with focused energy over a period of three years to execute the armor enterprise to perfection. Their remarkable collective accomplishments now allow the museum to return to our community in glorious fashion one of its defining civic experiences.

The Armor Court project represents a perfect confluence of aesthetic/scholarly imperatives and the public interest, precisely the goal of the Lila Wallace–Reader's Digest Fund's Museum Collections Accessibility Initiative that in 1995 provided a substantial grant to underwrite most of the project's costs. Recognizing that among our nation's premier cultural assets are the permanent collections of our distinguished art museums, the fund provided major grants to support innovative projects that extend the public impact of permanent collections, particularly to new or previously underserved audiences. The Cleveland Museum of Art is proud to be among the twenty-nine museums nationwide to have been awarded one of these competitive grants. The Armor Court reinstallation is the keystone of our museum's multifaceted endeavor, supported by the Lila Wallace–Reader's Digest Fund, which includes a wide range of other programs. To the fund we offer our sincerest gratitude, both for the support afforded our project and for the realization that museums' permanent collections are fundamental resources that can stimulate broad public cultural participation.

Both the conception of the new installation and this volume are due to the dedicated and effective efforts of Stephen Fliegel, assistant curator of medieval art, who provided intellectual leadership for the enterprise. I offer thanks and congratulations to him for a job well done. In subsequent pages Stephen acknowledges many members of the project team, to all of whom I extend our gratitude. The book was written as an introduction to arms and armor and should serve to enhance the visitor's experience of the Armor Court. Its approachable manner is underpinned by significant new scholarship, thus making the volume also of interest to more dedicated students of the subject. The emphasis on the book's visual quality—its rich mixture of color illustrations—should help to dispel any preconceptions about armor as being "dusty." Its concluding checklist is intended to provide a summary catalogue of the collection as a matter of record.

Publication of *Arms and Armor* is supported by a generous grant from The Reinberger Foundation, established and administered by one of Cleveland's truly public-spirited families. We are indebted to Robert N. Reinberger and William C. Reinberger, who have once again demonstrated their commitment to our museum and their dedication to fostering the arts and culture in our community.

May all those who read this volume be inspired to visit the new Armor Court, and may all who experience that glorious place be inspired to seek further joy and enlightenment from this book.

Robert P. Bergman, Director

Preface and Acknowledgments

This publication was planned to coincide with the 1998 reinstallation of the museum's arms and armor collection in the space known as the Armor Court. Architecturally unique and beloved by many, this space has included a display of European arms and armor throughout the museum's history. In large part due to the success of the original design, the basic installation of the collection was little altered for decades. The 1924 catalogue of the original bequest by Mr. and Mrs. John L. Severance has remained the only serious effort to publish this collection to date. A checklist of the Severance Collection appears at the end of this book, and a history of its acquisition and display will be found at the beginning.

While the present book may include some features of interest to the specialist scholar, the collector, and the educator, its intended audience is the general reader who aspires to know more about this fascinating topic. No work of art can be fully appreciated if divorced from the culture that produced it. I have thus endeavored (successfully, I hope) to present the highlights of the museum's arms and armor collection against a historical backdrop in an interesting and informative way. My desire is to induce those who read the following pages to explore the wealth of specialist literature by authors far more qualified than I; a bibliography can be found at the end of the book. And further, I would encourage those curious about the subject to visit this museum's collection, or that of another city which may be more geographically accessible to the reader. My aim throughout has been to respect the objects as works of art, and not merely as implements of warfare and sport—though they are at times certainly both.

Thanks to a generous grant from the Lila Wallace–Reader's Digest Fund and the insightfulness and enthusiasm of this museum's director, Robert P. Bergman, the possibility of a major reassessment and reinstallation of the arms and armor collection became a reality in 1995. The formidable tasks of re-evaluating the collection and establishing a suitable approach to its reinstallation were made less daunting by the interest and collegial support of many specialist scholars and professional curators working in the field, both in the United States and in Europe. Nor could either task have been accomplished without the skill, dedication, and professionalism of my colleagues at the Cleveland Museum of Art. This publication truly represents a collaborative journey.

Outside the Cleveland Museum of Art, I would first like to thank most warmly the following scholars, curators, archivists, and other professionals who have helped me by sharing their knowledge: At the Metropolitan Museum of Art in New York, Stuart W. Pyhrr and Donald J. LaRocca provided expertise and encouragement with considerable goodwill. William D. Wixom, chairman of medieval art and The Cloisters, read early drafts dealing with the Severance Collection during the 1960s and made valuable suggestions. I am also deeply indebted to Walter J. Karcheski Jr., curator of arms and armor at the Higgins Armory Museum, Worcester, Massachusetts; Guy Wilson, master of the armouries, Royal Armouries, Leeds; Christian Beaufort, director, and Matthias Pfaffenbichler, curator of arms and armor, Hofjagd- und Rüstkammer, Vienna; Heinz-Werner Lewerken, director, and Holger Schuckelt, curator, at the Rüstkammer, Staatliche Kunstsammlungen Dresden; and Lena Rangström and Nils Dreijholt, curators of the Livrustkammaren, Stockholm. At the Philadelphia Museum of Art, I am grateful to Dean Walker, curator of decorative arts, and P. Andrew Lins, conservator, for their time and encouragement. For assistance with comparative images reproduced here, I thank Liliane Bouillon-Pasquet, director, Tapisserie (Museum) de Bayeux; Siân Roberts, senior archivist public relations, Birmingham City Council (U.K.); Helga Schütze, Nationalmuseet, Copenhagen; Reinhart Dittrich, Steiermärkisches Landesmuseum Joanneum, Graz; Michael Stanske, Universitätsbibliothek Heidelberg; Chris Rawlings and Zoë Stansell, The British Library, London; Eugenia Alonso, Fundación Coleccion Thyssen-Bornemisza, Madrid; Alison Gallup, Art Resource, New York; Herman Maué, Germanisches Nationalmuseum, Nuremberg; Helga Jubitz, Stadtbibliothek, Nuremberg; Catherine Belanger and Christine André, Musée du Louvre, Paris; Guido Cornini, Archivio Fotografico, Musei Vaticani; Ulrike Berger, Österreichische Nationalbibliothek, Vienna; and Phyllis Harper, Hathaway Brown School, Shaker Heights, Ohio.

At the Cleveland Museum of Art I would like to thank Robert P. Bergman, director, and Diane De Grazia, Clara S. Rankin chief curator, for their confidence and warm support throughout the course of this project. I owe a profound debt of gratitude to Jonathan Kline, research assistant in medieval art, from whose consummate research skills this publication has benefited greatly. Conservators Nancie Ravenel and Jack Flotte played pivotal roles in analyzing and treating the arms and armor collection in preparation for both publication and installation. I acknowledge their skills and professionalism with warmest gratitude. The museum's chief conservator, Bruce Christman, entered the project at various junctures, offering sound and welcome advice. For the new Armor Court installation, I must thank the design team that invested its collective talent and countless hours of dedicated work to produce the stellar results: Jeffrey Strean, director of design and facilities; designers Russell R. Culp and Raymond Glover; and installation technicians David Geiger, Andrea S. Joki, Brian Ulrich, and Beth Wolfe. Assistant photographer Gary Kirchenbauer—with verve and humor—produced the beautiful color images of the collection illustrated within these pages.

The logistical difficulties of moving large numbers of objects throughout the building, tracking their whereabouts, and recording collections data were resolved by the museum's chief registrar, Mary Suzor, and her highly competent staff. Among them, I especially thank Victoria Foster and, for their help during the early stages of the project, Joanne Fenn and Andrea Bour. Art handler Joseph Brown was responsible for fabricating temporary mounts to facilitate ongoing photography of the collection. I thank archivist Ann Marie Przybyla and her assistants Dianne O'Malia and Phil Haas for the wealth of documentation they provided concerning the early history of the Severance Collection. I am grateful to Christine Edmonson, interlibrary loan librarian in the Ingalls Library. I thank my editor, Kathleen Mills, and would like to express particular gratitude to Laurence Channing, head of publications, not only for the quality design of this book, but for his valued insights and suggestions throughout.

S. N. F.

Armor Court, about 1916–17. Cleveland was only the second fine arts museum in the United States, after New York's *Metropolitan Museum of Art, to create a dedicated space within its galleries for the display of European arms and armor.*

The Severance Collection

I already have our former Court of Casts arranged in my mind's eye as a Court of Armor, and wish to make every possible effort to carry out this scheme, which I am sure will work out very beautifully.
—FREDERIC ALLEN WHITING, DECEMBER 19, 1914

In June of 1916, Cleveland's new art museum opened its doors for the first time, revealing among its newly acquired treasures a breathtaking installation of European arms and armor resplendent with colorful regimental banners and a set of magnificent seventeenth-century Flemish tapestries. This installation would evermore designate the museum's signature space as "Armor Court." With its pale sandstone walls, marble floor, skylight, and of course the much-loved collection of arms and armor given through the munificence of Mr. and Mrs. John L. Severance, the Armor Court represented for three successive generations of Clevelanders the symbolic heart and soul of the Cleveland Museum of Art. As the range and depth of the museum's collections grew over subsequent years, the Armor Court remained an unchanging island of stability, and the arms and armor collection was often the first introduction to the visual arts for Cleveland school-children.

Excavations for the museum had commenced in the spring of 1913, following in the wake of similar endeavors at Pittsburgh, Cincinnati, Toledo, St. Louis, and Chicago, and the somewhat older Metropolitan Museum of Art in New York and Museum of Fine Arts in Boston. All of these served as models for consideration for Cleveland's board of trustees. Pivotal decisions had to be made, beginning with the appointment of a nationally prominent leader who would take charge of the enterprise and mold the new institution. On June 5, 1913, Frederic Allen Whiting was formally named secretary of the building committee and charged with the formidable task of not only overseeing construction of the new museum, but also providing it with a collection and a program of operations.

An Enlightened Imagination

Whiting, who had been recommended to the Cleveland trustees by Henry Watson Kent, secretary of the Metropolitan Museum of Art, was a well-known educator and proponent of the Arts and Crafts movement. This movement originated in Britain during the nineteenth century as a reaction against the dehumanizing effects of industrialization which, according to the art critic and social reformer John Ruskin, by debasing the quality of the worker's life also debased art and craftsmanship. Ruskin therefore championed a "craft" as opposed to a "machine" aesthetic. Based principally on social and moral considerations, the Arts and Crafts movement aimed to improve society by elevating the quality of workmanship, informing and educating the worker, and thus instilling taste.

The movement advanced handmade, individually crafted products over factory-made goods. Essentially anti-academic, it celebrated the virtues of individualism and the designer's right to experiment and to explore the full possibilities of his materials. The most influential of these designers was William Morris. He founded his firm of Morris, Marshall, Faulkner and Company in 1861, working initially with stained glass but later incorporating furniture, metalwork, tiles, wallpapers, and fabrics, always advancing what he perceived as medieval craft techniques.

Whiting's views were less radical than those of Ruskin and Morris. He did not reject industrial products, for example, but felt that modern workmanship, product quality, and fine design could be fostered by knowledge of and exposure to historic arts and crafts. As a teenager he had lived for a time in the manufacturing town of Lowell, Massachusetts, where he belonged to clubs along with boys from working-class families. These formative years had planted in him the seeds of commitment and service among industrial, often immigrant communities, for whom Whiting saw education as the road toward a better future. In his initial presentation to the board as the museum's first director, he remarked: "The Museum of today is primarily an educational institution. . . . Closely allied to the educational function of the Museum is what may be called its social responsibility."[1]

In 1898 Whiting had sailed to Liverpool, England, to visit the utopian workers' community at Port Sunlight, and by 1900 he had been appointed secretary of the Society of Arts and Crafts, Boston—the leading arts and crafts group in the United States. He spent subsequent years organizing meetings and lecturing to the many smaller arts and crafts societies around the country. By 1911 Whiting had established a national reputation as a spokesperson for arts and crafts issues and the concomitant issues of education. He articulated his vision for a sensitized and discriminating American public capable of appreciating the "importance of beauty as a necessary element of daily life."[2] Whiting maintained that "this involves, in the end, a reorganization of society through a changed point of view as to the value of artistic work. It means an appreciation by the purchaser of his responsibility for the welfare and happiness of the producer of what he purchases."[3]

Whiting arrived in Cleveland in 1913 with a fully nurtured vision for the arts in an industrial age. Believing firmly that the educational mission of the museum should reflect the city's industrial heritage, five years later he would write in the museum's *Bulletin:* "Cleveland is one of the great iron and steel centers, and should own the most useful collection of fine examples of wrought iron and steel, cast bronzes, etc., as an inspiration to workers and designers in these fields. Due

As the museum's first director (1913–30), Frederic Allen Whiting (1873–1959) presided over the construction of the original neoclassical building and defined the themes—armor and tapestries—that continue to identify one of the museum's signature spaces.

to the generosity of Mr. and Mrs. John L. Severance the museum owns a notable collection of arms and armor, representing the high-water mark in the fabrication and decoration of this difficult material."[4] Whiting had clearly assimilated many of the reformist ideals of Ruskin and Morris.

As he wrote these words in 1918, the acquisition of the new "Severance Collection" was a *fait accompli*. However, Frederic Whiting knew early on—long before its scheduled opening—that the new museum must have a collection of arms and armor. The Metropolitan Museum of Art had a distinguished collection of this material, which Whiting knew and coveted. Indeed, in 1912 the Met had created a specialized department for arms and armor, with Bashford Dean as its first curator. That such a collection would have an important educational impact in a manufacturing city like Cleveland with its steel and emerging automotive industries was a given. The crafting of a suit of armor—annealed by hand, hand-hammered over anvils and dies, and hand-assembled and decorated—was, after all, a historic exemplar of the automobile. Why not provide Cleveland's new museum with a collection that could inspire its craftsmen?

Then, as now, historic arms and armor were demonstrably compelling to visitors, especially to young people. Whiting knew that armor would very likely be the first introduction for children (and for many adults) to the visual arts, a subject of study worthy in its own right but also a potential springboard to other decorative media as well as to sculpture and painting. The search for an armor collection began in earnest in 1914, the year the museum officially began to accept objects for its future collections.

Serious Disappointment: The Keasbey Collection

Archival evidence does not suggest precisely when Frederic Allen Whiting became acquainted with Bashford Dean, the Metropolitan Museum of Art's curator of arms and armor, a position created expressly for him. It seems reasonably safe to assume that the two men were introduced by Henry Watson Kent, who as secretary of the Metropolitan had been offered the directorship of the Cleveland Museum of Art in 1911. Kent declined the trustees' offer, but recommended

A zoologist by training, Bashford Dean (1867–1928) possessed a keen, if self-taught, knowledge of arms and armor, and took a methodical approach to his adopted subject. He became the first professional curator of arms and armor at an American museum (New York's Metropolitan, 1912–27) and eventually earned a distinguished international reputation for his expertise.

Whiting among others for the post and agreed to serve as a consultant during the building phase of the new museum. Whiting made numerous visits to New York to consult with Kent, and it seems likely that he was introduced to Dean on one of these occasions.

Dean had been formally trained as a zoologist with a specialization in ichthyology. He earned a doctorate from Columbia University in 1890 (writing his dissertation on "Pineal Fontanelle of Placoderm and Catfish") and held a succession of academic posts at Columbia through 1927, teaching both biology and zoology. In 1903 he was appointed curator of fishes and reptiles at New York's American Museum of Natural History, a post he held until 1914. Dean's parallel interests and dual careers in both zoology and arms and armor are remarkable even for his day. His expertise in arms and armor was apparently self-cultivated and certainly extensive. During his tenure at the Metropolitan (1912–27), he was considered America's pre-eminent authority on the subject and had established an international reputation, traveling and consulting widely. He built his own substantial private collection of arms and armor while simultaneously developing the Met's holdings to a high place among the collections of the world.

Interestingly, for a time (1912–14) Dean maintained simultaneous curatorial positions at the Museum of Natural History and the Metropolitan. He was equally brilliant in both capacities. His training as a zoologist provided him with a methodology for the organization and study of arms and armor, a branch of art historical scholarship still in its infancy. From 1925 until his death, Dean served as a professor of fine arts at New York University, in fact offering a course in arms and armor.

It stands to reason that Whiting would seek Dean's advice in finding a suitable collection of arms and armor for the Cleveland Museum of Art. By October of 1914 Dean had informed Whiting of the possible availability of one such collection, that of Henry Griffith Keasbey, an American by birth who had resided in Great Britain for some forty years. Keasbey had assembled a collection of more than seven hundred pieces of arms and armor with great love and care, and was a generous lender to both the London Museum and the Metropolitan Museum of Art. Undoubtedly Dean knew him well. Keasbey was elected a Fellow of the Royal Archaeological Institute and was always to be found wherever arms and armor were to be seen or bought. Many of the pieces forming his collection had derived from classic nineteenth-century collections—Meyrick, de Cosson, Brett, de Belleval, Gimbel, Magniac, Zschille, and so on.

Dean wrote to Whiting on October 10, providing brief descriptions of the collection's highlights and adding, "I'd buy it [myself] if I could now afford it. And I'll try and get . . . half a dozen of the pieces to fill gaps in my own collection. I advise quick decision for Mr. Keasbey may himself come over in November."[5] Whiting was undoubtedly compelled by the notion of acquiring Keasbey's collection for the museum's Inaugural Exhibition, then slated for early in 1916, and immediately took up the matter with the board of trustees. However, faced with limited resources, he was concerned not only about securing funding to make the purchase, but also with the expense of its installation and maintenance.

Whiting proposed that the collection be secured initially as a loan. He wrote to Dean on October 15, 1914: "I would like to know if, in your opinion, the acceptance of this collection as a loan would require the employment by us of a man experienced in the handling of armor to care for it and how expensive a man we would have to secure for this purpose. I am under the impression that when we talked the matter over in New York, you volunteered to write Mr. Keasbey of the possibility that we would be glad to take the collection as a loan for a term of two or three years in the hopes that we might find it possible to acquire it permanently."[6]

Negotiations proceeded rapidly with Keasbey, who was still in England, with Dean serving as go-between. Whiting was now corresponding almost daily with Dean and Kent. By late October 1914, Whiting and Kent were discussing the possible placement of the Keasbey Collection in the event it might be acquired. For the first time we catch glimpses of Whiting's aesthetic concerning the installation of an arms and armor collection. On October 26 he wrote to Dean: "When Mr. Kent was here a few weeks ago, I talked over the question of the collection with him and we decided that the room best suited for its exhibition was a gallery about 45 feet square which I have indicated on the enclosed plan [the present gallery 212]."[7] It is quite amazing in hindsight to imagine that Whiting ever believed that he could squeeze a collection consisting of about seven hundred objects into so small a space. In the same letter, he continued: "It was my idea to carry out the plan I suggested to you in showing these in connection with tapestries. . . . I should hope that Mr. Keasbey would have no objection to our using his collection in connection with other armor which might be supplemented as I hope to secure a few complete horse armors so as to have at least two or three mounted figures if the material can be found. . . . In this connection I hope that you will have us in mind for some battle flags either for purchase or loan, preferably the latter."

The eventual installation of armor, of course, featured the prominent juxtaposition of armor with tapestries and battle flags. Whiting had undoubtedly gotten the idea of using flags from the installation he had seen and admired at the Metropolitan. The space that would eventually be known as the "Armor Court" was on paper still known as the "Court of Casts," and was undoubtedly to be modeled after the well-known cast collection at London's South Kensington Museum (now the Victoria and Albert Museum). Such a collection consisting of plaster casts made from historic sculpture could be had readily and would have enormous teaching potential. The original idea of installing a cast collection was probably not Whiting's but rather Kent's, who had advised on installing cast collections in Springfield, Providence, New York, Pittsburgh, and Buffalo.

Henry Griffith Keasbey would prove himself in negotiation to be both exasperatingly wily and prone to changing his mind. Cleveland had now made it clear to him that it was interested in making an offer for the collection, and he in turn had made it clear that he was amenable to selling at the right price. Keasbey had planned to ship his collection from England to New York so that it might be examined by Whiting there. However, the vicissitudes of the world war made Keasbey reconsider. On November 4, 1914, Dean wrote to Whiting: "It appears now that the collection has not been sent. It is, however, so packed that it can be forwarded at any moment. I believe a question arose about insurance and Mr. Keasbey did not feel willing to pay the additional price which the new mine fields off the Irish coast seem to have caused."[8] Nevertheless, Keasbey was induced to visit Cleveland on November 19, where it was hoped that he might be favorably impressed with the city and the new museum then under construction. Keasbey

John Long Severance (1863–1936) was a member of the museum's board of trustees and one of Cleveland's great philanthropists. In 1916 Severance and his wife generously provided the gift of purchase funds for the acquisition of the museum's arms and armor collection.

was courted over lunch at the Union Club hosted by Judge William B. Sanders, president of the board. Present were some of the trustees and Whiting. While the lunch seems to have been pleasant, Keasbey proved noncommittal. "He tells me that two other museums have made inquiries regarding the collection," Whiting would report to Kent, "and that while we have first choice, other things being equal, he wants a few days to think the matter over before deciding."[9]

By December 2, Keasbey had not yet decided whether to sell. He sent Whiting a note asking for more time. "He intimated that his present feeling was that he would not be justified in lending the collection except upon pretty definite assurance of purchase, but did not give his final decision,"[10] Whiting reported to Dean. Whiting now found himself in a difficult position, having not actually seen the Keasbey Collection. On December 2, Whiting wrote Dean: "It would be very difficult, I fear, for me to get my Trustees to agree to buy the collection without first having seen it and without knowing something more definite about it as at present we are relying upon your statement that the collection has good things in it and would be a safe purchase. . . . Whether Mr. Keasbey has collected from the standpoint of design, as well as from the standpoint of mechanical appliances, I am not fully convinced."[11]

The point seemed moot, however. By early January Keasbey still had not provided Whiting with a firm selling price and had informed him that he was planning to leave his collection in England for the time being. Moreover, the death on January 6, 1915, of board member Dudley P. Allen, upon whom Whiting was relying for financial support, now made Whiting pessimistic about landing the Keasbey Collection. On January 7 he wrote to Dean: "It looks as if I will have to give up the idea of getting this collection, which is a matter of serious disappointment to me, as I had set aside the so-called Court of Casts for this purpose and it will be difficult to secure other material to take its place satisfactorily."[12] Interestingly, it is obvious that Whiting had now abandoned any notion of installing an armor collection in gallery 212, and that he considered the Armor Court as the appropriate place to display this material—from the standpoint of both the court's architecture and the floor space it provided.

Mounting Anxiety: The Macomber Collection

Bashford Dean was genuinely concerned by Whiting's plight and had offered to go on a purchasing trip to Europe to find armor for the Inaugural Exhibition to take the place of the Keasbey Collection, an offer that was politely rejected by Whiting due to the financial uncertainties of the purchasing budget following the death of Dr. Allen. It is clear from Whiting's correspondences during 1915 that he faced the Inaugural Exhibition, now scheduled for January 1916, with mounting anxiety. It is also clear that the installation of an armor collection had become a paramount objective for the "Armor and Tapestry Court." Whiting never entirely gave up on winning the Keasbey Collection, and in 1915 found in board member John Long Severance a sympathetic ear. Severance agreed to buy the collection from Keasbey provided that they could come to terms on the price. Sadly, Keasbey persisted in changing his mind and his asking price. Negotiations finally broke off once and for all. On October 29, Dean made an impassioned—almost desperate—appeal to Keasbey on Whiting's behalf:

> I am sorry, too, for many reasons that your collection will not go to Cleveland—indeed I am still hoping that you may see the way clear to let them have it, though I confess that I am hoping against hope. They depend, as I explained to you, upon the financial support of a single person in this matter, and as he has explained himself pretty clearly, I fancy there is nothing more to be done. Perhaps you might have an errand in town before you leave Princeton and would come in and have luncheon with me here. I'd like to be inspired with persuasive eloquence then and see what I can do! I feel that armor ought to be shown in the fine new building in Cleveland, and I'm even turning over the sad plan of dismantling my room at Riverdale for them for a year or two if the worst comes to worst. Do come in and let us have a final talk![13]

BRONZE PORTRAIT MEDAL OF FRANK GAIR MACOMBER (D. 1941), 1929 J. S. LARSEN (AMERICAN, 1876–1946) MUSEUM OF FINE ARTS, BOSTON 31.392

Macomber, a Boston attorney, investor, and collector, was the original owner of the arms and armor collection that would eventually be sold to the Cleveland Museum of Art in 1916. He formed his collection during the final decades of the nineteenth century largely from old European sources.

This letter reveals much about the personal commitment of Bashford Dean to Whiting and to the Cleveland Museum of Art: Dean was now considering the loan of his private collection. On November 1 he wrote Whiting: "So far as Mr. Keasbey is concerned, there is little to be done unless the Cleveland Museum can see its way to pay his new price. The alternative, it seems to me, is to see what the Macomber Collection can be gotten for."[14] Dean then went on to articulate a scenario for lending his private collection for a period of two years, discussing the need for cases and technical support and further suggesting that he might be appointed curator of armor in Cleveland for the duration of the loan period. Whiting responded on November 5 that he would prefer for the moment to explore the possibility of acquiring the Macomber Collection of Boston, and informed Dean of his intention to write Mr. Macomber to this effect.

Frank Gair Macomber was a wealthy Bostonian who, like Keasbey, had built his collection during the final decades of the nineteenth century and had, in fact, acquired pieces from the same classic armor collections. He bought heavily from the famous London dealer S. J. Whawell, including much of the Franz Thill collection which Whawell had purchased in 1902.[15] Macomber, an attorney, had originally made money in the insurance business and had developed a self-cultivated connoisseurship in various branches of the decorative arts. His collecting interests, like many others of his era, were eclectic—furniture, tapestries, Chinese porcelain, and arms and armor. As a collector he would prove to be a major donor to Boston's Museum of Fine Arts. In 1910 Macomber persuaded that museum to create an honorary (i.e., unpaid) curatorship for him in the department of Western art with responsibility for decorative arts—a position he held there for thirty-one years. Many arms and armor items from Macomber's collection were lent to Boston's museum in 1899 and were listed in a small catalogue. Eventually, wishing to divest himself of this material, he offered to sell his armor collection to that institution, but the deal never came to fruition.

As the Cleveland winter approached in November 1915, Frederic Whiting was fixated on the Macomber Collection and the ever closer Inaugural Exhibition. On November 15 he wrote to Dean: "I had hoped to hear this morning from Mr. Macomber in reply to my letter but have no reply as yet. . . . It seems to me too bad to have aroused Mr. Severance's interest so thoroughly and to fail to find the material which he is willing to buy, but I have a feeling that the matter will come out satisfactorily if we keep our eyes open and are not in too much of a hurry."[16] Whiting now realized that the museum could never open in late January or early February as he had planned. He continued to Dean, "I have about decided that we cannot have our opening until March or April so that we have a little more leeway for our negotiations than we anticipated."

By November 22 the Macomber deal seemed to have foundered as well. Dean, now feeling as anxious as Whiting, began to press the Cleveland director for a decision: "I am sorry that Mr. Macomber does not seem in a receptive mood—evidently he isn't for he is emphatic. If you still feel the need of armor to give allure to your great Tapestry Hall perhaps I can help you out as I suggested some time ago. . . . But if you and I take this matter seriously it means now a final decision and the date of opening—for every day will count, and at the best there isn't much time between now and, say, April, when one has armor to mount and repair."[17] Then, on December 2: "It would be a *travail du chien* to open the gallery by the first of May."[18]

On December 24, 1915, Dean wrote to Whiting informing him that he had consulted with his director at the Metropolitan, Dr. Edward Robinson, to seek approval of his scheme to "lease" his private collection of arms and armor to the Cleveland museum for a period of two years—with Dean as its curator. Dean had imagined that he could serve in both capacities simultaneously: "But when I expounded my subject it became clear to me that Dr. Robinson thought it inexpedient for me to serve on your staff while holding my post here. . . . So there we are! . . . So what can be done now in the direction of arranging your new gallery with armor I don't for the life of me know."[19]

After a meeting on Christmas Eve with the museum's executive committee, Whiting had reset the date for the opening to May 3, giving him four months to find a collection to fill what was now called the "Court of Tapestry and Armor." He preferred to close the year on a note of optimism and replied to Dean: "It seems to me that the matter need not be considered as impossible despite what you say. . . . Meanwhile, I want to make this suggestion—that you learn if you can secure from the Metropolitan Museum a leave of absence of from four to six months and that instead of being appointed curator of our collection of armor, if this seems to Dr. Robinson unwise, that we simply engage you for an honorarium . . . to secure and install for us as adequate a collection of armor as the time will permit to be ready by May 3rd."[20]

Whiting had in mind the use of Dean's collection for a two-year period while the search for a permanent acquisition of arms and armor went forward. Indeed, Whiting was now more committed than ever to filling the great hall with arms and armor: "Mr. Severance is not prepared to say formally to the Committee that he will spend [x number of dollars] during the next four to five years in building up an armor collection, but he told me I could say to you [Dean] that he would undoubtedly be interested to do so. It seems to me that this opens up a very alluring and promising prospect. . . ."[21]

Dean was pessimistic regarding the chances of installing his collection in Cleveland's new Armor Court in just under four months. He now politely rejected Whiting's new proposal but offered to "chip in" a few suits of armor for Cleveland's opening year, expressing the hope that Whiting might eventually find his coveted armor collection. Whiting and Dean continued their correspondences through the winter months of 1916, speculating as to possible sources of an armor collection for Cleveland's opening, considering the Joubert Collection briefly— this came to naught—and at one point considering reopening negotiations with Henry Griffith Keasbey.

In late March came word that the Macomber Collection in Boston was now for sale, but at a high asking price. "Mr. Mitchell Samuels [a dealer from the firm of French and Company, New York] was out here . . . seeing Mr. Severance," wrote Whiting to Dean, "and brought up to Mr. Severance the fact that he now had the Macomber collection for sale and that he had explained to Mr. Macomber that the price he had been asking was altogether too high for it . . . but Mr. Samuels had the idea that Mr. Macomber knew that many of the pieces were not right and that he thought he would be able to get it down to a good deal lower figure than the last price he stated . . . and that many of the pieces could be disposed of afterwards to still further reduce the net cost."[22] This is a remarkable revelation given the formal deaccessioning of so much of this collection by the museum in 1960. Dean's interest, however, was piqued by this unexpected turn of events: "I am interested in what you write about the chance of getting Mr. Macomber's Collection, which for the most is very nice. It could certainly make an attractive showing in your gallery."[23]

Events now occurred quickly. Whiting and John L. Severance traveled to Boston to view the Macomber Collection. With Mitchell Samuels acting as agent for Frank Macomber, the two parties came to terms—consummating the deal in late April 1916 with purchase funds formally provided by Mr. and Mrs. Severance. John L. Severance was one of the city of Cleveland's foremost humanitarians, philanthropists, and patrons of the arts of his day. His affiliation with the museum began in 1914 when he was elected a member of the advisory council, and the following year he succeeded his brother-in-law, Dr. Dudley P. Allen, as a member of the board of trustees. In 1920 he was made a member of the accession committee and in 1926 was elected president of the board, continuing in office until his death in 1936. His gift of purchase funds for acquisition of the Macomber arms and armor collection was typical of a generous legacy of giving to citywide philanthropic projects, including the gift of $1 million toward the building of Severance Hall as a permanent home for the Cleveland Orchestra. At his death, his entire art collection, including old master paintings, was bequeathed to the Cleveland Museum of Art. Severance's gift of an arms and armor collection to the young museum—of paramount importance to its first director—was the first of many civic-minded philanthropic acts from which the museum would benefit.

On April 27, 1916, Whiting immediately telegraphed Dean to apprise him of the closure of the deal with Macomber. The museum's opening was now about a month away. It is clear from Whiting's telegraph that he expected the collection to be shipped to Cleveland within a matter of days. An exchange was also worked out with Dean at this time which sent elements of the Macomber Collection to him in return for three equestrian armors, a few suits, and ten regimental banners from Dean's private collection that would go to the Cleveland museum.

Ever cognizant of Whiting's state of anxiety over meeting the opening deadline, now set for June 6, Dean wrote Whiting on May 9, 1916: "I am carrying a full head of steam to try and have everything out to you on time but it is going to be difficult. I will however be sure to get the three mounted horsemen and one of the other suits, but my effort is to have them *all* there at the time of your opening. I am depending upon the word of the freight people here to the effect that there is no delay in transporting the cases to Cleveland. My impression is that if the objects leave here by the 22nd there will be ample time to have them in order by the opening. It will be my plan to run on to Cleveland about the 27th so as to lend a hand in case you need me."[24] Dean enclosed with this letter a drawing for placement of the ten banners within the Armor Court. He was now working intensely in New York upon the preparation of the armor designated for Cleveland, designing mounts, pedestals, cases, and other hardware needed to make the display a reality. Despite this breakneck pace, Dean found time to report to Whiting almost daily by letter, detailing the preparation of horse mannikins and the crating of his objects for shipment.

Meanwhile, in Cleveland the museum had now formally accessioned the magnificent set of seventeenth-century Flemish tapestries given as a gift by Mrs. Dudley P. Allen as a memorial to her husband. The tapestries were being installed in the Armor Court in preparation for the armor's arrival. On May 20 Whiting wrote to Dean: "The Macomber Collection finally arrived late yesterday afternoon after the [railroad] car was lost for four or five days within five miles of Cleveland. . . . To our dismay we found that almost all of the suits had been very largely dismembered and that Mr. Macomber had not taken the precaution to put temporary tags on the various pieces so that we have a puzzle, which I fear [we] will not be able to solve in getting these suits together again. . . . I wired you last night asking if it might be possible for you to come out for Sunday or if not, suggesting that you might be able to help us with the suits when you do come."[25]

In 1930, the year of Whiting's retirement from the museum, a staff member would reflect upon the collection's installation: "Not the least of his [Whiting's] brilliant achievements was the installation of the Armor Collection which was obtained at so late a date that no one without the energy of a dynamo would have thought its exhibition for the opening possible."[26] After his death in 1959, Whiting's obituary in *The Plain Dealer* would recount the final sequence of events:

> At the last moment he heard of a great armor and tapestry collection in Boston. He was told he could never get it installed in time. But he hurried to Boston, had it packed in a van and put on a train for Cleveland. Mr. Whiting hurried back home, but the treasure did not arrive. He sent railroad officials flying up and down the line, looking for the van. There was no trace of it. He went back and forth interviewing officials. One night, discouraged, Mr. Whiting took a train home. He couldn't sleep, and he lay in his berth with the curtain raised. Just outside Geneva, Ohio, he saw the van on a siding. He got it here. Crews worked all night to get it inside and ready. Clevelanders, when their museum was opened for the first time, jammed traffic. They expected to find a new empty building. Instead, they discovered every room filled with priceless works of art. They were enchanted.[27]

The actual mounting and installation of the Macomber Collection, however, was achieved by Dean, who had arrived in Cleveland about a week before the opening and had "literally taken off his coat and attacked the Chinese puzzle of some hundreds of unconnected pieces of iron strewn over the floor of the Armor Court."[28]

Cataloguing the Collection

The opening of the museum on June 6, 1916, was a great success, and the new Tapestry and Armor Court had made exactly the impression with the Cleveland audience that Frederic Whiting had wished. The Armor Court immediately defined itself as the museum's signature space, and Whiting's judgment of hanging tapestries in juxtaposition with arms and armor provided the visual mix that would remain its hallmark through the present day. Whiting continued to add a few items to the Severance Collection, as it was now popularly called, first in 1919 and again during the early twenties, largely through Bashford Dean, upon whom he continued to rely for advice regarding mounting, display, and labeling issues. While he was undoubtedly pleased with the collection, it is evident from his continued correspondences with Dean that he was still seeking additions.

Whiting had very early on recognized the need for publishing a catalogue of the new museum's arms and armor collection. Having survived the inaugural festivities, he queried Dean in September 1916: "I am beginning to think about the question of a catalogue for the armour collection and I am wondering what your recommendation would be about this. I should like very much to have an accurate catalogue prepared and to print a catalogue of the collection in an abbreviated form. Would it be possible for you to undertake this and on what basis. . . . I presume Mr. Severance would be willing to pay the expenses of preparing such a catalogue. . . ."[29]

Dean responded that he was interested in the cataloguing project but was overloaded with work, including a course he was preparing for New York University, and suggested that someone else might be found for the task. He advised Whiting to begin photographing the collection in anticipation of the publication of an arms and armor catalogue, and both men agreed to return to the subject as time permitted. "The armour continues to attract a good deal of attention," Whiting wrote Dean, "and I think Mr. Severance continues happy in his gift. Mr. Carter, Assistant Director of the Boston Museum was here for a short time yesterday, the first of the Boston officials to see the Museum, and I am sure he will carry back to Mr. Macomber a pleasant word as to the installation of his old treasures."[30] It is interesting that Whiting's correspondences now refer to the exhibition space solely as the "Armor Court," having dropped "Tapestry" from the nomenclature.

In 1917, as World War I raged in Europe, Dean was commissioned a major in the ordnance department of the U.S. Army. On November 2 he reported to Whiting: "I do not know now when I will have the opportunity of seeing you. There is more than a chance I am to go abroad on an armor errand for the Government and I am expecting my credentials any day. . . . This will mean an absence of two months (or longer if I am submarined!)."[31] The subject of an arms and armor catalogue nevertheless remained very much on Whiting's agenda, and he frequently broached the issue with Dean during 1918 and thereafter, as time and occasion permitted. Whiting rightfully felt a great sense of personal accomplishment in the impressive new Severance Collection and was clearly anxious to promote it both nationally and internationally. A catalogue would lend not only legitimacy to the collection itself, but would also establish the Cleveland Museum of Art's commitment to scholarship.

Helen Ives Gilchrist would eventually be the person invited by Whiting to write the catalogue of the Severance Collection. A 1905 graduate of Cleveland's Western Reserve College, her affiliation with the museum began in 1916 as a docent providing tours of the new collections. Her interests were primarily in the culture of the Middle Ages, but she had a particular penchant for the subject of arms and armor. Gilchrist became a staff member of the museum, working in the education department in 1917 and 1918, taking a brief leave of absence to volunteer in the YMCA support huts in Europe, then serving U.S. troops stationed there. She apparently was conducting research on the arms and armor collection during 1918, germane to her teaching responsibilities, and had suitably impressed both Whiting and Dean with her written reports on works in the collection. Shortly after 1918, Gilchrist left the museum for New York to pursue a master's degree at Columbia University. While in New York, she took courses in arms and armor under Dean.

In 1919, as Gilchrist studied in New York, a young curator at the Metropolitan Museum of Art—William Matthewson Milliken—was departing New York to take up a new appointment in Cleveland. Milliken's arrival at the Cleveland Museum of Art would fundamentally affect the future direction of the institution, and in a significant way establish Cleveland's international reputation as a repository for medieval art. While working in the Metropolitan's decorative arts department, Milliken had honed both his connoisseurship and his knowledge of the art market. Whiting now appointed Milliken as Cleveland's first curator of decorative arts, with responsibility for the ancillary collection of arms and armor. However, Milliken's primary interests did not include arms and armor, an area where he would have gained little experience at the Met, as this collection was curated by Bashford Dean. Milliken's interests lay in the field of medieval decorative arts, particularly small, finely crafted treasure objects, of which none was then represented in the Cleveland collections. Ironically, upon Milliken's arrival, for all practical purposes—including teaching—Cleveland's "medieval" collection consisted principally of its arms and armor.

While the museum during its first years possessed a few minor examples of medieval sculpture and decorative arts, the Severance Collection remained the core collection for teaching the crafts and culture of the Middle Ages well into the early twenties. In 1919 the great medieval treasures with which the Cleveland Museum of Art gained its international reputation still lay a few years in the future: in 1922 Milliken's first acquisition, the eleventh-century Rhenish morse ivories; in 1923 the great twelfth-century Limoges "Spitzer" cross; in 1924 came the eleventh-century Byzantine ivory (Bethune) casket as well as the French Gothic table fountain; and in 1925 the exquisite eleventh-century Byzantine ivory plaque of the *Virgin and Child* (the "Stroganoff" ivory). It was 1931 that brought both the milestone of Milliken's career and the museum's establishment of an international reputation: the acquisition of nine objects from the Guelph Treasure, the former ecclesiastical treasure of Germany's Brunswick Cathedral.

As incredible as it may seem, the installation in the Armor Court was still lacking gallery labels as late as 1921. On October 7 of that year, Whiting wrote to Dean: "I have recently learned that Miss Helen Gilchrist, who was formerly in our Education Department, has received the M.A. degree in New York for a thesis on arms and armor and I am wondering if you would consider that she would be qualified to prepare labels and brief descriptions of the armor collection. . . ."[32] Dean affirmed that she was able to do the job and that he would give her work space in the arms and armor department's library at the Metropolitan. He also agreed to oversee her progress. Milliken also agreed to help with the cataloguing where he could, though it is clear that his role was minor. Publication costs of the catalogue were, once again, borne by Mr. and Mrs. Severance.

Gilchrist began preliminary cataloguing as well as the preparation of labels in January 1922, working in Cleveland during the first three months of the year, then moving to New York to complete her research. Between 1922 and 1924, she managed to publish a number of small articles related to arms and armor in the Cleveland museum's *Bulletin*.

Gilchrist's progress on the catalogue was rapid, and in the fall of 1924 it was finally published under the title *A Catalogue of Arms and Armor Presented to The Cleveland Museum of Art by Mr. and Mrs. John Long Severance*. The catalogue, featuring photographic reproductions of the majority of the collection, was organized typologically with reproductions of inscriptions, town, arsenal, and makers' marks drawn by Theodore Sizer of the museum's staff. It included a short

introductory essay by Bashford Dean, "On the Appreciation of Armor." Unfortunately, despite the potential benefit to the museum, only 300 copies were printed and the catalogue was never sold commercially. Instead, copies were presented to libraries, museums, and collectors in the field. Specially bound volumes were presented to Mr. and Mrs. Severance, Frank Gair Macomber, Bashford Dean, Miss Helen Frick in New York, and the museum's trustees.

The results, however, were laudatory. As *Art in America* reported in February 1925, "This handsome illustrated catalogue of the Severance Collection introduces a new authority in this special field in the person of the author, Miss Helen Ives Gilchrist. It also calls attention to a very noteworthy group of objects unsurpassed in historical interest by any similar collection in this country, with the exception of . . . the Metropolitan Museum in New York."[33] Sadly, Gilchrist never returned to her study of armor, but chose other literary pursuits.

Devastating News

With the publication of the Gilchrist catalogue, Cleveland's arms and armor collection officially became the "Severance Collection" in tribute to the munificence of its donor. As time passed, the name of Frank Gair Macomber was gradually forgotten in connection with these objects, save among specialist scholars. The association of the Severance name with Cleveland's arms and armor collection led some to the erroneous impression that John L. Severance had actually collected arms and armor in the manner of C. O. von Kienbusch, William Randolph Hearst, or George F. Harding. Such, of course, was not the case, and armor never stood at Severance's Longwood estate in Cleveland Heights.

The museum's Armor Court, as conceived by Frederic Allen Whiting in 1914, had been brought to successful fruition. The coming decades saw the nurturing of an audience which came to regard the space with special fondness. The Armor Court became the most requested focus of tour requests for the museum's educators. With its skylight and the natural sculptural quality of armor, the court was also a favorite place for drawing classes. And those who reached their seniority in the 1990s would look back with a particular nostalgia to their childhood introduction to arms and armor at the museum. This, it would seem, is the ultimate tribute to the foresightedness of Whiting and the largesse of the Severances.

*Children visiting
the Armor Court
about 1950.*

*The Armor Court as
it appeared in the
early 1960s, following
deaccessioning.*

In November 1924—in the wake of the Gilchrist catalogue—Henry Griffith Keasbey finally sold his arms and armor collection at auction, the sale taking place at the American Art Galleries in New York. A second sale followed a year later. With an ironic twist, the introduction to the auction catalogue noted: "It is only to be deplored that some American museum could not have secured the collection *en bloc*. In fact, the Cleveland Museum is known years ago to have tempted its owner to part with it, making him a generous offer, which the owner declined."[34]

In 1928 Bashford Dean took ill and died unexpectedly at the age of 61 at the sanitarium operated by Dr. Kellogg in Battle Creek, Michigan. Whiting grieved the loss of his old friend and associate, as did a grateful board of trustees, and two years later, in 1930, resigned his post as museum director to become president of the American Federation of the Arts in Washington. His successor was William Milliken. That same year, John L. Severance—Cleveland's "Grand Old Man"— died suddenly and was mourned not only by the museum, but by an entire city to which he had given so much. Helen Ives Gilchrist became the librarian of Cleveland's Hathaway Brown School; she retired in 1956 to San Diego, where she died in 1964.

With the resignation of Whiting, the arms and armor collection now entered a long period of inactivity. For Milliken, who would leave a great legacy of medieval treasures during his directorship, the Armor Court was probably deemed largely satisfactory and representative. He made no further efforts to enhance or develop the armor collection, preferring to invest the museum's resources in other areas. For all practical purposes, the Severance Collection was now a closed collection. And so it remained during the Milliken years. The regimental flags that Whiting had acquired from Dean, and which he so keenly wanted for display in the Armor Court, were removed in the late 1940s, having suffered the untoward effects of ultraviolet light emanating from the skylight.

In 1958 the Milliken years ended. As the directorship of Sherman E. Lee began, it became painfully obvious to him and his new assistant curator of medieval and Renaissance decorative arts, William D. Wixom, that the Severance Collection of arms and armor contained pieces that were not what they seemed. Wixom had a connoisseur's eye and a particular love of late Gothic German sculpture. Like Milliken before him, Wixom would play a major role during the next twenty years in continuing to build Cleveland's already significant medieval holdings in a variety of media. Though not a specialist in European arms and armor, Wixom inherited the Severance Collection as ancillary material with curatorial responsibility for its proper care, study, and display.

Given the limited size of the Severance Collection—around four hundred objects—it had never warranted a specialist curator. The Metropolitan Museum of Art was and remains to this day largely unique among major U.S. museums in having a specialized and dedicated department for arms and armor. (Although it must be added that the Higgins Armor Museum of Worcester, Massachusetts, remains the only museum on this side of the Atlantic to focus exclusively upon arms and armor.) After nearly forty years, however, and despite brilliant activity in other collecting areas, Cleveland's arms and armor collection had received little by way of new scholarship, labeling, or reinstallation. It remained installed essentially along the same plan as laid out by Dean and Whiting in 1916. It was apparent to Sherman Lee that action was warranted. Once again, the museum turned to America's foremost collection of arms and armor—the Metropolitan—for assistance and technical advice.

On September 3, 1959, Lee wrote to his counterpart at the Metropolitan, James J. Rorimer, inquiring whether it might be feasible to borrow the expertise of one of the Met's arms and armor curators to "vet" Cleveland's collection. Rorimer suggested Stephen V. Grancsay, who arrived in Cleveland in early December to spend a week critically evaluating the museum's armor. The results, more or less what Lee and Wixom had anticipated, were devastating. Some thirty-five percent of the collection was either modern or, if original, of weak quality. Lee moved swiftly. The questionable pieces were removed from display and by May 1960 had been presented to the board of trustees for deaccessioning.

William H. Riggs, former owner of the Field Armor for Man and Horse with Arms of the Völs-Colonna Family, *now in the Cleveland Museum of Art (see page 20). Riggs is pictured here with the armor in his Paris townhouse in the rue Murillo about 1910.*

Unfortunately, from the aesthetic, collecting, and educational standpoints, the Armor Court had now lost its centerpiece: four equestrian armors.

Steps were needed that would put the Armor Court back in order and provide a sense of visual focus, aesthetic harmony, and completeness. The remainder of the collection, which was still of considerable size though lacking balance, was cleaned and remounted, and new cases were designed, including two large L-shaped vitrines near the museum's south entrance. Moreover, a new equestrian armor was secured as a centerpiece to the display. This armor, a North Italian ensemble for man and horse, decorated with the arms of the Völs-Colonna family of South Tyrol, was secured as a two-year extended loan from the Metropolitan. Lee had not only wished to continue the tradition of displaying arms and armor in the Armor Court, one which had been uninterrupted since 1916, but also recognized the collection's importance for teaching. He lamented in a letter to James Rorimer that "one of the by-products of this [removal of unauthentic armor] is much embarrassment to the Educational Department since one of the great drawing cards for the school visits was the armor, particularly the horsemen."[35]

Eventually, in 1964, the equestrian armor would be acquired from the Metropolitan by purchase. Today, this armor for man and horse remains a valued centerpiece in the Armor Court and a favorite of school tours. In addition to new armor cases and wall panoplies consisting of edged weapons and pole arms, Wixom and Lee integrated period furniture and Spanish pictures by Goya, Murillo, and El Greco, to create a design that would serve the institution for the next thirty years.

The deaccessioned pieces of armor from the Severance Collection were included in an involved trade with the firm of French and Company in New York. Together with minor deaccessioned works of European decorative arts, textiles, and Asian art, the armor was exchanged for one hanging of a set of three French, late Gothic, allegorical tapestries from Chaumont dating to about 1500–10.[36] The remaining two tapestries were purchased with monies drawn from the museum's Severance and Hanna funds. The museum, it would seem, was well served by the involved exchange. Ten years later, in a letter of May 2, 1974, to Mr. Milton Samuels of French and Company, Lee would reflect: "I am delighted that you feel so sympathetically towards the Chaumont tapestries and I can assure you that we are eternally grateful to French and Company for working out the complicated transaction that made it possible for us to acquire them."[37]

A Continuing Legacy

In retrospect, the acquisition of the Macomber Collection by Whiting and Severance remains a solid and important investment for the museum. The remaining core includes valued and important examples of plate armor, mail, edged weapons, pole arms, crossbows, and firearms (a checklist can be found at the end of this book). That spurious pieces should have entered the collection in 1916 is not surprising, given that armor scholarship was in its infancy and still lacked the technical methodologies available to modern conservators and curators. A corpus of critical catalogues and technical studies simply did not exist in 1916. It must be pointed out that the Cleveland Museum of Art was only the second major American museum, after the Metropolitan Museum of Art in New York, to assemble a collection of arms and armor of any significant size. The museums of Philadelphia, Detroit, and Chicago have acquired their fine collections in the period only since 1950.

In the late 1990s, Cleveland's collection of arms and armor continues to provide a prized and major presence in the grand space of the Armor Court. As this publication goes to press, the museum—under its fifth director, Robert P. Bergman, and with the benefit of a major grant from the Lila Wallace–Reader's Digest Fund—prepares its second major reinstallation of the Severance Collection of arms and armor. As it has captivated audiences for eighty-two years, so this treasured collection will continue to serve the museum's new audiences of the future—a continuing legacy of vision, education, and service established by Frederic Allen Whiting and John Long Severance.

1. Evan H. Turner, ed., *Object Lessons: Cleveland Creates an Art Museum* (Cleveland: The Cleveland Museum of Art, 1991), 39.

2. Frederic Allen Whiting, transcript of a lecture, Records of the Society of Arts and Crafts, Boston, 1902 (Archives of American Art, Smithsonian Institution, microfilm roll 300, 37).

3. Whiting, "The Arts and Crafts Movement in the United States," Records of the Society of Arts and Crafts, Boston, 1903–4, 2 (microfilm roll 300, 151).

4. Whiting, "The Relation of the Museum to Local Industry," *Bulletin of The Cleveland Museum of Art* (December 1918): 123.

5. Dean to Whiting, 10 October 1914, CMA Archives.

6. Whiting to Dean, 15 October 1914, CMA Archives.

7. Whiting to Dean, 26 October 1914, CMA Archives.

8. Dean to Whiting, 4 November 1914, CMA Archives.

9. Whiting to Kent, 20 November 1914, CMA Archives.

10. Whiting to Dean, 2 December 1914, CMA Archives.

11. Ibid.

12. Whiting to Dean, 7 January 1915, CMA Archives.

13. Dean to Keasbey, 29 October 1915, CMA Archives.

14. Dean to Whiting, 1 November 1915, CMA Archives.

15. The author is indebted to Stuart W. Phyrr, curator-in-charge of arms and armor at the Metropolitan Museum of Art, New York, for this information.

16. Whiting to Dean, 15 November 1915, CMA Archives.

17. Dean to Whiting, 22 November 1915, CMA Archives.

18. Dean to Whiting, 2 December 1915, CMA Archives.

19. Dean to Whiting, 24 December 1915, CMA Archives.

20. Whiting to Dean, 29 December 1915, CMA Archives.

21. Whiting to Dean, 25 December 1915, CMA Archives.

22. Whiting to Dean, 21 March 1916, CMA Archives.

23. Dean to Whiting, 21 March 1916, CMA Archives.

24. Dean to Whiting, 9 May 1916, CMA Archives.

25. Whiting to Dean, 20 May 1916, CMA Archives.

26. Turner, *Object Lessons,* 11.

27. *The Plain Dealer*, Cleveland, 23 December 1959.

28. Turner, *Object Lessons,* 11.

29. Whiting to Dean, 9 September 1916, CMA Archives.

30. Whiting to Dean, 16 October 1916, CMA Archives.

31. Dean to Whiting, 2 November 1917, CMA Archives.

32. Whiting to Dean, 7 October 1921, CMA Archives.

33. *Art in America* XIII, no. 2 (February 1925): 104.

34. American Art Galleries, New York, sale 29–30 November 1924.

35. Lee to Rorimer, 14 December 1959, CMA Archives.

36. The three panels are said to come from the Chateau of Chaumont: *Triumph of Eternity* (CMA 1960.176), acquired by exchange; *Youth* (CMA 1960.177), Severance Fund; and *Time* (CMA 1960.178), Hanna Fund. France, Valley of the Loire, c. 1500–10.

37. Lee to Samuels, 2 May 1974, CMA Archives.

A Descriptive

History of Arms and Armor

FIELD ARMOR FOR
MAN AND HORSE
NORTH ITALY,
C. 1575
CMA 1964.88 [6]

As suggested by an etched coat-of-arms that appears seven times, this armor for man and horse was probably made for an unknown member of the Völs-Colonna family of the South Tyrol. It seems to have formed part of a "garniture"—an armor with multiple customized exchange elements which could convert the basic suit to various field or sporting configurations. With different pieces of the garniture attached, this suit could have been worn for either cavalry or infantry use in the field.

20

Introduction

We have come to think of the craft of arms and armor as a uniquely medieval tradition associated exclusively with the culture of European knighthood, conjuring images of chivalrous deeds, of courtly love, of chansons and troubadour poetry, of tournaments and deeds of valor. While this romantic dreamscape frequently overlaps with historic truth, it is often conditioned by nineteenth-century fiction and twentieth-century film. The reality is that most plate armor surviving into the twentieth century is more properly a product of the Renaissance than the Middle Ages. In fact, about ninety-five percent of today's surviving armor comes from the period *after* the Battle of Agincourt (1415), and European armor achieved its technical and aesthetic perfection during the two centuries between 1450 and 1650. Nevertheless, while much of the last century's fictional literature and today's popular imagination is replete with myths about armor, the emergence of the knight, fully clad in plates of steel, toward the end of the fourteenth century is truly and clearly a medieval phenomenon.

Warfare, of course, has been endemic to the human condition since time immemorial. Integral to the study of human conflict is the concomitant history of arms and armor, and the relentless quest to achieve advantage as well as invulnerability in battle. For the warrior, ancient or modern, martial supremacy was secured not only through skill, discipline, and training, but also through the possession of superior arms. Thus, the ultimate challenge for the armorer was to render his warrior-client impervious to harm through ever-improving defensive armor. The weaponsmith's goal, in turn, was to devise new and increasingly efficient weapons to defeat those defenses. Since offensive weapons and defensive armor were frequently the arbiters of life and death, it was essential that they be constructed with the greatest technical knowledge, care, and skill—a process that often resulted in objects of great beauty.

Over the ages, a special relationship has evolved between man and his weapons. Arms, which provided their owner with life-supporting nourishment and protection for one's family and people, became associated with such noble virtues as bravery, loyalty, self-sacrifice, and solidarity. Thus, arms and armor have long been considered worthy of decoration and fine design, becoming artistic creations in their own right intended both to embellish their owner and to provide him with status and authority. The Greek poet Homer described the practice (which still survives) of preserving weapons as souvenirs or trophies, particularly those of distinguished warriors or vanquished foes, or those which played a role in important struggles. We are told, for instance, that Ajax and Odysseus quarreled over who would possess the arms of the dead Achilles. In a sense, armaments must be considered among the earliest of man's collectibles.

Systematic collections of European arms and armor, some of which have survived into our own day, were actually begun in the age of armor by historical figures who were both connoisseurs and patrons: King Charles VIII of France (ruled 1483–98), the Holy Roman emperors Maximilian I (ruled 1493–1519) and Charles V (ruled 1519–56), and King Philip II of Spain (ruled 1556–98), for example. The Hapsburg Archduke Ferdinand II (ruled 1529–95) is perhaps typical of many princely collectors of his age. After inheriting Tyrol and the outlying Austrian possessions in Swabia, Ferdinand moved into the tenth-century castle of Ambras, which he then renovated into a fashionable Renaissance palace capable of housing his vast art collections. These collections were divided into three main sections: arms and armor, pictures (including portraits), and a *Kunstkammer* comprising eighteen cabinets. Most of today's surviving armor has passed down through ancestral collections, princely armories, and municipal arsenals. Some of these remain relatively intact, such as the family armory of the Vogts (a church bailiff) of Matsch at Churburg in Austria. Other collections, however, have been dispersed in the last century through war, theft, and the auction block, only to once again be incorporated into new public or private collections.

It is only within the past fifty years or so that the study of historic arms and armor has been recognized as a serious and specialized branch of art historical research. While armor was certainly of interest to nineteenth-century collectors, military historians, and fiction writers it was either ignored or overlooked by contemporary art historians, who preferred to focus on the more intellectually acceptable study of painting, sculpture, and architecture. Even among those art

RED-FIGURE
LEKYTHOS
(OIL JUG)
ATTRIBUTED TO
THE OIONOKLES
PAINTER
GREEK, ATTIC,
C. 480–70 BC
CHARLES W.
HARKNESS
ENDOWMENT
FUND
CMA 1928.660

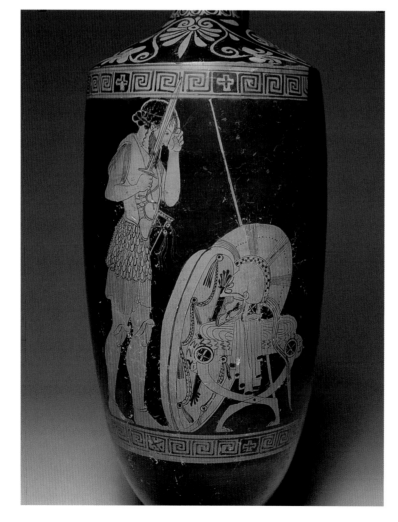

The scene depicts a young warrior cutting a lock of his hair with his sword. The youth is presumed to be one of the Seven Against Thebes, *a legend recorded by Aeschylus in 467 BC which tells of warriors tying hair locks to the chariot of their leader to be used as mementos in case they died on the field of battle. He is shown wearing a formfitting breastplate (or "muscle-cuirass") and greaves (shin defense). This type of armor required very careful fitting to the individual owner. On the stool to the right is a beautiful crested helmet and shield.*

historians who were beginning to establish European decorative arts (furniture, ceramics, glass, etc.) as a serious field of study during the nineteenth century, arms and armor were still usually neglected as being of lesser importance. This practice continued until the 1930s, when a few distinguished German art historians began to treat arms and armor with the same scholarly erudition as that applied to other branches of the visual arts. Today, the subject is accepted as representing an important chapter in the history of the decorative arts.

Ancient armor is among the most beautiful ever made. This handle from a cylindrical bronze cista, a box for holding cosmetics and jewelry, shows two winged figures carrying off the body of a slain youth. The group perhaps represents the twin brothers Sleep and Death with the body of the hero Sarpedon, who, according to Homer's Iliad, *was killed by the Achaians and stripped of his armor as battle trophies. Sarpedon's body was then taken by the twins to be cleansed, anointed, and given a hero's burial. The handle shows beautifully delineated crested helmets with hinged cheekpieces folded in the upright position.*

CISTA HANDLE
ETRUSCAN, 4TH
CENTURY BC
PURCHASE FROM
THE J. H. WADE
FUND
CMA 1945.13

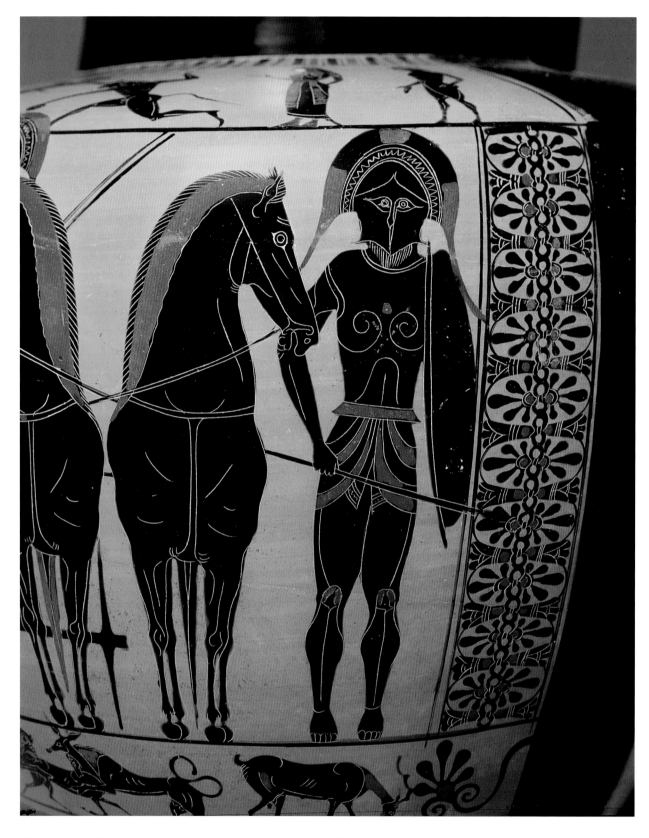

The warriors flanking the chariot wear metal cuirasses with swirling decoration over the chest and full-face Corinthian helmets. Greek helmets followed a number of designs, beautifully shaped and skillfully wrought. Crested combs like those shown here were added as extra protection against sword strikes and also for decoration. The helmet worn by the figure on the right has a transverse crest, a feature later adopted by the Romans as a sign of rank.

Ancient Armor

Patróklos now put on the flashing bronze.
Greaves were the first thing, beautifully fitted
to calf and shin with silver ankle chains;
and next he buckled round his ribs the cuirass . . .
then slung the silver-studded blade of bronze
about his shoulders, and the vast solid shield;
then on his noble head he placed the helm,
its plume of terror nodding high above.

—HOMER, *THE ILIAD*

The craft of the armorer and that of the weaponsmith are among the world's most ancient. Arms and armor-making techniques had, in fact, reached a high level of sophistication during the Roman Empire, as adduced by the reliefs on the Column of Trajan (AD 114). In classical mythology, the goddess Minerva (Pallas Athena), the patroness of institutions of learning and the arts, was clad in armor with spear, shield, and helmet. Vulcan, the god of fire and inventor of smithing and metalworking, was the armorer to the gods, notably Achilles, Aeneas, and Mars.

For the earliest armor, however, we must look to the Egyptians, Babylonians, and Hittites. All had well-developed armies from around 2000 BC and employed armor of scale and fabric construction: small pieces of overlapping metal sewn onto fabric as a kind of overlay. They were sometimes padded for comfort. Bronze helmets were customarily worn with these early armors.

However, it was not before the rise of the Greek city-states and the emergence of classical Greek civilization around the eighth century BC that technology became sufficiently developed to permit the shaping of large metal plates to fit the human body. Prior to this, early attempts at creating body armor were usually limited to a heavy bronze cuirass, a roughly formed bronze cylinder intended to protect the torso and upper thighs. Such armors were heavy, cumbersome, and of limited value to their users. In the so-called heroic period, Greek warfare consisted of a "free-for-all" style of combat in which highborn leaders riding in chariots led lightly armed troops into battle. With the emergence of the Greek city-states around 800 BC—Argos, Athens, Corinth, Thebes, and, of course, Sparta—military service became both a right and a duty for the soldier citizen. The Spartans were legendary for their harsh discipline, which started at childhood. Military obligations for Sparta's male citizens lasted from the age of twenty to sixty.

In ancient Greece, armies of foot soldiers now became organized into close-rank regimented systems of combat. The most important infantry unit was the *locho,* which consisted of about a hundred fighting men acting in unison under a *lochagos.* The locho could be further subdivided into two *pentekostyes* or four *enomotias.* Much of our knowledge about Greek armaments derives from vase painting, which reveals that a further innovation, the Argive shield, emerged around the same time. This shield was large and circular, covered with oxhide, and designed to protect the warrior from chin to knee. Its weight was supported by means of a central strap for the forearm, with a grip for the hand. The Greek word for the foot soldier armed in this way was *hoplite,* meaning "shield bearer."

Greek vase painting is an important source of knowledge about ancient armor and weapons. In this combat, the warriors field large Argive shields painted with distinctive devices and carry long thrusting spears.

Short swords were carried for close combat. These heavily armed hoplites wear full-face helmets of the Corinthian type, two with high crests.

Since the Argive shield covered not only its user but also the unprotected side of the man to his left, its introduction permitted certain tactical changes in the conduct of Greek warfare. Hoplites were organized into phalanxes, or compact blocks of troops that functioned as a single unit. The phalanx was literally a dense wall of shields bristling with spears. It presented a formidable adversary not only on land but also on board ships, where hoplites were capable of fighting as marines. Provided that he had the necessary degree of protection and fought in a particular way, a warrior remained a hoplite. This did not preclude local variations in the style of his equipment, particularly his helmet.

The faces of Greek shields customarily were painted or applied with distinctive devices—sometimes designed to identify whole units of troops, on other occasions different for each individual fighter. Throwing spears were eventually superseded by thrusting spears, about ten feet long, which now accompanied the Argive shield. An additional weapon for Greek infantry was a sword carried for hand-to-hand combat. Foot soldiers were supported by other fighters such as archers and slingers. During the fifth and sixth centuries BC, Greek armor assumed its recognizable form as depicted on countless amphorae and other painted ceramic wares. Body armor consisted of a bronze cuirass handsomely fashioned as breastplate and backplate to cover the upper body as far as the waist. Conversely, a corselet of leather or thick layers of linen might also be worn. A pair of bronze greaves, essentially "shin armor," were worn to encase the legs from knees to ankles. These beautifully contoured elements were generally made so skillfully that they fit the wearer exactly, without the need for attachment straps or buckles.

Known to the Greek writers after the sixth century BC as Keltoi, *and feared by the Romans as formidable warriors, the ancient Celts appear to have inhabited the temperate areas of Europe from Asia Minor to the British Isles. While Celtic warriors are often described by classical writers as fighting naked, the evidence of this silver vessel, found in a Danish bog, suggests that some were clothed and armored. The infantry (below) wear shirts and breeches, perhaps made of a type of mail, while carrying spears and long shields with round bosses. Above, the cavalry wear "jockey-cap" helmets with crests of boars or birds of prey and seem to have spurs on their feet.*

Greek helmets are among the most beautiful ever made and follow a number of different forms. Hammered from a single sheet of bronze, in their simplest and most austere form they were designed as a simple conical hat—a translation in metal of the *pilos,* the felt hat favored by the Spartans. The most elaborate helmet was the Corinthian which encased the whole head in a smooth shell, leaving only small slits for the eyes and mouth. Crested combs could be added as additional protection against sword strikes and for embellishment.

The most worthy adversary faced by the Greeks was the Persians (centered in what is now Iran). Under Darius I (ruled 521–486 BC), the Persians systematically assembled an empire by conquest, eventually extending their territories from India in the east to the Aegean Sea, the Danube, and Egypt in the west. The Persian army's superiority over the peoples of Asia Minor was due largely to battle techniques adopted from the people of the Steppes: the rapid attack of horse-mounted warriors armed with heavy composite bows as their principal weapon. The backbone of the Persian army was its magnificent cavalry, wearing little or no armor so as not to weigh down their horses or encumber their movement. Persian warriors astride their horses provided a splendid spectacle, bedecked in brightly colored clothes and glittering with gold jewelry and appliqués. The skill of archery was so admired in Persian society that the great kings had themselves portrayed as archers on their coins. In addition to the bow, fighters carried wicker shields, with some carrying a short sword tied to the right thigh, and short spears suitable for throwing. The crack troops of the Persian army were the 10,000 warriors known as the "Immortals," who comprised an elite corps provided the best equipment. The Immortals carried both bow and spear. Their spears had a metal ball at the end to serve as a counterweight, embellished with gold and silver.

Between 500 and 479 BC a series of battles took place between the Greek city-states and the Persians—at Marathon, Thermopylae, Salamis, and Issus—resulting in the Persians' eventual expulsion. Darius I had crossed the Bosphorus twice with his army, once to invade Scythia and again to invade Greece as a reprisal for the help given by mainland Greeks to the city-states in Asia Minor, which had revolted against their Persian overlords. In 494 BC, faced with a common threat from the Persian Empire, the Athenians and Spartans buried their own rivalry in an attempt to expel the invaders. These events, and the defeat of Darius when the Athenian general Miltiades led the much smaller Greek forces at the Battle of Marathon in 490 BC, are described in the histories of Herodotus and account for some of the most heroic military feats in ancient history.

GILT-SILVER DISH
WITH KING
HORMIZD II OR
HORMIZD III
HUNTING LIONS
IRAN, SASANIAN,
AD 400-600
JOHN L.
SEVERANCE FUND
CMA 1962.150

The Sasanian kings, the last dynasty of native rulers to reign in Persia, were much occupied with war, especially with Rome and later with Byzantium. They were eventually overthrown by the Muslims. Their craftsmen were renowned for exquisite vessels in silver, like this dish showing a king engaged in a lion hunt, traditionally the royal sport of the Sasanians. Like their Persian ancestors, the Sasanians were crack archers as well as consummate horsemen. Here, the king's equipment—a bow, sword, and ornate helmet—and the horse's trappings have been delineated in crisp detail.

The Roman Celtic Tradition

Originally a colony of the more northerly Etruscans, Rome was traditionally held to have been founded by Romulus in 753 BC. By the third century BC, however, Rome dominated the Italian peninsula from which it would eventually conquer and rule most of the known world. Over time the Romans would develop classic armors and weapons that would leave an indelible mark on methods of conducting warfare. For example, heavy armored cavalries were in use by the Romans by the fourth century AD, as were the lance, the pike, the bow, chain mail, and articulated metal body armor. While these did not immediately survive the breakup of the Western Empire in the fifth and sixth centuries, they would reappear later in medieval guise. The artists and armorers of the Renaissance would, in fact, use the classic Roman cuirass and helmet, as interpreted from Roman sculpture, to epitomize the perfect heroic figure.

The Roman army developed by adaptation and innovation. From the numerous military systems with which the Romans came into contact, notably those of the Greeks and the Celts, they adopted tactics and weaponry. The Greek historian Polybius, writing in the second century BC, observed that the Romans adopted both the equipment and deployment of armored cavalry from the Hel-

The soldiers shown here are legionaries. One, at center, is clad in a scale shirt, while the man to the right wears the lorica segmenta, an armor for the upper body made up of overlapping bands of iron. The Roman legions were aided in tactical maneuvers by their extensive use of battle standards, some of which are visible here.

IMPERIAL FIELD ARMOR AS SHOWN ON THE AURELIAN PANELS OF THE ARCH OF CONSTANTINE ROME, AD 176–82 (DEDICATED AD 312–15)

lenistic Greeks, substituting, for example, long spears in place of the javelin (called the *pilium*). Long spears are better suited to mounted combat.

In the early days of Rome's history, Roman warriors wore little armor. A helmet and a breastplate were used in conjunction with a small round shield, usually made of wood and leather. More elaborate bronze shields have been found from this early period, but these seem to have served a mainly ceremonial function. The favored swords were a long slashing type of Celtic origin (the *spatha*) and a much shorter stabbing sword called the *gladius*. By the third century BC, Roman troops were protecting themselves with a kind of linen cuirass covered with thin metal plates called *lamellae*. They were also using by this time mail shirts made of thousands of small interlocking rings of metal. The evidence seems to point to the Celts as the inventors of mail armor.

The Celts were among the most formidable enemies the Roman legions would have to fight. They lived throughout Europe in what is now France, Spain, and Britain, and as far east as Hungary. There are reports by some of the classical writers that many of the Celts went into battle naked from the waist up adorned with torques—heavy metal neck rings made of silver, gold, or bronze and worn as badges of honor. In 55 BC a Roman expeditionary force led by Julius Caesar

BRONZE
GLADIATOR'S
HELMET
ROMAN, FOUND
POMPEII, 1ST
CENTURY AD
MUSÉE DU LOUVRE,
PARIS
INV. MNC 1674

At brutal spectacles in Rome, professional combats (often fought to the death) became wildly popular, and eventually were held in other towns of the Roman Empire. This style of helmet, with its wide brim and tall comb, became associated with those gladiators known as mirmillones. *They carried a short sword and shield and were armed with a greave on the left leg as well as a jointed guard on the right arm.*

landed on the south coast of England. This initial attempt and another the following year toward subjugating the ancient British Celts failed. The spectacle that Caesar encountered apparently left its mark, for the Romans abandoned Britain for another century, returning in AD 43.

In his accounts, Julius Caesar portrayed a terrifying warrior-class society predicated upon bravado and military prowess: "All of the Britons dye their bodies with Woad [the juice of the isatis] which produces a blue color and gives them a wild appearance in battle. They wear their hair long; every other part of the body, except for the upper lip, they shave." That the British Celts who occupied these islands were related to those on the Continent was taken for granted by Caesar. Indeed, the ancient Britons shared many of the same religious beliefs, rituals, art forms, and military tactics as the Celtic-speaking peoples of the Continent. Caesar, for instance, in his *De Bello Gallico* noted the use of battle chariots in which "they swarm round enemy lines, hurl their missiles and, with the terror aroused by their horses and the clatter of the wheels, cause confusion in the ranks; they push forward between their own cavalry squadrons and jump down from the chariot to carry on fighting on foot." The Roman landing forces were notably impressed by such tactics.

However, despite such descriptions of the Celts as seminaked warriors, there exist depictions which show Celtic warriors fully clad and possibly armored in mail. On the Danish *Gundestrup Cauldron* of around 200 BC, Celtic cavalrymen are shown wearing crested metal helmets and carrying spears while Celtic infantry are represented with long shields adorned with large metal bosses. Celtic shields were large and generally oval in shape. Examples of ceremonial shields and metal helmets have been dredged from the Thames River in London and are today preserved in the British Museum. By the third century BC the Celts favored the long slashing sword, the spatha, as their principal weapon (which was later adopted by the Roman cavalry). Other favorite weapons were the spear, usually made in two distinct forms—one with a broad, leaf-shaped head, made for thrusting, and a lighter version made for throwing—and the sling, used to propel small pebbles or prepared clay "shot" at high velocity.

As the Roman armies advanced throughout Europe and the Mediterranean basin, their conquered foes became subject peoples of Rome. Some of them were thoroughly integrated as administrators, citizens, or troops in the Roman army— with the exception of the Celts, whom the Romans systematically massacred. Through their wars of conquest, the Romans were brought into contact with new styles of warfare, as well as armor and weapons technology. By about AD 160 the principal infantry force was now the Roman legion, comprising some four thousand men. The legion was subdivided into classes according to wealth and age, with three main battle divisions—the *velites, hastati,* and *principes*—forming the first- and second-line infantry. The *triarii* were a smaller body made up of the oldest veterans. However, the smallest tactical unit was the *maniple* (or handful)—consisting of two centuries, or two hundred warriors. The Roman legions were highly organized and motivated. Their tactical maneuvers were facilitated by extensive use of distinctive battle standards which served as both rallying points and signaling instruments. A legion was composed of ten cohorts, each of which carried its own standard on a long staff, the *signum*. The Roman legionary wore a bronze helmet with a crest indicating his unit and rank. Officers wore elaborate bronze cuirasses and decorated helmets with the crest worn transversely across the head.

The Roman legions were now armed principally with the short sword (the gladius) and the javelin (or pilium). The javelin, essentially a light spear for throwing, featured a small barbed head attached to a wooden shaft by means of a long rod-like socket. The legionaries would hurl their javelins in a series of volleys. The danger to the enemy was that even if the javelin only hit a wooden shield, its barbed head was designed to stick fast so that it could not easily or quickly be pried free. Its long metal socket meant that an enemy soldier could not hack it off, but was left with his shield dragging the full weight of the javelin. Roman weaponsmiths ingeniously designed the javelin so that it could be thrown only once. Any impact usually bent the thin iron shaft behind the javelin's head, thus rendering it useless to an enemy who might conceivably retrieve it and throw it back. This was accomplished by leaving the shaft untempered during the forging process. In another version of the Roman javelin, the head is held in place only by a wooden peg designed to break upon impact.

Having thrown their javelins, the Roman legions made the final onslaught with their short swords, the warrior being protected by his large rectangular shield (the *scutum*). The gladius was worn on the right-hand side so that it could be withdrawn with ease, unencumbered by the shield. The Romans were excellent engineers and devised various instruments for siege and field use, including battering rams, ballistae for hurling large darts, and catapults for throwing rocks.

Unfortunately, actual Roman arms and armor survive in relatively small numbers today. Unlike the Greeks and Etruscans, the Romans did not bury their dead warriors laid out with their arms. Instead, a trooper's armor and weapons were recovered and sent back to the depot, where they were repaired and issued to the next recruit. Our knowledge of Roman arms and armor is based on Roman art, primarily sculpture, and to a lesser degree on documentary evidence—descriptions and references in Roman literature. With the close of the Republican era, and the establishment of Roman supremacy over much of the Mediterranean world, Rome under the emperors is generally better documented. It is thus possible to gain a clearer picture of the Imperial Roman army and its armor and weaponry.

Today's popular image of the Roman soldier is largely conditioned by the panoply of his arms and armor. Trajan's Column was erected in Rome in AD 101–102 to commemorate the Roman victory over the Dacians (modern-day Romania). The column's relief sculpture shows the various stages of the Dacian War and, with its representations of the Roman military, serves as an important source of information about how these celebrated warriors looked. The legion had by this date been reorganized yet again, with the distinctions between hastati, principes, and triarii largely eliminated. Light infantry and some cavalry were now composed of *auxiliares,* or non-Roman troops.

The principal body armor now worn by legionaries was the classic *lorica segmenta,* clearly shown on Trajan's Column and certainly the best known of all Roman armors. It featured a series of overlapping iron bands linked on the inside by means of leather straps and fastened on the outside with laces, buckles, and straps. The lorica segmenta protected the upper body, including the shoulders. Other forms of armor still in use were mail (*lorica hamata*), made of interlinked iron rings, and scale armor (*lorica squamata*). Trajan's Column represents the emperor himself wearing a muscle-cuirass—an anatomically shaped bronze breastplate and backplate. The muscle-cuirass frequently occurs in Roman portraiture for representations of the wealthy and powerful, and clearly was a mark of status.

Bronze helmets evolved in various styles and materials; however, helmets of the *coolus*-type had become common for most legionaries. This was essentially a "jockey-style" helmet with a stunted peak, wide neck skirt, and shaped earflaps. It is likely that much local variation existed in the crafting of military helmets throughout the Roman Empire, with stylistic idiosyncracies and local preferences. While helmets may have been crafted in bronze in one part of the empire, iron may have been employed in another.

Muscle-cuirasses were worn by Roman emperors and important generals to signify status and military prowess. They were highly favored in imperial portraiture, as revealed in the relief sculpture of Trajan's *Column (AD 101–102) in Rome and on this marble sculpture of Emperor Augustus (ruled 27 BC–AD 14). The emperor's breastplate is beautifully embossed with Roman gods and mythological figures.*

AUGUSTUS OF
PRIMA PORTA
ROMAN,
1ST CENTURY
VATICAN MUSEUMS

BARBUTE (FROM THE VENETIAN GARRISON AT CHALCIS) NORTH ITALY, C. 1350–1420 CMA 1923.1065 [68]

This helmet and a small number of others were apparently excavated from the Venetian garrison at Chalcis on the Greek island of Euboea. A rare early survival, this type of helmet was characterized by its high conical apex. Italian chronicles refer to the professional men-at-arms who wore such helmets as barbuti. *The word derives from the Italian* barba—*meaning "beard"—and refers to the curtain of mail (camail) often attached to these early helmets. The small holes along the face opening and neck were for the attachment of the camail and the lining.*

34

Medieval Armor

*He was fitted with a cuirass . . . whose double layer of mail could be pierced with no lance
or javelin. . . . On his head was placed a helmet, resplendent with precious stones.*
—JEAN OF MARMOUTIER, ON THE KNIGHTING OF GEOFFREY OF ANJOU IN 1128

The period immediately following the fall of Rome is customarily referred to as the Dark Ages—not because of any innate chaos, but rather for want of records, scholarship, and information about the migration cultures that occupied the north and east of Europe. Despite these gaps in our knowledge, it is clear that Europe's migratory tribes, mostly Germanic, had developed consummate metalworking skills. These skills encompassed coinage, jewelry, and ornate vessels, as well as weapons and to some extent armor.

The armor worn by these Germanic tribes was minimal. A conical helmet, finely crafted and sometimes lavishly decorated with inlaid silver, typically was used in conjunction with a round shield and long sword. From these misty centuries survive some impressive examples of the armorer's craft. For example, the *Sutton Hoo Helmet,* dating to about 625 and distinguished by its ornamental "eyebrows," was found in the burial chamber of an Anglo-Saxon chieftain. Another Anglo-Saxon find, the *York Helmet* of about 775, was discovered during building operations in the city of York in 1982. This helmet consists of a skullpiece, two hinged cheekpieces, a fixed noseguard, and a curtain of mail (or camail) to protect the neck. Both of these rare survivals illustrate the accomplished metalworking skills of early northern armorers as well as the love of adornment and importance attached to personal arms.

YORK HELMET
ENGLAND, ANGLO-
SAXON, LATE 8TH
CENTURY
YORK CASTLE
MUSEUM

This rare helmet was excavated in the northern English city of York in 1982, providing an extremely important reference to armor technology and aesthetics in Anglo-Saxon England. The skullpiece is decorated with stylized eyebrows much like the more fragmentary Sutton Hoo Helmet *in the British Museum. It includes a guard to protect the nose, hinged cheekpieces that could be folded up out of the way, and a mail neckguard. An inscription on the crossbands of the skullpiece indicates that the owner of the helmet was a Christian.*

Mail Armor

The history of European armor from the Migration Period onward can essentially be divided into two periods—the age of mail and the age of plate—with an intervening century of transition. From the fall of Rome through about the middle of the thirteenth century, body armor basically consisted of surviving Roman and Celtic techniques adapted by the migratory tribes who eventually established their

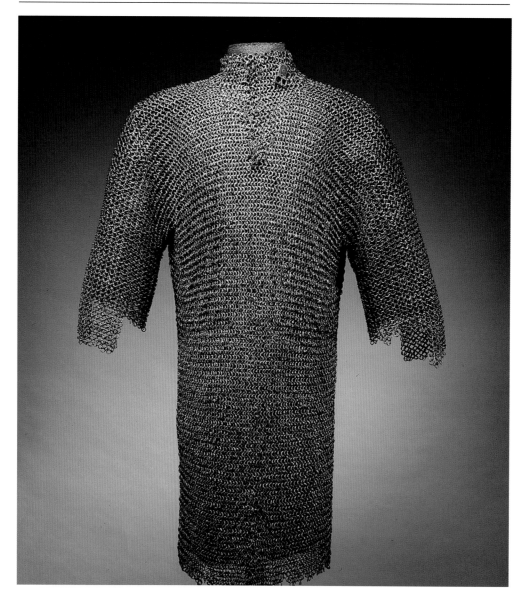

A hauberk is a mail shirt that generally extended between the hip and the knee. European knights wore mail over a padded undergarment known as an aketon. After the development of full plate armor, mail continued to be a linking element or accessory well into the 1500s.

own kingdoms throughout Europe and proliferated this technology. By around 1250, the European knight was still effectively protected in much the same way as the fifth- and sixth-century horsemen who wandered across Europe. He wore a mail shirt (a *hauberk*)—the predominant form of metal body defense throughout Europe until about 1350—supplemented by a metal helmet and a shield. Though precious little early mail has survived, it is well represented in artistic representations from the period, chiefly in manuscript illuminations, seals, sculpture, and brass tomb effigies.

The famous *Bayeux Tapestry,* probably commissioned by Bishop Odo for the newly dedicated abbey at Bayeux in Normandy around 1077, remains one of the best sources of information, not only for mail, but also for arms and armor of the period generally. The tapestry presents the viewer with a pictorial narrative of the Norman Conquest of England of 1066, in which Duke William of Normandy defeated King Harold near the town of Hastings. In the tapestry, we are shown Norman knights wearing mail hauberks and round conical hats with noseguards.

The Bayeux Tapestry *(actually an embroidery) provides a visual narrative of the invasion of England by the forces of William of Normandy, the battle near the town of Hastings, and William's decisive victory over King Harold of England. It was probably commissioned by Bishop Odo for the new abbey at Bayeux in Normandy shortly after the actual events.* The Bayeux Tapestry *stands as the single most important source of information for arms and armor of the period. The English and Normans were similarly equipped—in mail hauberks with conical helmets and either kite-shaped or round shields. A variety of weapons are shown: swords, bows, spears, lances, and the English specialty, the battle axe.*

The knights ride stirruped horses and carry long oblong shields with long pointed bottoms. They carry couched lances and long swords as their primary weapons, and some carry lighter spears or javelins.

It is known from other sources that the Normans took crossbows with them to England, but none has survived and none is depicted in the *Bayeux Tapestry*. Nevertheless, within seventy-five years of the conquest, crossbows were considered sufficiently deadly that they warranted a specific papal ban on their use against

The scramasax, a single-edged knife, was a general-purpose implement. It could serve equally well as a tool or as a weapon and generally did not exceed twelve inches in length. As with most objects dating to the Migration Period, iron weapons such as these survive as excavated grave goods and tend to be heavily corroded. The grips, now missing, would probably have been fashioned from wood or bone. Silver inlay is used to decorate the pommels while ornamental gold foil bands, perhaps from the original scabbards, have survived relatively intact.*

Christians. William's archers, armed with the shortbow, were an important element of the invading army but, unlike the mounted knights, wore little or no armor. The Norman archers came from the ranks of the lower social orders and, not being members of the noble classes, fought exclusively on foot. They are shown wearing simple tunics, sometimes with a padded cap. A few wear mail hauberks, perhaps acquired as war booty. The shortbow, which unlike the later longbow could not penetrate mail, was nevertheless a formidable weapon in large numbers; the *Bayeux Tapestry* shows numerous arrows embedded in or passing through the English shields. Duke William himself is shown wielding a mace, probably more a symbol of his authority than a functional weapon. The tapestry depicts the Norman knights attacking the "Saxon" shield wall adopted by the En-

This famous image provides a wealth of information about the use of mail during the thirteenth century. Because mail was expensive to make, its use generally was limited to warriors of noble birth. Others might hope to obtain mail as war booty, *removing it from the corpses of fallen knights. Most of the knights shown here wear a complete hose of mail. These were probably tied onto a waist belt or perhaps laced to the undergarment known as an aketon.*

STRIPPING THE DEAD: A SCENE FROM THE MACIEJOWSKI BIBLE

FRANCE, C. 1250 THE PIERPONT MORGAN LIBRARY, NEW YORK M. 638, FOL. 35R

glish. The two armies were largely similar in equipment, but varied in tactics: In contrast to the Norman knights, the English army fought entirely on foot and fielded no mounted warriors. Though in the tapestry they are shown similarly clad with mail, helmet, and kite-shaped shields, the English are often seen wielding axes, considered their particular specialty.

Mail armor is believed to have originated with the Celtic peoples of Europe after the fifth century BC. The term itself is derived from the Old French word *maille* (meaning "mesh"), which correctly implies a protective textile, and mail was precisely that—a garment constructed of large numbers of small interlinked rings of steel (each ring linked to four of its neighbors). Mail was extremely flexible and thus could be worn with relative comfort, though it was susceptible to rust and could become extremely hot in the sun. It was normally worn over a quilted undergarment, which protected the skin from chafing and helped to absorb light to moderate blows to the body. Mail for the torso, the head, the legs, and the hands was constructed as separate pieces, each "woven" specifically to the shape and size of that part of the body it was intended to protect. Miniatures in thirteenth-century manuscripts routinely show mail sleeves terminating in integral fingerless

TOMB SCULPTURE
OF A RECUMBENT
KNIGHT
FRANCE,
NORMANDY,
C. 1230–40
PHILADELPHIA
MUSEUM OF ART
1945.25.72

This unknown French knight, represented in effigy, is clad entirely in mail, over which he wears a surcoat cinched by a belt. The surcoat helped preserve the mail from the damaging effects of rain and provided relief from the heat of the sun while in the field. It also provided a place to display heraldic arms. The knight's coif, or hood, has been pulled down from the head and gathered at the neck to better reveal his face.

mittens, which allowed the knight sufficient dexterity to wield a sword or a lance but presumably little else. Mail hoods are sometimes shown drawn backward over the head while not engaging an enemy.

Mail was expensive to make, which generally limited its use to warriors of noble birth who had the means to pay for it, or to others who could obtain it as war booty. In 805 an edict of Charlemagne established a link between the right to own land and the obligation to own a mail shirt. This was a fundamental component of the feudal system in which the warrior classes held their land from the king in return for military service. At the time of the Norman Conquest in 1066, the price of a mail shirt was twelve *solidi,* or roughly the cost of a battle charger.

BISHOP'S MANTLE
(CAPE)
EUROPEAN
(GERMAN OR
SWISS?), C.1520–30
CMA 1921.1256 [91]

Mail capes known as "bishop's mantles" were popular with German mercenary foot soldiers during the first half of the sixteenth century. They were often the only element of armor worn.

Mail-makers are documented in the city of Cologne as early as 1293, and a surviving charter of the mail-makers' guild of Cologne dates to 1391. We know very little about these early makers of mail armor. Beginning in the early fifteenth century, however, occasional drawings and engravings portray such craftsmen at work, allowing us to extrapolate the manufacturing process which must have continued relatively unchanged down through the centuries.

The craft of mail-making was obviously quite distinct from the process of constructing plate armor. The maker of plate armor began with a billet of steel and literally hammered it into its final form, say a breastplate or a helmet. In constrast, the skill of mail-making lay in the final linking of thousands of metal rings into a finished product. A hauberk, for example, might include as many as a quarter million steel rings. Since so much mail armor was made, it can be deduced that there was great division of labor in the workshops and that the manufacturing process went fairly quickly. We can assume that the master craftsman was kept supplied with a fairly constant supply of steel rings and rivets from which he "wove" the finished product—each ring being interlinked with its four neighbors and riveted closed. The laborious early stages of the production process, the manufacturing of the iron or steel rings (both were used) from drawn wire, were probably entrusted to dozens of journeymen and apprentices.

The advantage of mail was that it provided excellent defense against the sword cut, though only limited defense against crushing blows from weapons like the mace or the battle axe. Mail was also capable of stopping low-velocity missile weapons like arrows and spear thrusts. The medieval knight needed to supplement his mail defense with a metal helmet and a shield. At first shields were either round or oval, but by the year 1000 they had been lengthened with a pronounced lower point to protect the left knee of the mounted knight, as shown in the *Bayeux Tapestry*. The beginning of the thirteenth century introduced the surcoat, which was worn over mail to preserve it from rain and to offer relief from the sun. The surcoat also allowed the display of heraldic arms to identify the knight on the battlefield.

With time the increasing effectiveness of the longbow, which could punch through mail rings with its arrows, exposed the deficiencies of mail armor. It was the crossbow, however, that brought about its final decline. Improvements to the crossbow's spanning mechanism enabled it to fire bolts at three to four times the velocity of the longbow, thus rendering mail armor useless. The solution was to devise a deflective surface off which bolts would glance with little or no damage. Thus was born plate armor.

Despite its deficiencies, mail remained in widespread use for many centuries and never entirely ceased to be made throughout the age of armor. Even during the sixteenth century, it was often worn underneath full plate armor as additional protection, and continued to be made in Europe until the seventeenth century.

The task of the mail-maker involved linking thousands of small rings of steel to create a mail garment. This mail-maker is using a pair of riveting pincers to join the rings. A finished hauberk hangs in the background.

The hauberk on page 36 weighs thirty pounds. By the early fifteenth century mail was being worn as an accessory to supplement full or partial plate armor. It continued to afford a secondary level of protection for areas not fully covered by plate armor, such as the armpit and groin.

The hauberk on page 36

A MAIL-MAKER
(FROM THE
HAUSBUCH DER
MENDELSCHEN
ZWÖLFBRÜDER-
STIFTUNG)
GERMANY, 1435–36
STADTBIBLIOTHEK,
NUREMBERG
MS. AMB. 317

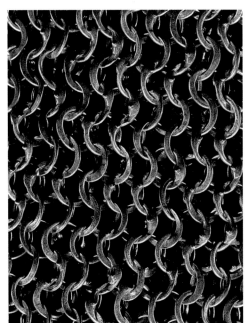

HAUBERK (DETAIL)
EUROPEAN
(GERMANY?),
15TH CENTURY
CMA 1923.1120 [92]

SWORD
WESTERN
EUROPEAN, C. 1400
CMA 1921.1252 [195]

A KNIGHT WITH HIS
SQUIRE (FROM THE
MANESSE CODEX)
GERMANY, C. 1320
HEIDELBERG
UNIVERSITY
LIBRARY
MS. COD. PAL.
GERM. 848,
FOL. 149V

This page from the Manesse Codex *clearly shows the importance assumed by spectacular heraldry once the knight had concealed his face within an enclosed helmet. This knight has affixed a pole-shaped crest to the sides of his great helm. Shield, crest, and banner all carry the same design. At courtly events like the tournament, the beautiful and sometimes witty designs of a knight's coat of arms would have been greatly appreciated.*

Plate Armor in the Gothic Age

In the three centuries following the landing of Duke William's forces at Hastings, the physical appearance of the European knight steadily evolved. Shields became shorter and flatter and, while the lance and the sword remained the primary weapons of the noble warrior, the sword became slightly more decorative with elongated quillons or "Brazil-nut" pommels. The sword retained its long straight blade, which by the twelfth century was often decorated with religious inscriptions. The pommels of these knightly swords were usually made of iron, but sometimes of bronze. Even more rarely, exotic materials like rock crystal, semiprecious stones, or holy relics were mounted into sword pommels. The sword remained the knightly weapon *par excellence,* with an almost religious significance due to its cruciform shape symbolizing the Christian cross.

(Facing page) The principal weapon of the European knight was his sword—a simple weapon with a broad, two-edged blade, a straight (or slightly curved) crossguard, and a round pommel (or counterweight). The pommel gave the knight full mastery of a perfectly balanced weapon (the basic shape of which did not change significantly between 1200 and 1500). Since the steel used in making swords and that used in armor required different qualities and properties, the major swordsmithing centers of Europe are usually different from those that specialized in making armor.

More noticeable is the development of helmet styles. The conical helmet worn by the Normans gradually yielded to a more rounded version, which in turn was ultimately replaced in the thirteenth century by a flat-topped helmet. These helmets are illustrated in countless manuscript illuminations of the period, and one can only assume that the style must have been extremely popular. The sides of the helmets are either perfectly vertical or else taper toward the base. By the end of the thirteenth century these flat-topped helmets assume iron faceguards pierced with sights and ventilation holes, eventually leading to the development of a form known as the "great helm"—an all-enclosing cylindrical helmet. With his face now totally obscured, the knight chose to mount a decorative crest (initially made of leather, and later of wood) on top of his helmet as an aid to identification in tournaments.

A knight's emblazoned shield and his helmet with crest, mantling, and wreath were integral parts of the personal insignia that came to be known as a coat of arms—a term deriving from the decorated surcoat once worn by medieval soldiers on top of their chain mail. The coat of arms was therefore, at one time, literally a protective coat. After about 1250, the helmet and crest were regarded as so important in Germany that they appeared on seals instead of the complete coat of arms. With the end of the age of chivalry, the value attached to the helmet declined in Germany as elsewhere. Yet in heraldry, the helmet with its crest remained an essential part of the full achievement of arms, and even into modern times the armored helmet continued to denote rank.

It was the fourteenth century, however, that saw the most profound changes in the physical appearance of the knight. Overlapping plates of steel were developed as a viable alternative to mail for covering the entire body, and it was not until after about 1350 that Europe received its first glimpse of "the knight in shining armor." The rigidity of plate gave greater protection than the by-then penetrable surface of mail. In fact, this had been recognized by European armorers before the fourteenth century, though not successfully implemented. Indeed, elements of plate armor had existed in the thirteenth century to encase the knees (*poleyns*) and to protect the lower legs (*greaves*), parts of the body especially vulnerable during battle on horseback. The fourteenth century was a time of transition in the development of body armor, during which plates of steel were worn in conjunction with mail. First, small plates gradually were added to cover the limbs, then larger ones to protect the torso, until by the fifteenth century the entire body was

BARBUTE (FROM THE VENETIAN GARRISON AT CHALCIS) NORTH ITALY, C. 1350–1420 CMA 1923.1065 [68]

The strength of armor plate came primarily from its shape, not the thickness or weight of the steel from which it was made. The streamlining of this helmet, with its conical apex, was functional and would have protected the wearer from downward glancing blows to the head.

ASSOCIATED
GOTHIC
BACKPLATE AND
PAULDRONS
GERMANY AND
ITALY, LATE 15TH
CENTURY
CMA 1916.1613 [23];
1916.2080.1–2 [24]

Over time, the increasing effectiveness of the crossbow and longbow made mail armor vulnerable. The European knight responded by gradually adding steel plates to supplement his mail defense, and by around 1400 he was protected almost entirely by plate armor. The elements shown here, with their sculptural line and fan-shaped pauldrons, illustrate the beauty of plate armor from the Gothic age.

encased in steel. Around 1415, by the time King Henry V of England invaded France, mail was either completely covered or replaced by plates of steel.

When the armorer had mastered the craft of shaping plates of steel to allow mobility of the limbs by articulation, and to provide for turning joints, the transition of plate armor was complete. The armor plates were ingeniously pivoted to each other at the sides by sliding rivets that moved in slots. The elements of a suit of armor were never riveted directly to each other (since this would render them inflexible), but were made to overlap slightly. Within the concealed areas were the

This elegantly constructed breastplate consists of two primary plates of steel fastened at the center by a rivet. The lower plate is embellished with a border of embossed flutes that converge upward and terminate in a fleur-de-lys. Gothic plate armor achieves its beauty not by surface decoration but by the simple elegance of its line, seemingly inspired by contemporary architecture. It was the streamlined shape of the armor with its glancing surface that afforded protection to its owner.

rivets securing them to interior leather straps. The exterior rivets were either sliding rivets or nonfunctional ornamental rivets. Exterior and concealed hinges were also essential functional accessories for attaching movable parts. Tubular arm canons were attached by means of tongue-and-groove construction.

Around 1350 a new approach was taken by the armorer in the fashioning of armor plates. Instead of making steel thicker to prevent penetration, the plates were fashioned at angles to ward off crossbow bolts or sword thrusts. The breastplate, for example, assumed a pronounced vertical ridge down the center, while helmets such as the basinet assumed a more conical shape to deflect downward blows to the head. Plate armor also became more formfitting, allowing greater comfort and mobility. The shaping of armor plates in this way anticipated streamlining and re-

sulted in armor with sculptural definition and compelling beauty. As a result of the introduction of plate armor, the shield was made superfluous and gradually disappeared from use.

The forging of steel, a very hard material, into precisely fitted, interconnected plates was a task requiring great skill and patience. With the passage of time, the craft of the armorer was to become concentrated in specific centers in Europe, usually areas that were accessible to the ore required for making steel. Each center acquired certain characteristics of its own. While it is true that arms and lower-grade munition armor were produced throughout Europe during the late Middle Ages, it is equally true that the specialty craft of plate armor-making, including the finest armor technology available at the time, was concentrated in but a few important centers with access to international trade routes and natural resources such as ore, charcoal, and running water. By the beginning of the fifteenth century, divergent armor styles were detectable in South Germany and North Italy. The chief armor production centers were found at Nuremberg, Augsburg, Landshut, Innsbruck, Milan, and Brescia. The products of these centers gained international renown and were exported throughout Europe. While the manufacture of low- to middle-quality plate armor flourished in other European cities, such as

GOTHIC
PAULDRONS
DETAIL OF
ARMORER'S
MARKS
CMA 1916.2080.2 [24]

When the elements that made up a suit of armor had been forged, shaped, and polished, they were inspected for fit and finish. At this stage, the master armorer would use a punch to stamp each element with his maker's mark. Other associated marks might include a town or guild mark, depending on the city of origin. The set of three marks shown here are of a type known to be Milanese. The upper mark seems to show the letters GAN beneath a crown and probably refers to the armorer's familial name, while the mark below, twice repeated, is a split cross with the letters YA. These probably refer to the armorer's Christian or first name. The marks are apparently unrecorded.

Cologne, Genoa, and even Florence, generally speaking their products did not achieve the same success or, like the Royal Armouries at Greenwich, England, not until the sixteenth century.

In the early Middle Ages, the makers of armor were very likely to have been blacksmiths and metalworkers by trade. By the thirteenth century, however, armor-making had emerged as a specialized craft in its own right. Like other medieval crafts, armorers formed trade guilds to regulate competition, product quality, and the entry of apprentices into the trade, and to provide security for their members. Admission to an armorer's guild was not easy. The would-be member was required to demonstrate a consummate knowledge of his craft and a high degree of proficiency that could be obtained only through years of training as an apprentice. A prospective armorer would have to work his way up through the various stages of apprentice, journeyman, and finally master armorer. His status as a master was achieved only after proving his skill by making a trial piece of a complete suit of armor, which then had to be approved by five masters in the guild.

It is the second half of the fifteenth century, however, that is regarded as the greatest period of the armorer's craft. During this century armor elements assumed a slender, streamlined look with sharp, pointed, and cusped edges. This was particularly true in Germany, where elements such as sabatons, elbow-cops, and shoulders appeared to be inspired by contemporary Gothic architecture. For this reason, the style is usually referred to as "Gothic" armor. Gothic armor was not, as yet, encumbered by excessive surface decoration but was confined to smooth polished surfaces embellished by subtle, elegantly curved flutings or ornamental borders of pierced or brass-overlaid steel. The beauty was achieved by sublime purity of line. The play of light on the various surfaces of steel emphasized in ever-changing ways the subtle shapes of the armor plates.

Armor of this period, which today may appear drab, was originally polished mirror-bright and was accompanied by accessories such as colorful plumes and heraldic devices. The typical helmet of fifteenth-century Gothic armor was the *sallet* or *salade,* characterized by its rounded top, keel-shaped ridge, long tail extending down over the back of the neck, and general grace of line.

ST. MAURITIUS,
CAST ABOUT 1507
PETER VISCHER
THE ELDER
(GERMAN,
NUREMBERG,
1460–1529)
GERMANISCHES
NATIONALMUSEUM,
NUREMBERG
INV. PL 2226

This black-patinated brass statuette of the warrior-saint is modeled fully in the round and is remarkable for its accurate and highly detailed treatment of the saint's Gothic armor. The city of Nuremberg was a major center for the production of armor during the late fifteenth and early sixteenth centuries. It concentrated on high-quality armor for a noble clientele and possessed a highly structured guild system. The breastplate and gauntlet worn by the saint can be generally compared with the illustrations on pages 46 and 47.

TILTING SUIT
(COMPOSED)
SOUTH GERMANY,
C. 1560–80
CMA 1916.1502
(HELMET);
1916.1511.A–L [1]

Chivalry and the Tournament

And they gave each other such great blows that they thrust through each other's shields and tore their mailcoats. . . . They dented and bent their helmets and sent the rings of their mailcoats flying until they drew blood enough; for their hauberks were so hot from their own heat that they were scarcely more use than a coat.
—CHRÉTIEN DE TROYES (DIED C. 1183), *YVAIN OR THE KNIGHT WITH THE LION*

Chivalry is an evocative word—conjuring images of knights clad in gleaming plates of steel, carrying swords and shields emblazoned with heraldic devices. The word connotes castles, prowess in battle, adventures in foreign lands, and, of course, courtesy toward women. While all these images help to define the essence of chivalry, its meaning was often abstracted by writers during the Middle Ages. Sometimes they might use the term simply to describe a group of heavily armed horsemen; other times it might refer to a religious order, implying a system of ethics and a code of values. These values were usually deeply interwoven with the Christian faith.

In most European languages, the word for "knight" is literally connected to horses and to horsemanship (*chevalier* in French; *Ritter* in German). Chivalry thus implies a man of aristocratic standing and noble ancestry who is capable of equipping himself with a warhorse and heavy arms, the cost of which would have been prohibitive to anyone outside the ranks of the nobility. The word chivalry cannot be divorced from this martial world of the mounted warrior, nor from the aristocratic world that nurtured him and made him, through the conduit of certain rituals, what he was: the knight, a professional warrior.

Nobility itself did not automatically confer knighthood. Once earned, however, it became a jealously guarded class privilege. The status and honor of knighthood rendered to it the character of an international brotherhood, which very often transcended national boundaries. The would-be knight could begin his arduous quest as young as seven years of age, when he might serve his father as a page. In this role he was taught polished manners and personal grace, learning among other skills how to select wine and serve at table. At about fourteen, he might join a different noble household as a squire where he would receive training in martial arts, the care of horses, and the proper techniques and etiquette of the hunt. When judged ready, the young man would be permitted to go to war as a shield-bearer or squire for his lord. Only when he had acquired the necessary fighting skills and could afford to outfit himself and a horse with armament and equipment was he considered ready to become a full-fledged knight. The "dub-

The illustration at left shows the asymmetry of jousting armor. The participants rode along a wall-like barrier known as a "tilt" with their left sides facing. Consequently, armor on that side of the body tended to be thicker. Note the larger reinforcement plate (called a grandguard) over the left shoulder for extra protection. Also, the breath holes in the helmet were placed on the right side (farthest from an opponent's lance) to avoid injuries from splinters. The bracket attached to the right breastplate is called the lance-rest, a shock-absorbing support designed to accommodate the lance when "couched" under the right armpit.

This unknown knight wears armor of the Venetian fashion of about 1520. The artist has faithfully painted the armor's details, such as rivets and the attachment straps and buckles for the leg elements. The breastplate and sabatons have abandoned the pronounced points characteristic of earlier Gothic armor and favor the more rounded forms fashionable during the Renaissance. The squire in the background rides the knight's horse while wearing his helmet and carrying his lance.

bing" or initiation ceremony was often held on a battlefield and consisted of a knight touching the shoulder of the squire with the flat blade of a sword.

Since ownership of a trained warhorse and its contingent equipment was the minimum worldly possessions required of a knight, the animal represented an enormously valuable asset, both for the practical purposes of fighting and as a status symbol. In accordance with its value, a horse was often decked out in sumptuous

CURB BIT
ITALY, LATE 16TH
CENTURY
CMA 1916.1581 [71]

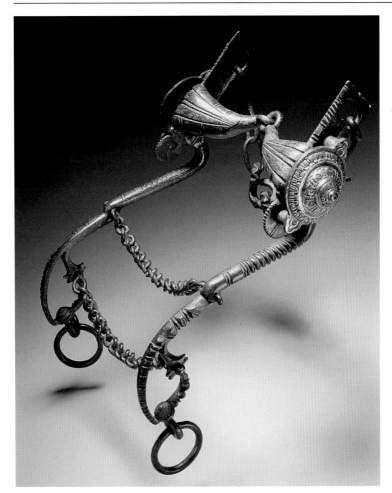

A well-constructed curb bit was an essential piece of equipment for keeping a powerful battle stallion under control. Like other horse trappings, bits were often elegantly fashioned and ornamented. This example has applied and gilded bosses.

trappings of velvet or brocade with the armorial bearings of its master embroidered in gold or silver thread. Gilt spurs were a well-guarded privilege that distinguished knights from other riders. Horsemen of lesser rank, such as sergeants or men-at-arms, were permitted only iron or brass spurs. Squires, as knights in training, however, had the right to wear silvered spurs.

Knights often maintained their martial skills during times of peace by competing in tournaments. Much surviving armor appears to have been made specifically for use in tournaments—the great sporting and social events of the

Fastened to a knight's heels by means of straps and buckles, the spur was used to prod the horse into action. These examples are of the oldest type known. The "prick" spur was so called because its neck terminated in a spike.

PAIR OF PRICKED
SPURS
SPAIN(?),
13TH CENTURY
CMA 1916.1953 [74];
1916.1611 [73]

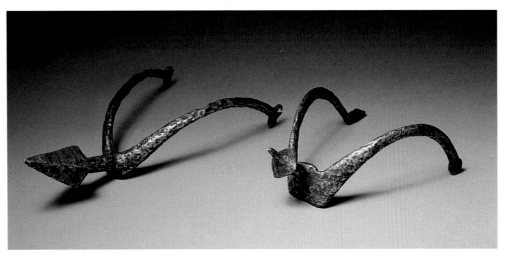

Middle Ages—and might be compared with the protective gear worn by today's hockey or football player. Historically, tournaments seem to have begun around 1100 as a mock combat between two groups of mounted warriors for the purpose of warfare training. On these occasions, the same armor and weapons were used as in battle, often with fatal results. Despite initial disapproval by the Church, tournaments flourished and placed special emphasis upon individual knightly prowess. The losers in such early tournaments were not "killed" but "captured" by the victor, who might demand as his ransom the loser's horse, armor, and a payment of money. By the end of the twelfth century, Richard I of England had legalized tournaments and introduced certain controls. They were now held by permission of the king and were subject to a special tax.

By 1200, however, the tournament had become a purely sporting occasion at which knights displayed their courage and skill. The growing emphasis on the

Der Weisskunig *(Story of the White King) is the illustrated autobiography of Maximilian I—a somewhat fanciful account commissioned in 1505. The popularity of tournaments peaked around 1500, and by Maximilian's reign there were at least eleven different forms of mounted jousts. This scene depicts tilting in the background, and in the foreground a form of jousting without a tilt barrier that was popular only in the Germanic lands. Blinders over the horses' eyes prevented distraction.*

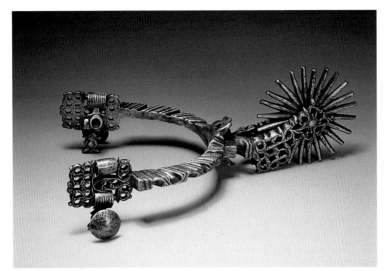

Instead of a "prick" terminus at the neck, the rowel spur had a rotating wheel installed between two prongs. This type of spur gradually supplanted the prick spur as a safer and less severe alternative for the horse. Rowel spurs first appeared during the thirteenth century and were in general use by the fourteenth century.

prowess of the individual knight fostered new forms of combat, such as the duel on horseback called the joust, or the duel on foot. In the joust, blunted lances were increasingly used; the objective was usually to break lances, but in some forms the aim was to unhorse one's opponent. The tournament evolved mainly into a social event after 1400, in which actual combat was combined with feasts, pageants, music, and dance, all with some common theme of romantic chivalry. Only the monarch himself could afford to stage such a festival, and only the great nobility could afford to take part.

Emperor Maximilian I, from 1493 to 1519 the ruler of much of central Europe as well as the Low Countries, surpassed every other monarch in the extravagance of his tournaments. Among the many forms of the joust which he devised was a combat with sharp lances in which the jousters were protected by great shields of wood and leather. These shields were bolted to the armor by the large guards on the knights' lances, and by metal plates or sockets hanging from

Images of the trials and tribulations of love were readily appreciated by the noble, secular clientele of medieval France, for whom this casket was intended. The original owner would have been steeped in romantic tales of chivalry. At center, two knights in mail, surcoats, and helms joust with blunted lances "for courtesy"—a version known as the Joust of Peace. Spectators watch from the balcony above. To the right, soldiers attempt to scale the walls of the Castle of Love while others launch a catapult filled with rose petals. This siege is known to have been enacted in Treviso, Italy, in 1214.

THREE VIEWS OF A
JOUSTING HELM
(STECHHELM),
C. 1498
ALBRECHT DÜRER
(GERMAN,
NUREMBERG,
1471–1528)
CABINET DES
DESSINS, MUSÉE DU
LOUVRE, PARIS

This distinctive jousting headpiece, known as a "frog-mouthed" helm, had to be securely fastened to the cuirass with strong mounts in order to withstand the massive shock of the pointed lances. The combatant would have worn a padded cap within the helmet to further cushion the blow. Many artists of the day, including Dürer, provided sketches or working designs for interested clients.

the saddle over the thighs. Such sporting combats necessitated the development of special armor such as the distinctive "frog-mouthed" helm, which the armor workshops of Nuremberg specialized in making. A drawing of one of these helmets made by Albrecht Dürer in 1498 has survived along with a number of actual examples. As the combatants approached each other in a joust, they leaned for-

PAIR OF BRASS
STIRRUPS
ENGLAND(?),
17TH CENTURY
CMA 1919.49.1–2 [80]

With the aid of stirrups, the knight could rise (especially during jousts) and, buttressed against the high cantle of the saddle, was able to bend forward in order to gain the full advantage of the weight of his own armor and that of his horse. The footplate of the stirrup gradually became wider, as shown by these seventeenth-century examples.

FIELD ARMOR FOR
MAN AND HORSE
WITH THE ARMS OF
THE VÖLS-
COLONNA FAMILY
NORTH ITALY,
C. 1575
CMA 1964.88 [6]

A knight depended on his horse as both a weapon and a means of defense, and thus went to great lengths to care for and protect his charger. From the 1100s on, knights first covered their steeds in trappings of fabric and later of mail. By around 1400, full steel plate armor for horses was complete. The total combined weight of the armor shown here is 114 pounds.

ward in order to see through the sights at the top of their helms. Just before they met, each straightened so that his face was completely protected against a possible lance blow. The thickness of the steel plates composing these helms is suggested by the weight of one example in Nuremberg: twenty-three pounds. A complete suit of tournament armor could total more than one hundred pounds. However, such suits were worn for relatively short periods of time.

Although the tilt was the most popular type of jousting practiced in the sixteenth century, the *mêlée*—fought between two teams of contestants in a confusing jumble of horses and riders—remained in widespread favor and often formed the climax of the greatest tournaments. It was fought in what was basically ordinary field armor fitted with special reinforcements on the left-hand side. Sometimes, after contestants had broken their lances, they discarded their reinforcements before continuing to fight with blunted swords. The German artist Lucas Cranach

This armor was designed specifically for the foot tournament, an event separate from the equestrian jousts. The original owner of this suit would have worn it with colorful puffed and slashed britches and hose.

The use of accessories such as a large ostrich feather plume and red velvet pickadils between the steel plates would have provided additional sartorial splendor.

the Elder was fond of sketching colorful tournament scenes, which he often transferred in faithful detail to woodblocks.

Another tournament contest was the foot combat, which may have originated as the continuation of the joust after one of the combatants had been unhorsed. It later developed into a separate event with its own forms of armor and weapons (the two-handed sword and the pole axe being particularly popular). After a time, combats on foot came to be fought over a barrier that separated the combatants and protected their legs, and thus a half-armor became sufficient. From about 1500, instead of wearing specialized armors for each form of combat, the wealthiest patrons began to use the same basic field armor for each, with reinforcing or alternate pieces added according to the nature of the contest. This type of armor, known as a garniture, could be assembled in different ways for use in battle or tournaments.

PORTRAIT OF
LUCIO FOPPA
(DETAIL)
AMBROGIO FIGINO
(ITALIAN, MILAN,
1548–1608)
PINACOTECA DI
BRERA, MILAN

The growing relationship of armor to costume is suggested by this portrait in which the sitter's armor is etched with the same motif that is embroidered on his trunk hose. Armor could be worn with costume accessories to provide a look of great ostentation, which was of paramount importance for public spectacles such as tournaments or parades. Most wealthy patrons could afford the additional expense of embellishing their armors. The armor by Pompeo della Cesa (opposite page) may have been worn in such a fashion.

A TOURNAMENT
SCENE, DATED 1509
LUCAS CRANACH
THE ELDER
(GERMAN, SAXONY,
1472–1553)
DUDLEY P. ALLEN
FUND
CMA 1927.204

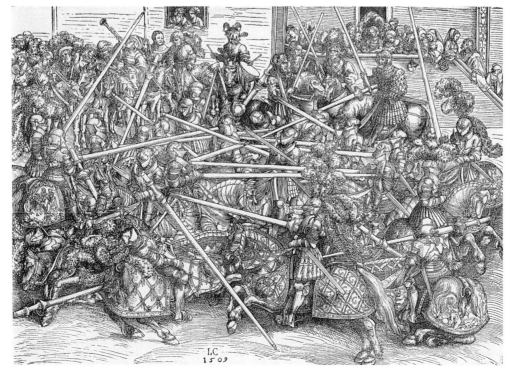

Group engagements known as the mêlée, fought between two teams of contestants, gained favor during the sixteenth century. These events were often fraught with confusion and chaos, as shown in this woodcut.

WAR HAT (OR
KETTLE HAT)
MISSAGLIA
WORKSHOP
ITALY, MILAN,
PERHAPS 1475–1500
CMA 1916.1565 [50]

Open helmets like this one were in use from the thirteenth through the fifteenth centuries and are the ancestor of today's common military helmet. Such helmets were worn by foot soldiers as they attempted to scale the walls of an armed

town. The slight ridge, or comb, down the center served to improve deflection and increase strength. The rivets along the rim were not only decorative, but a means of attachment for a liner.

Medieval Warfare

I love the gay Eastertide, which brings forth leaves and flowers. . . . It gives me great joy to see, drawn up on the field, knights and horses in battle array. And it delights me when the skirmishers scatter people and herds in their path.
—BERTRAND DE BORN, LATE TWELFTH CENTURY

The Role of Cavalry and Infantry

The conventional picture of medieval warfare is one of "mounted shock combat" in which heavy cavalry armed with couched lances decided the outcome of a battle in a single glorious charge. While such images are certainly rooted in historical reality, medieval military campaigns were normally complex exercises involving large infantry corps, laborers (who carried no weapons), foragers, and fireraisers, in addition to elite cavalries composed of wealthy knights. It has been traditionally held by historians that the introduction of the stirrup in western Europe around AD 700 made mounted shock combat possible by literally anchoring the knight to his charger, thus allowing both to function as one irresistible unit. This point of view, however, has been largely superseded. Historians now recognize that the Roman cavalry saddle provided considerable support and that the stirrup made far less difference than previously supposed. There is also no evidence for the couched-lance technique (jousting) before the late eleventh century, nor was the stirrup introduced in a revolutionary instant, but rather in a gradual and patchy way. Nevertheless, the couched-lance technique, especially when combined with the "wraparound" saddles of about 1100, made European cavalries more potent. The primary function of mounted shock combat was to neutralize an opponent's cavalry. These tactics required tremendous discipline, patience, and impeccable timing if a charge was to be successful. Properly executed, the charge or "joust" was capable of shattering any body of troops.

Knights tended to fight in small tactical units of "friends" who had trained together in tournaments—units that formed the basic components of larger battles. Cavalries were expected to keep close order and to endure the enemy's provocative taunts pending the charge, which was conducted in line. The joust was only the first round in a battle. Fighting then continued with sword and mace, on foot if necessary. From around 1300 onward, the lance became much heavier and required the use of a lance-rest affixed to the knight's steel breastplate in order to hold it steady at speed.

Such clashes between heavy cavalries were far rarer than medieval writers—who tended to concentrate upon the exploits and heroic deeds of the nobility—would have us suppose. During the Middle Ages unsupported cavalries were never superior forces. Only when combined with large numbers of infantry, particularly archers, did they play a significant role in warfare. The Welsh chronicler Geoffrey of Monmouth (c. 1100–1154) in his *History of the Kings of Britain,* written about 1138, describes the battle fought between King Arthur and his nephew Mordred. In his text Geoffrey conveys the effectiveness of a combined infantry and cavalry in his own day:

> Profiting from their long experience in warfare, [Arthur's men] drew up
> their troops most skillfully. They mixed their infantry with the cavalry

The Battle of Nancy on January 7, 1477, between the forces of the King of France and the King of Feuereisen (the fictionalized name for Charles the Bold, Duke of Burgundy) involved early artillery, visible in the distant background. The cavalry, heavily armored in close helmets, fight with lances and swords. Of particular interest is the unarmored infantry's use of the pike, a long, small-headed spear, as a lethal hedge against cavalry charges.

and fought in such a way that when the line of foot soldiers moved up to the attack, or was merely holding its position, the cavalry charged at an angle and did all that they could to break through the enemy lines and to force them to run away.

By the fourteenth century, densely packed infantries armed with "hafted" weapons such as spears, halberds, and pikes had demonstrated success in defeating armored cavalries at Courtrai (1302) and Bannockburn (1314). At the Battle of Crécy in 1346, the massed ranks of the English infantry used one of the most potent weapons against "the flower of French knighthood": the longbow. These bows, made of six-foot-long staves of yew or elm, fired steel-tipped armor-piercing

(Right) In 1346, in the small town of Crécy in northern France, the English forces of Edward III (at right) met and defeated the French armies of Philip VI in a major battle of the Hundred Years' War. French nobles were decimated by the English longbows (lower right), which appeared for the first time on the Continent. Note the use of crossbows by the French, a slower and less accurate weapon.

CLOSE HELMET
GERMANY,
C. 1510–30
CMA 1923.1067.A [5]

A helmet of true "close-helmet" construction, pivoting open at the rivets on the sides.

THE BATTLE OF CRÉCY, 1346 (FROM *FROISSART'S CHRONICLES*)
FRANCE,
15TH CENTURY
BIBLIOTHÈQUE
NATIONALE DE
FRANCE, PARIS
MS. FR. 2643,
FOL. 165V

arrows with great accuracy. The effect against the French at Crécy was devastating: fifteen hundred knights and squires killed as opposed to English losses of only one hundred men. The French crossbowmen at Crécy had to laboriously prime their weapons by hand-cranking a windlass each time they wanted to fire a single bolt. By contrast, the English longbowmen could shoot ten arrows per minute and with far greater accuracy. With time, the increasing use and effectiveness of gunpowder began to affect armor and weapons. Firearms eventually replaced the longbow and crossbow, but certain hafted weapons such as the pike, a steel-tipped staff weapon measuring from twelve to twenty-two feet in length, remained effective through the end of the seventeenth century.

Fortifications and Siege Warfare

Medieval society was held together by a web of personal relationships among kings, noblemen, and clergy. Nothing epitomized strength, authority, and security more than the castle, with its crenelated towers, moats, and impregnable walls. Thousands of these residence fortresses were built throughout the Middle Ages all the

FRONT PANEL OF A BRIGANDINE (FRONT AND BACK VIEWS) ITALY(?), C. 1500–25 CMA 1921.1250 [39]

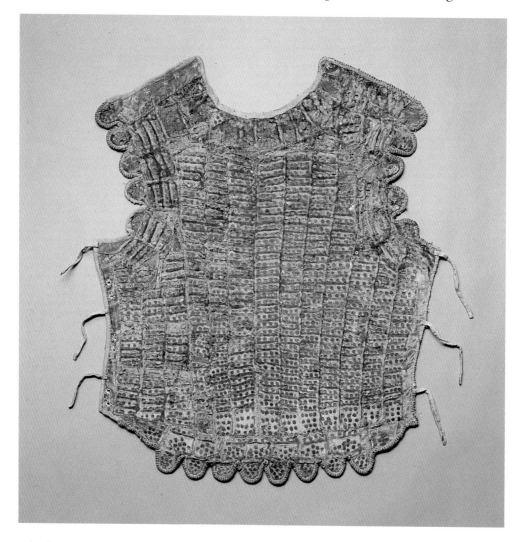

The brigandine was a vest-like body defense popular with both knights and infantry from the 1400s through about 1550 (see previous illustration). It is constructed of multiple small steel plates riveted to the interior of a cloth covering. Finer examples, like this one, are faced in velvet or even fabric made of gold thread. The brigandine gave some protection from the elements and was relatively light and extremely flexible.

way from Ireland to Palestine. The simple truth is that the conduct of warfare during medieval times depended on the control of fortifications such as castles or towns fortified by walls. Frontier areas in particular were often heavily fortified as a means of putting down popular resistance as, for example, the Welsh borders under King Edward I's reign (1272–1307). Latin Syria, Spain, the Baltic lands, and other territories on the periphery of Christendom were similarly dotted with castles. Thus, in order to control territory, it was incumbent upon the occupier to fortify its strategic places: sites overlooking coastal areas, rivers, plains, or mountain passes. In addition to serving as bastions of defense, castles could provide forward support bases for armies on the move. During peacetime they were administrative centers, residences for Europe's aristocratic elite, treasuries, prisons, and munitions depots. In the medieval world, military success was often defined by an army's ability either to defend or to capture a castle or a fortified town.

The quickest method of attack for an army was to simply storm the defenses of a fortress using siege ladders to scale the walls. This was not always possible, however, since the architecture of fortification is based on the principle of plac-

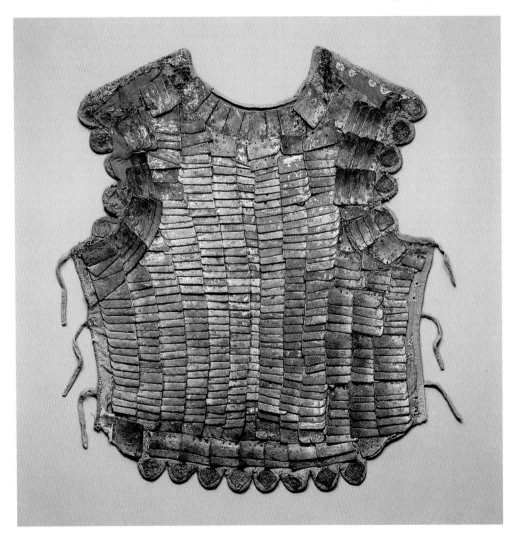

ing a series of obstacles in the way of an attacker. As assault soldiers overcame each of these obstacles, the defenders were theoretically able to reduce the overall number of attackers. Moats and ditches prevented progress up the outer walls where protruding towers, manned by defending archers and crossbowmen, could rain down a hail of flanking fire. Stones and other heavy projectiles could be hurled down on the attackers, as could boiling tar, pitch, or water, thus either slowing or preventing their progress. Should the walls be breached, castle design, especially after the thirteenth century, featured a series of gateways and passageways protected by movable grills called portcullises. These could be lowered at strategic places to entrap enemy soldiers, who could then be picked off by defenders firing above from apertures known as "murdering holes" (*meurtrières*). At the very center of the castle would be found the keep, an immensely strong tower intentionally difficult to access. The keep served as a final defensive position for the defenders. Siege warfare developed as a response to these gradual improvements in defensive fortifications, which in turn led to new and innovative siege weapons and techniques.

To evade these defenses and prevail, an attacker had to go over, through, or mine under the walls of a fortress. Generally, castles were so well fortified that such methods were difficult and costly. An alternative was blockade. Indeed, some besieging armies elected to allow starvation, disease, or treachery bring about the surrender of the occupants. By strict definition, a siege is a passive operation. It requires that the besieging army surround the fortress, cut it off from communications and supply, and wait for lack of food, water, or ammunition to compel surrender. Given sufficient time and patience, this system does not fail. However, patience was usually lacking among medieval armies, whose ranks would frequently lose interest and return home during harvest time. Attacking armies,

This miniature from a manuscript made for Philip the Good, a Burgundian duke, provides a graphic glimpse into medieval siege warfare. The use of mobile siege towers is clearly visible as the attacking army attempts to breach the town's walled defenses. While the scene is meant to represent Jerusalem, it could easily be any fortified town in French Flanders or the Lowlands.

THE STORMING OF JERUSALEM (FROM THE *CHRONIQUE DE JERUSALEM ABRÉGÉES*), C. 1450
MASTER OF THE GIRART DE ROUSSILLON (FRENCH, ACTIVE C. 1450–70)
ÖSTERREICHISCHE NATIONAL-BIBLIOTHEK, VIENNA
MS. 2533, FOL. 7V

THREE HALBERDS
GERMANY AND
SWITZERLAND,
16TH AND 17TH
CENTURIES
CMA 1916.1562 [105];
1916.1559 [103];
1916.1554 [101]

The halberd was a favored and highly specialized staff weapon of central European infantries. Its axe blade was used for hacking, the spike for thrusting, and the beak either for piercing armor plate or for pulling a knight from his saddle. It was wielded with great effect by Swiss and German mercenaries.

therefore, had various techniques and siege machines at their disposal to hurry the process along and to bring about faster capitulation.

As a first measure, attackers could begin by filling in the ditch with brushwood and earth to allow access to the outer wall. They might then choose to surmount the wall using various scaling ladders, some of which were expandable in height. Another alternative was the use of a mobile siege tower on wheels called a *beffroy,* or belfry, which carried assault soldiers and crossbowmen within its wooden interior. These towers, covered in wet hide to protect them from fire, could be pushed up against the defenders' wall. At this point the tower's drawbridge was released and the attackers raced out to engage in hand-to-hand combat with the wall's defenders. If successful, the attackers could secure a position and eventually open the castle's gates for the main force waiting outside. The *Gesta Francorum* provides the following description of the siege of Jerusalem in 1099 and the crusader army's use of such devices:

> Then our commanders made arrangements for Jerusalem to be captured with siege engines, so that our men could enter to worship at the church of the Holy Sepulchre. They made two wooden siege towers, and many other devices. Godfrey of Bouillon made his own siege tower with machines in it, and so too did Raymond of Toulouse; the wood for these things had to be dragged from a considerable distance away. The Saracens inside the city, seeing that our men were making these devices, made remarkable improvements in its fortifications and had the towers nightly increased in height.

The danger in using these scaling towers lay in their vulnerability to fire from incendiary arrows from above. Belfrys were literal deathtraps for the assault troops crammed within their wooden interiors. They were also susceptible to bogging down on uneven terrain or even toppling over.

It was also possible to breach a fortified wall at ground level through "mining." Specially trained soldiers or "miners" could work with picks at the base of the wall to engineer a breach or a collapse of a section. Movable shields or sheds were specially designed to provide cover for the besieging soldiers as they picked away at the foundations of a castle's walls, as illustrated in countless medieval miniatures. Above, the defenders would hurl heavy stones or incendiary materials onto the men below. The main technique for mining, however, involved digging an underground tunnel up to the wall or tower, then digging a hollowed chamber beneath it. The chamber was shored up by wooden beams which at the appropriate moment were set alight, thus collapsing the chamber and the masonry above it. The only countermeasure available to the fortification's defenders was to dig a second tunnel in the hope of intercepting the attackers' tunnel.

Instead of going over or under the defenders' walls, the final option was to go *through* them using a variety of rams and catapults. This was the third line of attack. Used effectively and given enough time, such "siege machines" were capable of reducing a section of wall entirely or punching a hole through it. The ram was a thick beam of wood with a pointed iron head, suspended from an armature with thick ropes and swung back and forth by a team of soldiers against the masonry in order to break it down on impact. The soldiers deploying a ram usually required protection from defenders hurling heavy projectiles or flammable pitch down upon them. The solution was to house the ram within a wheeled shed with an armored roof. The soldiers themselves wore heavy armor and special helmets for additional protection.

For battering an enemy's walls from a safer distance, various artillery pieces called "siege engines" were devised, though in truth the attackers would attempt to bring these devices as close to an enemy's walls as possible for greatest effect. The oldest of these (used at Paris as early as 885–86) was the *ballista,* a kind of giant crossbow. Using torsion, the bolts, stone balls, and javelins that the ballista hurled generally did little to breach a fortified wall, but the device was a weapon of terror capable of inflicting horrible, usually fatal, wounds upon the defenders. The *mangonel* was a large catapult which, like the ballista, used torsion to project a missile from the end of a beam—usually large stones capable over time and in sufficient numbers of damaging fortifications. The *trebuchet* was another form of the catapult. Instead of torsion, the trebuchet depended on a heavy swinging beam with a counterweight to launch stones or flammable objects. Trebuchets were considered the most useful form of artillery before the development of gunpowder weaponry. Attackers would sometimes resort to a kind of "biological warfare" and hurl unspeakable objects—rotting corpses of men or animals, severed heads of slain or captured enemy troops—into the castle or town. These tactics were meant to spread disease and to demoralize the defenders into submission.

Gunpowder had begun to reach western Europe by the middle of the twelfth century, and with the introduction of siege guns the advantage in fortification warfare began to move from the defenders to the besiegers. Siege engines like the trebuchet were gradually supplemented by and eventually replaced by gunpowder artillery. The earliest cannons, often pictured in fifteenth-century miniatures

This woodcut shows armored cavalry with lances approaching from the left. The town itself is ringed by artillery, as attacking infantry rush through the breached fortifications. Note the use of halberds and pikes.

and woodcuts, were little more than simple tubes of no great size. They were probably cast in bronze or iron using technology already mastered in bell foundries. The cannons used at Crécy in 1346 were made of iron bars welded together and bound by hoops. Not surprisingly, these early cannons were as dangerous to the gunners as they were to the enemy. Barrels often exploded or fired their projectiles so inaccurately as to kill friendly troops.

By 1400 a bewildering variety of guns existed in Europe, ranging from *culverins* to huge *bombards* that were moved by water or on four-wheeled carts. Wrought iron cannons could now fire balls weighing two hundred to more than four hundred pounds. High stone walls that for many centuries defied stone-throwing engines now collapsed under the high-velocity impact of large siege guns like the bombard. One such iron bombard, known as "Mons Meg" and cast in Burgundy in 1449 (now at Edinburgh Castle), is fifteen feet in length and weighs eight and a half tons. It used more than one hundred pounds of gunpowder to fire a ball weighing over five hundred pounds. The Ottoman Turks used guns like "Mons Meg" with devastating effect at the siege of Constantinople in 1453, in which the city's heavy walls were eventually breached after continuous bombardment.

PARTIAL SUIT OF
ARMOR IN
MAXIMILIAN STYLE
GERMANY,
NUREMBERG,
C. 1525
CMA 1916.1714.A–J
[2]

70

Manufacture and Decoration

And a helmet well beaten
From steel soft and malleable,
Many markings so beautiful
Thereon were found,
By the smith's masterly hand
Strewn in the metal's sheen.
—*BITEROLF UND DIETLEIB, C. 1250*

A complete suit of plate armor was designed not only for personal protection, but also for weight and comfort. It was constructed from numerous individual plates of steel, sometimes more than two hundred, of which no two were identical. Making a suit of armor was thus a tedious, labor-intensive, time-consuming, and strenuous process that required the skills of a number of craftsmen: an armorer to forge the plates; a polisher (or "millman") to polish the plates; a finisher to assemble the plates into a suit and fit the pieces with fasteners, pads, and straps; and, finally, a decorator—a goldsmith or etcher—to embellish the armor.

The metal used in armor construction did not necessarily need to be of great weight and thickness to provide effective defense. It is erroneous to assume that fine suits of armor are extremely heavy, or to associate strength with great weight. However, the construction of a suit of armor required considerable technical skill and experience, as well as a substantial knowledge of metal.

Making the Steel

The medieval armorer began the long process of making a suit of plate armor with a "billet," a small unfinished bar of iron or steel, usually less than twenty-five square inches in area. Billets were not made by the armorer himself but rather in iron-producing centers, which by necessity were located in ore-bearing regions. It is thus not by coincidence that the major armor-producing workshops at Nuremberg, Augsburg, and Milan were situated near the source of the raw material. The ultimate quality and reliability of a suit of armor rested not only on the skills of the armorer, but also on the hardness of the steel. Medieval metalworkers were adept at refining iron into steel, and at strengthening steel through the technical processes of quenching, tempering, and case hardening.

While some armor was wrought from iron, steel—recognized very early to be harder and more durable than iron—was the preferred material for plate armor. The raw material for steel was iron ore, which was mined and then melted

Distinguished by its regularly fluted surfaces, which created a dazzling effect in sunlight, armor in the "Maximilian" style (left) was popularized in South Germany and Austria during the first decades of the sixteenth century. The style's name derives from its introduction during Maximilian I's reign as Holy Roman Emperor (1493–1519). Perhaps originally meant to imitate the pleatings of contemporary male costumes, the flutings were also a strengthening device similar to corrugated metal. This enabled the armorer to use plates of thinner and thus lighter steel. Such suits of armor demanded time-consuming and highly precise work, which quickly drove production costs high enough that the fashion disappeared by 1540.

The chanfron consisted of a plate of steel contoured to the horse's head from its ears to its nostrils. Normally, holes were cut at each side of the forehead for the ears, and earpieces were sometimes riveted around their edges. This example, however, was forged in one piece. It belongs to the transitional period between the Gothic and the fluted armors introduced by Emperor Maximilian. The hinge at the top is for attachment of the crest plate.

in a furnace to produce a "bloom"—a spongy piece of newly made iron ready for further working. To prepare steel for the armorer's workshop the direct method was used, in which the iron bloom was not removed immediately from the furnace and allowed to cool but remained in the furnace longer to be exposed to hot carbon monoxide gas. The iron absorbed the gas and resulted in a bloom of higher carbon content (that is to say, steel).

The quality of medieval steel varied considerably. While numerous legends arose in the Middle Ages and after as to secret, almost alchemic, processes for making hardened, superior steel, the real secret lay in the ore itself. Some regions produced iron ore suitable for armor making, while other regions were home to ore completely ill suited for this purpose. We know, for instance, that the excellence of steel made at Innsbruck was the result of the manganese in the ore. Konrad Seusenhofer, Maximilian I's court armorer, complained that his mine master was supplying him with inferior metal. Seusenhofer believed that this metal would detract from Innsbruck's reputation as a leading center for armor production, and suggested that it be classed as "Milanese," after a competing city.

One of the advantages of using steel to make armor was that its hardness could be improved by the quenching process, which involved plunging red-hot steel into a cold medium like water to induce rapid cooling; the more rapid the cooling, the harder the steel. This process resulted in extremely hard steel that unfortunately was often also brittle. An improved method was to quench the steel, then reheat it gradually to temper it and reduce its brittleness. Many of these technical processes for making steel and hardening it through quenching and tempering are described in medieval "recipe" books. Ultimately, the armorer's success at working the steel depended on his ability to control the temperature of the steel while forging it.

Forging the Plates

The next step was to hammer the billets into flat plates, which in turn could be shaped into the required armor elements. This was strenuous work carried out by hand, although eventually water-driven tilt hammers were used for the preliminary work. It seems that while some armorers did this job themselves, the usual practice was for the steel-making center to hammer the billets into plates for shipment to the armorer's workshop.

The armorer would cut the steel plates into the rough shape needed to form a specific armor, such as a helmet or breastplate. An armorer made patterns much like those used by tailors in order to see the flat shape of the various pieces before hammering. He would then begin to work the steel in its cold state by hammering it out until a basic shape was achieved. It appears that the plates were subsequently hammered over metal formers or "dies" corresponding to the final shape desired. These formers, in use after the thirteenth century, essentially func-

Maximilian established his court armory at Innsbruck in 1504, and by 1508 Konrad Seusenhofer was supervising six journeymen, four polishers, and two apprentices. In this woodcut, the forge and its bellows are seen at the right, while the *master himself works alongside two journeymen at a common workbench littered with anvils of various forms and sizes. In the background are finished products.*

Popular throughout the sixteenth and seventeenth centuries, the burgonet was a light, open headpiece favored by cavalry and infantry alike. Its main features are a peak over the eyes and hinged cheekpieces that fasten with a strap or lace under the chin. The basic helmet lent itself to variations of design or ornamentation. This version, with its triple crests, is known to have been produced in Augsburg. The style was worn by the personal bodyguard of Emperor Charles V (ruled 1519–56).

tioned as anvils of varying shapes and sizes onto which the armorer hammered the now-hot metal. Large numbers of them were kept in the workshop to accommodate the many types, styles, and sizes of armor elements. According to woodcut illustrations such as Hans Burgkmair's depiction of Seusenhofer's workshop, these anvils could be inserted into a hole in the armorer's workbench and changed as needed.

Though no medieval treatise on the making of armor has survived, we know much about this process from illuminated miniatures in early books, woodcut illustrations like Burgkmair's, and a few paintings such as *Venus at the Forge of Vulcan* by Jan Breughel. In many of these illustrations the armorer is shown holding the metal with his bare hand while hammering with the other, a clear indication that the metal was cold at the time. Most representations of armorers' workshops show a nearby forge (a special furnace or hearth used to heat metal for shaping), indicating that the armor plates, while worked cold at various stages, were often

BURGONET
("CASQUETELE"
TYPE)
ITALY, MILAN(?),
C. 1510–40
CMA 1916.1642 [51]

reheated during this process. Heat was needed both to anneal the metal and to render it malleable for working such details as fine rope edges.

The shaped plates were graduated in thickness according to the vulnerability of different body parts. Not only did the thickness of individual plates vary, but so did different areas of the same plate. Thus, a breastplate was made thicker than a backplate, and the breastplate was made thicker at its center to protect vital areas such as the heart. The individual pieces also were fashioned to present a glancing surface to an opponent's weapon. With the advancing sophistication of firearms in the sixteenth century, so-called "armor of proof" was developed. Simply put, armor of proof was guaranteed to resist contemporary firearms. To test the armor plates, the armorer fired a pistol from twenty paces at his finished pieces. The resulting dent from the bullet was left in place as "proof" of the armor's soundness.

Once all the plates constituting the soon-to-be suit of armor had been forged, the pieces could be assembled on a trial basis to check the exactness of the fit. This was an important stage. It was essential that all the pieces functioned with precision, allowing the wearer to move with articulation. Unless pieces overlapped correctly, dangerous gaps would appear as the wearer moved. These flaws were corrected by repeated filing and hammering until the fit was precise.

Polishing, Fitting, and Assembling the Armor Plates

After the trial fitting, the unassembled pieces would be passed to the next crafts-man, the polisher (called a "millman" in England). At this stage the pieces were still blackened from repeated heating in the forge and covered with dimple marks from hammer blows. The larger armor workshops such as those at Innsbruck, Augsburg, or Greenwich employed several of these specialized craftsmen to smooth the metal surface of the armor and polish it to a silver-bright finish. Most

Etching, by far the most common technique for armor decoration, involved the use of a graving tool assisted by acid to create a design. The etched design could be blackened to create contrast, as shown here. This field armor, now lacking its lower elements, has been etched along its borders.

On the breastplate, pauldrons, and tassets, etched medallions enclose profile busts reminiscent of Roman portraiture. This decorative style was commonly found on armor produced in Milan and Brescia during the second half of the sixteenth century.

BREASTPLATE WITH
ETCHED FIGURE
KNEELING BEFORE
THE CRUCIFIXION
GERMANY,
NUREMBERG,
C. 1550
CMA 1916.1647 [30]

This breastplate exemplifies the superb sculptural forms achieved by Renaissance armorers. During the mid-sixteenth century and later, South German armorers frequently used the etched motif of a kneeling knight before the Crucifixion, perhaps as a personalized devotional image for the warrior in battle.

of the polishing was first done by hand. In the larger workshops, however, rapidly turning water-powered polishing wheels expedited the process, illustrated occasionally in miniatures and drawings from contemporary sources.

Next, the polished pieces were delivered to the finisher or perhaps to the master armorer for assembly. Each of the individual pieces (sometimes as many as two hundred) had to be attached to one another in the correct order to ensure a perfect fit and ease of movement. The plates were attached by rivets, either plate to plate or, as in the case of *lames*—overlapping plates of metal that formed a flexible defense—to leather straps running along the inside of the plates. Another means of achieving mobility was through use of "sliding" rivets, an arrangement whereby rivets on one piece worked in a slot on the next.

BURGONET, BUFFE,
AND BREASTPLATE
WITH ETCHED
BANDS OF
TROPHIES AND
MEDALLIONS
NORTH ITALY,
C. 1550–1600
CMA 1916.1653 [56];
1916.1930 [37];
1916.1654 [31]

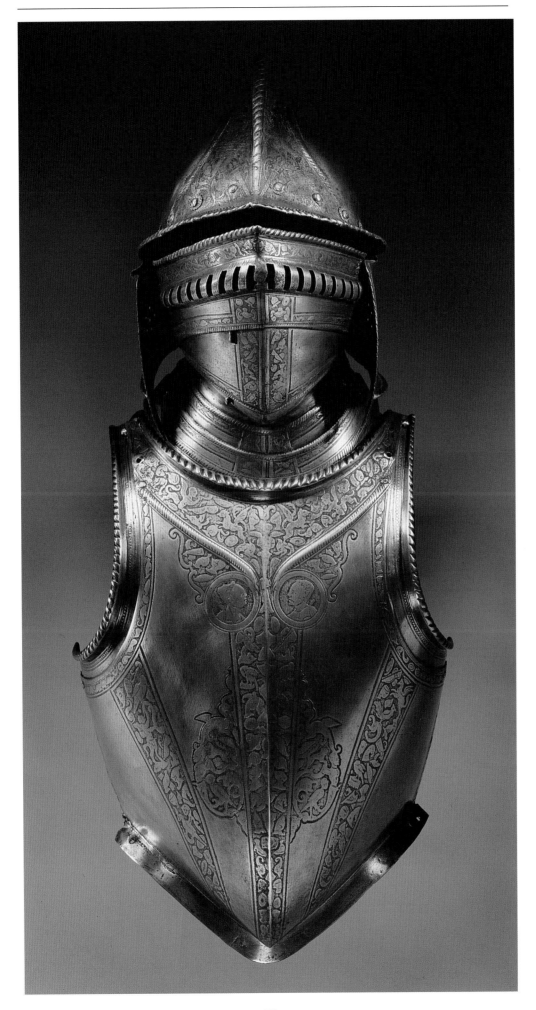

At this stage of the finishing work, hinges and buckles also were applied. Initially, brass hinges were affixed to the outside of the plates, but later on they were made of steel and riveted to the interior in order to save them from damage in combat. Straps and buckles were first used as fasteners to allow the wearer to get in and out of the armor. By the sixteenth century, a system of staples and holes had replaced straps for securing the pieces to the owner. The staple on the inner plate passed through a hole on the outer plate and was then fastened with a hook to prevent the two pieces from sliding apart.

Finally, various components of the suit of armor—the helmet interior, breastplate, and tassets, for example—were fitted with padded linings or velvet pickadils. These made the suit more comfortable to wear and prevented the plates from scratching during movement. The completed suit was inspected once again for fit and finish before the master armorer stamped his mark. The suit might then be subjected to yet another inspection by city examiners to ensure that it met set standards of quality. At Nuremberg, the final examiners stamped the city's half-eagle coat of arms on approved armor.

The sixteenth century saw the finest achievements of armor design. With the lavish patronage of princes and nobles, the fashion was set for extravagantly

Pompeo della Cesa—the most renowned Italian armorer of the late sixteenth century—maintained a large workshop in Milan's Sforza Castle. His wealthy clients, which included some of the most celebrated noblemen of their day, generally wanted their armor embellished. The etched and gilded decoration of this armor features vertical bands of strapwork enclosing cartouches, which in turn contain allegorical figures, classical warriors, and trophies. This represents Pompeo's classic style of armor decoration, found on more than forty surviving suits. These and other decorative designs were normally recorded in pattern books from which the prospective client made his selections.

HALF-ARMOR FOR THE FOOT TOURNAMENT,
C. 1590
POMPEO DELLA CESA
(ITALIAN, MILAN, ACTIVE 1572–93)
CMA 1996.299 [7]

BREASTPLATE (DETAIL)

decorated parade armors to be worn on official occasions, at court festivals, and
in official portraits. Almost all fine-quality armor now received decoration.

Engraving

Engraving, one of the oldest techniques for decorating metal objects, was used
throughout the seventeenth century to embellish both armor and arms. In antiquity, an incised pattern made with a pointed tool provided the simplest method
of decoration for bronze swords, axes, and spearheads. The technique involved the
manual incising of lines into the surface of the metal to create a pattern or image.
The artist used a sharp pointed instrument called a burin in what was a technically
difficult and laborious process requiring much skill. Engraving an iron or steel
surface is even more demanding, and thus its use for the decoration of armor was
limited. When engraving did appear on armor, it tended to be confined to borders made of latten, a brass-like alloy.

Nonetheless, in the hands of a skilled craftsman the burin and chisel could
be used effectively on steel plate. An armor made for Henry VIII of England in
1514–19, for example, was superbly engraved by Paul van Vrelant of Brussels with
entwined roses framing Saints George and Barbara (Royal Armouries, London).
The engraving technique was more frequently used to embellish the metal parts
of high-quality firearms. Its most common use, however, was for decorating bone,

MORION

NORTH ITALY,

C. 1575–1600

CMA 1916.1808 [60]

staghorn, and mother-of-pearl inlays on the stocks of firearms and powder flasks, where the artist could achieve a high level of contrast by filling the incised lines with black ink.

Etching

The most common decorative technique for armor was etching, particularly from the late fifteenth through the seventeenth centuries. In this technique either the design or its ground was "bitten" into the metal surface with acid, the rest being protected by a protective wax or varnish. Technically, etching steel was far easier than engraving or chiseling. It also enabled the artist to make changes or corrections while preparing the surface for the chemical process. Two forms of the technique were practiced: line etching and raised etching.

Line etching was developed in the late fifteenth century, though Italian books show that the method was known as early as the late fourteenth century. While in some cases this decorative technique might have been executed by the armorer himself, it usually was carried out by a specialized craftsman. First, the metal surface to be decorated was covered with an acid-resistant coating such as wax, varnish, oil paint, or even tar. Next the design was scratched into the metal through the protective medium, and the metal plate dipped into an acid bath. The acid would bite into the unprotected areas, leaving a permanent design. The coating was then removed with turpentine and the etched design was blackened, perhaps with a mixture of lamp black and oil. The decorative pattern now stood out in contrast against the burnished steel ground.

The technique of line etching on arms and armor was actually the precursor of printed etching since the etched design, with the application of printer's ink, could actually be printed on paper. Designs for decorative motifs were frequently published in pattern books, then copied or adapted by arms etchers. While the technique was understood and used in late medieval Italy, it was the German etchers of the sixteenth century who perfected the technique. One such master was Daniel Hopfer (c. 1470–1536), who along with his large family of arms etchers and printmakers made Augsburg famous for this decorative technique.

In the first quarter of the sixteenth century, the German etchers developed a variation of line etching known as raised etching. In this version of the technique, the design stands out in slight relief, with the background recessed and darkened. The protective wax or varnish was applied with a fine brush to those areas that were to be decorated with the elevated design. The background was usually decorated with small raised dots, formed by applying the protective medium with a quill. When the metal plate was exposed to a strong acid, the unprotected background area was eaten away, leaving the design in slight relief. This technique was preferred by arms etchers. The raised motifs could be further enlivened by gilding and blackening.

The morion was an open helmet characterized by a tall comb and curved brim peaking before and after. While popularly associated with the Spanish conquistadors in the New World, they were in fact worn by infantry and light horsemen throughout Europe. They also were commonly worn by palace guards and thus often were decorated. The Italian example at left has been beautifully etched over its entire surface.

Coloring: Gilding, Silvering, Bluing, Russeting

Gilding, a technique whereby a surface is embellished with gold, had been used to decorate armor since the thirteenth century. The most common application method was by firing, an extremely toxic process. In the fire-gilding method, the metal surface was prepared with a copper solution. Onto this was applied an amal-

CLOSE HELMET
AND GORGET
HOLLAND(?),
C. 1590–1625
CMA 1916.1787,
1916.1806 [57]

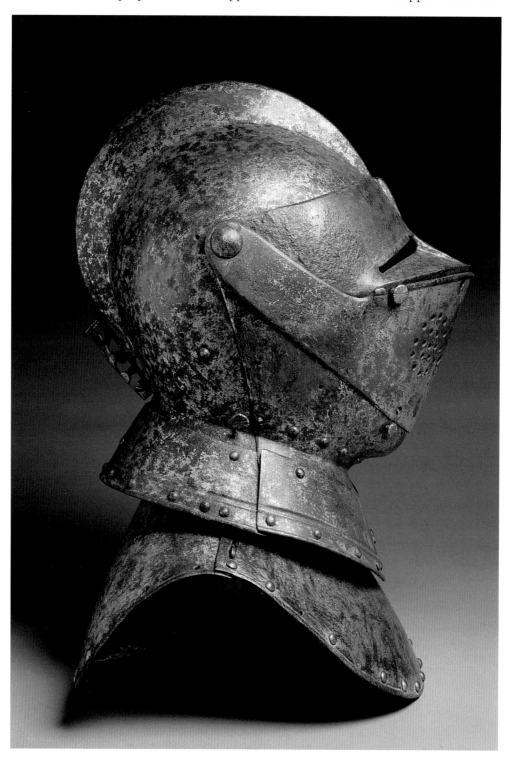

This helmet and gorget have been decorated by fire-gilding, an extremely toxic process that produced a look of great luxury. While originally part of a field armor, the pair appear to have later served a funerary purpose. They were probably suspended over a knight's tomb as "achievements"— a rich and imposing symbol of the dead man's social rank and authority.

gam of mercury and gold, which was then subjected to heat by firing. This firing process evaporated the mercury and left the gold adhering to the metal. It was also possible to apply gold to armor as "leaf," or foil. The gold leaf was applied to a freshly varnished surface with a paint brush. The piece was then heated slowly to dry the varnish and make the gold adhere. The gold leaf could then be burnished

PAULDRON FOR THE
RIGHT SHOULDER
(EXCHANGE PIECE
FOR FOOT COMBAT)
ITALY, C. 1600
CMA 1916.1524 [20]

This element for the shoulder once belonged to a suit decorated by the bluing technique, a process of superheating armor

plates to achieve a deep blue color. Gilding the borders created additional contrast for a refined appearance.

to a high luster. More rarely, armor was "silvered" by substituting silver foil for gold. In the "painter's gilding" method, a solution of varnish and gold dust was applied to the armor's surface and permitted to dry.

Gilding could be applied to the entire surface of a suit or, more commonly, to highlight selected areas such as crests of helmets or borders of breastplates. Gilding was commonly used in conjunction with other decorative techniques such as engraving and etching.

To coloristically tint armor by the bluing process, the metal plates were heated to an extremely high temperature—590 degrees Fahrenheit and above. At this temperature oxidation occurs and the metal turns a deep shade of blue; the steel is then quenched immediately. If only a partial bluing of the armor was required, the surface could be etched with a mild acid or warm vinegar to remove the coloration. The bluing of arms and armor—a technique used in German workshops from the fifteenth century onward—reached its height of fashion under the

BREASTPLATE

FROM A HUSSAR'S

CUIRASS

GERMANY
(AUGSBURG) OR
HUNGARY, C. 1580
CMA 1916.1521 [19]

This style of breastplate, with its numerous articulating lames, was probably used by Hungarian hussars, a type of light cavalryman. The steel plates were originally blued, now turned russet, and etched and gilded with strapwork bands, while the rows of vertical holes once provided gilt-brass settings for stones or glass-paste jewels. The effect would have suggested the semi-oriental costume and armor of the Near East favored by Polish and Hungarian armies of the late Renaissance.

Hapsburgs, particularly in Augsburg. It was often combined with border etching and gilding to achieve a stunning look of luxury, as on the suit made for Maximilian II (1527–1576) at Augsburg in 1557. Gilding and bluing gave armor a certain amount of protection against rust, and both techniques were frequently used to embellish sword blades during the eighteenth century.

A final technique for coloring armor plate was "russeting," or russet patination. This method, favored in France and England, imparted a pleasing brownish color to the metal surface. It was achieved by a chemical process that involved treating the steel surface with a mild corrosive medium. Like bluing, russeting provided the additional practical benefit of rust protection.

Damascening

Damascening originated in the Near East and was largely perfected by Muslim craftsmen, who disseminated it among Italian artisans. By the end of the fifteenth century, the technique was in use throughout Europe. It was eventually applied to arms and armor, first in Germany around 1520.

In damascening, gold and/or silver, which are relatively soft, are inlaid into the surface of a harder metal (bronze, iron, steel) for contrast and enrichment. This form of decoration—used to embellish not only armor but also weaponry such as sword hilts and gun barrels and locks—could be accomplished by one of two methods. The more refined method was to engrave a pattern into the surface of the metal to be decorated using a burin. Gold or silver wire was then hammered into the recesses and the entire surface polished. The silver and gold was held securely in place and might be allowed to stand out slightly in relief. In a variation of this technique known as stuck damascening, the steel surface was prepared by roughening or crosshatching. Gold and silver foils were then hammered into the metal surface and polished.

Embossing

The sixteenth century saw the revival of the ancient technique of embossing (*repoussé*). This technique had been used by goldsmiths throughout the Middle Ages and, with the advent of highly enriched and specialized parade armors, was gradually applied to the armor-making craft. In embossing, the pattern is first drawn onto the surface of the armor component. The plate is then hammered and punched from the inside to gradually shape the desired raised design on the outer surface of the metal.

In 1477 the Augsburg armorer Lorenz Helmschmid had embossed a horse barde fashioned for Emperor Frederick III. In the sixteenth century, however, only the costliest of armors were embossed. The technique was usually carried out in a highly specialized way to emulate the antique (*all'antica*) style harking back to the classical heritage of Greece and Rome. Outstanding but very expensive embossed suits—commonly enriched with gold and silver—were fashioned for the most wealthy of patrons. The embossed decoration of the famous "Hercules Armor" of Emperor Maximilian II, for example, was carried out by Eliseus Libaerts of Antwerp in the middle of the century. Other embossed armors were made for

BLACK AND WHITE ELBOW GAUNTLET FOR THE RIGHT HAND
NORTH GERMANY, C. 1570
CMA 1916.1082 [12]

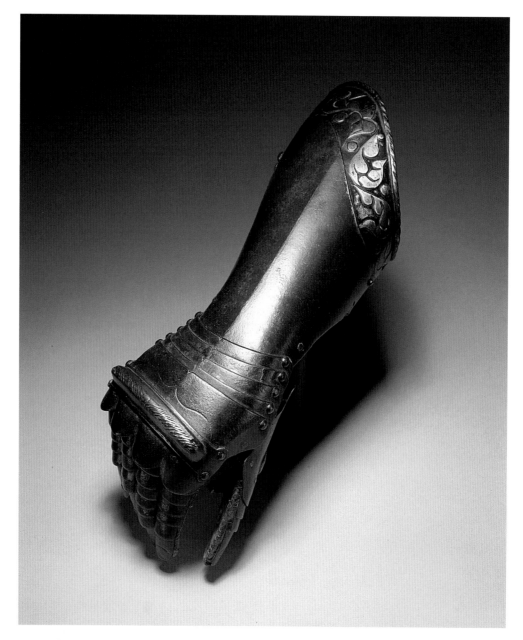

the kings of Portugal, Sweden, and France between the middle and end of the century.

Embossing was sometimes used in conjunction with other decorative techniques. An example is the "Lion Armor" made in Italy or France around 1550 and today preserved in the Tower of London. The suit is so named because of its embossed lions' masks, but is also decorated with gold damascening set against a black ground.

Plate armor alternately decorated with brightly polished ("white") and darkened ("black") surface areas is commonly referred to as "black and white" armor. The black color results from painting the surface areas, or merely leaving them dark from the forging process. The gauntlet illustrated below and at left has been additionally embellished with an embossed cuff.

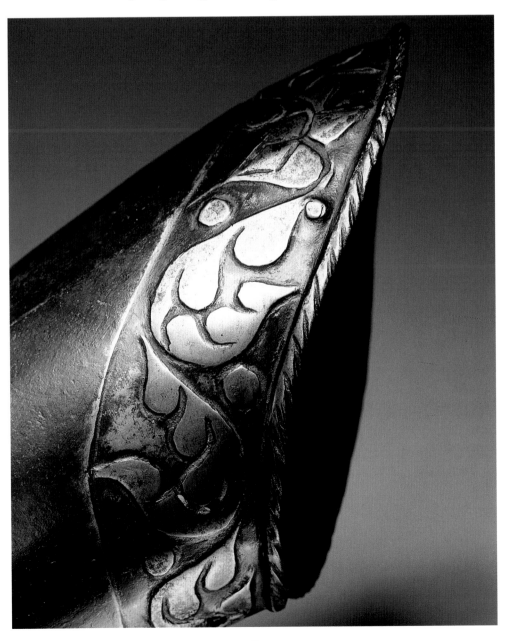

The Waning of Military Armor

It will kill a man to serve in a whole cuirass. I am resolved to use nothing but back, breast and gauntlet. If I had a pott for the head that were pistol proof it may be that I would use it, if it were light, but my whole helmet will be of no use to me at all.
—SIR EDMUND VERNEY (1636–1688)

During the course of the sixteenth century, the increasing use of firearms in conjunction with new tactics in the battlefield gradually undermined the importance of the fully armored warrior. Notwithstanding the abandonment of armor's utilitarian function—defense for the body—the prestige that fine armor bestowed upon its wearer was slow to disappear. For those who could afford it, emphasis shifted toward ownership of highly expensive "dress" or "princely" armors, which were decorated through various forms of surface ornamentation and intended principally to convey rank and authority.

Fine armor continued to be an expression of its owner's wealth, taste, and standing in society. Consequently, it was important to an owner that his armor conform to the highest standards of fashionability, as did his civilian dress, and that it reflect the finest workmanship and materials his means would allow.

Around 1500, armor styles began to depart radically from the Gothic harnesses and sallets so highly favored during the second half of the fifteenth century. In keeping with the new Italian fashion, German armorers began to emphasize rounded forms and surface ornamentation, and the Gothic vertical line gradually gave way to the horizontal. A transitional period between these two styles saw a combination of features striving to imitate "puffed and slashed" contemporary costume while at the same time preserving established technical reliability.

In essence, sixteenth-century armor combines the fashionability of Italian rounded forms with the technical and structural features of German armor. An early example is the narrow-ribbed fluted style usually called "Maximilian" after Emperor Maximilian I, whose patronage of armor workshops at Innsbruck and Nuremberg resulted in dazzling innovations. The fashion of rippling the surface of the armor plates with channels and fan-like ridges may have been meant to imitate the pleatings of contemporary costumes. The chief reason for this style of construction, however, was the armorer's desire to minimize weight and maximize strength. Since steel plates were strengthened by this "corrugated" effect, they

Painted during his exile in Saint-Germain, the portrait at left shows Charles in a typical French cuirassier's (cavalry) armor of blued and gilded steel. Because the armor is clearly French and of a style made around 1630 (the year Charles was born), this suit was obviously not crafted specifically for him. It very likely was lent or given to him, perhaps by his cousin, the *French king Louis XIV, for this very portrait. The evidence would suggest that Charles's taste in armor did not favor that of English make. At the age of fourteen, he was painted by William Dobson in a suit of armor of Dutch manufacture which survives today at the Royal Armouries in the Tower of London. Charles II was the last English monarch to own a complete suit of armor.*

"WAISTCOAT"

CUIRASS

NORTH ITALY,

C. 1580

CMA 1916.1721 [33]

This specialized form of costume armor was meant to simulate the civilian doublet with its row of buttons down the front. The owner could have opened it like an ordinary doublet since the two halves were hinged to a narrow backplate. While the waistcoat cuirass afforded protection to the torso and was generally light to wear, fashion—not function—was clearly the prerequisite. Such cuirasses tended to be more popular in Italy than elsewhere.

could be made appreciably thinner and lighter. Maximilian armors typically had round helmets, globular breastplates, and broad-toed sabatons (defense for the feet), illustrating the influence of Italian fashion.

Throughout the sixteenth century, armor styles continued to respond to changes in civilian costume and patrons' ever-changing whims. At the beginning of the century, three categories of plate armor had been delineated. The first was field armor, for use in battle. This armor was fairly light, averaging from forty-five to sixty-five well-distributed pounds. It was also strong and maneuverable with smooth, glancing surfaces. The second category was tournament armor, highly specialized for various forms of the joust and other sporting combats. Tournament armor was constructed of heavy, often reinforced, plates of steel. A complete suit could weigh more than one hundred pounds. The third category was parade armor, used for ceremonial occasions and made purely for personal embellishment. Since parade armor was not intended for use on the battlefield, it was made of thinner and softer metal, usually lavishly decorated.

In 1478 Maximilian married Mary of Burgundy, daughter of Duke Charles the Bold and heiress to the most sophisticated court in Europe. Playing a prominent role in the history of armor, Maximilian initiated the buildup of an armaments industry and fostered the modernization of the armorer's craft. In 1504 he installed a court workshop at Innsbruck. Known as "the last knight," Maximilian was an enthusiast of tournaments and hunting. In this imposing woodcut, the emperor wears the type of fluted armor that later would be named for him.

The Aesthetic of Ornament in Renaissance Armor

Until industrialization brought mass production to the manufacture of armaments, martial implements enjoyed a close relationship with the fine arts. Historically, the decoration of armor and weapons has served to manifest the culture that produced them. Indeed, as symbols of abstract concepts such as authority, power, and justice, arms came to convey ideas that far surpassed their original function. They acquired an ideological significance that in turn encouraged the practice of treat-

Duke of Ferrara after 1505, Alfonso I devoted his considerable energies to statecraft and war, leaving much of the cultural and social life of his brilliant court to his second wife, Lucrezia, daughter of Pope Alexander VI. He was fascinated by the new technology of firearms and

established a celebrated foundry for casting huge cannons. Throughout the Renaissance it was customary for nobility to be portrayed with the full panoply of war and leadership. Alfonso's armor and the symbolic mace held in his right hand bear witness to his authority and generalship.

PORTRAIT OF
ALFONSO I D'ESTE
(1476–1534)
DOSSO AND
BATTISTA DOSSI
(ITALIAN, FERRARA,
ACTIVE 1512–42)
GALLERIA ESTENSE,
MODENA

PHILIPPE DE CROY,
DUKE OF
AERSCHOT
(1526–1595)
FLANDERS, C. 1575
THE EDWARD B.
GREENE
COLLECTION
CMA 1940.1222

Heir of an illustrious Flemish family and a member of the Order of the Golden Fleece, Philippe de Croy held the position of governor of Antwerp and governor-general of Flanders. As such, he repeatedly served the interests of the Hapsburg emperor Charles V and King Philip II in the Spanish Imperial Army. He is represented in this vellum miniature wearing the ceremonial parade armor befitting a great general. His blued, etched, and gilded armor is probably of Augsburg make, a center favored by many of the Hapsburgs for its production of deluxe armor.

SEVEN-FLANGED
MACE
ITALY, C. 1540–50
CMA 1916.1589 [122]

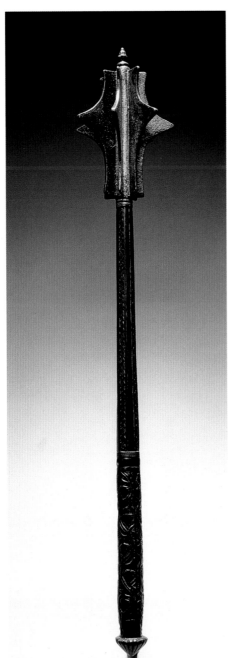

In use throughout the Middle Ages, the mace became increasingly popular in the fifteenth and sixteenth centuries due to the ineffectiveness of edged weapons against fully developed plate armor. Designed for use in both combat and courtly contests, it was regarded as a knightly weapon. Arming oneself with a mace eventually came to be regarded as a badge of rank, as this example must have been, to be carried by its owner in parades and on other ceremonial occasions.

SIR ANTHONY
MILDMAY, C. 1590–93
NICHOLAS
HILLIARD
(ENGLISH, LONDON,
1547–1619)
PURCHASE FROM
THE J. H. WADE
FUND
CMA 1926.554

This vellum cabinet miniature portrays Anthony Mildmay, the son of England's chancellor of the exchequer, in what appears to be his field tent. Wearing trunk-hose and a peascod doublet, he is in the process of dressing in armor, probably for the tournament. On the ground are strewn the leg elements from what is clearly a luxurious Greenwich-made suit. Behind, on the table to his right, is his right gauntlet, plumed helmet, and a holstered wheel-lock pistol. Mildmay's left hand clasps the hilt of an elegant rapier. The sitters who commissioned this very expensive form of portraiture were noted for their wealth, ostentation, and concern with image.

ing them decoratively. Thus, the aesthetic value attached to arms and armor, reaching a high point during the Renaissance, became directly relevant to the social status and artistic taste of the owner.

Armor decoration employed virtually every technique used in contemporary metalwork: etching, gilding, damascening, embossing, engraving, even enameling. Such expressions of virtuosity on the part of the armorer and armor decorator (usually separate persons) appealed to the individuality of wealthy Renaissance princes. There evolved at this time a stock vocabulary of ornamental details and motifs, often abstruse, that came to be used for the decoration of arms and armor with increasing extravagance. This ornamental vocabulary ultimately derived from or reflected other branches of Renaissance decorative arts, chiefly goldsmithwork, enameling, and ceramic decoration, but also print etching.

Classical works of art inspired Italian Renaissance decorative artists, whose designs were gradually adopted by their counterparts north of the Alps. The most important source of decoration on which Renaissance artists drew were grotesques, so called because they were found in Roman ruins belowground in what were thought to be grottoes. These fanciful mural or sculptural decorations consisted of interwoven human, animal, and plant forms. The Renaissance adaptation of grotesque ornament was recorded in prints like those of the Italian artist Nicoletto Rosex da Modena, or the Germans Daniel Hopfer, Wenzel Jamnitzer, Peter Flötner, Virgil Solis, Matthias Zündt, and Paul Flindt.

Such designs were readily studied via prints and pattern books (originally published for use by goldsmiths). From the early sixteenth century onward, pat-

The ornamental demi- (or half) chanfron covered the forehead of the horse but extended only halfway down the animal's nose. The edges of this piece and its wide central band have been skillfully etched with stylized floral motifs and then gilded.

tern books supplied fashionable ornamentations that could be either copied directly by arms decorators, or used as a basis for evolving their own compositions. Due to the widespread dissemination of ornamental prints, either loose or bound into pattern books, the forms and motifs developed in one country were easily spread to others. There was in addition a constant international exchange of artists. Several German and Flemish goldsmiths, for example, worked in Florence at the court of Cosimo I de' Medici, while Italian artists, such as the famed Benvenuto Cellini, were invited to France.

Metalsmiths and goldsmiths in particular have historically played an important role in the development of decorative forms and motifs for armor and

During the Renaissance, ornaments such as this were recorded via the print medium (here, an etching), often assembled into pattern books, and disseminated to goldsmiths and arms etchers throughout Europe, who in turn adopted them for their clients.

ROUND SHIELD
(RONDACHE)
ITALY, MILAN,
C. 1570
CMA 1916.1504 [93]

Radiating bands of etched decoration enliven this shield. The decorative vocabulary includes classical warriors represented within a setting of trophies of arms and grotesques. The escutcheons contain scenes of mythical combats. The inspiration is the antique, a typical preoccupation of the Renaissance.

weapons. At no time was this relationship more obvious, or more significant, than during the High Renaissance of the late sixteenth and early seventeenth centuries. Besides working with precious metals, some goldsmith-etchers—like Augsburg's Daniel Hopfer—decorated arms and armor for princely clients before turning to print etching. It is during this period that armor construction saw the culmination of a trend toward extravagant richness and the use of costly materials.

As the sixteenth century proceeded, goldsmith-designers and arms decorators began to reject classical ideals of harmony and proportion and to experiment with more adventurous and "mannered" forms, partly to satisfy the increasingly sophisticated tastes of their patrons. The penchant of these princely clients for mannered ostentation eventually resulted in armors and personal weapons designed for aesthetic and ideological purposes rather than practical use. Surviving examples of finely decorated arms and armor are replete with a broad range of ornamental motifs and subject matter, which—in addition to grotesques—include conventionalized foliate patterns (like the acanthus), arabesques, strapwork, animal themes, heraldry, biblical and mythological themes, classical history, and trophies. In some instances armor was embellished using symbolic and apotropaic (meant to ward

PORTRAIT OF HENRY
II, KING OF FRANCE,
AT THE AGE OF 28
NICCOLO DELLA
CASA
(FRENCH, ACTIVE IN
ROME 1543–47)
IN MEMORY OF
RALPH KING, GIFT OF
MRS. RALPH KING,
RALPH T. WOODS,
CHARLES G. KING,
AND FRANCES KING
SCHOTT
CMA 1946.308

POMMEL PLATES
FROM A SADDLE,
1571
ANTON
PEFFENHAUSER
(GERMAN,
AUGSBURG,
1525–1603)
CMA 1916.1888.1–2
[77–78]

At a time when the taste for armors in the antique fashion (all'antica) was at its height, the French king is shown sporting a Roman-style muscle-cuirass (see illustration on page 33). Such armors were expensive to produce and would have been worn only by European princes in pageants and on special occasions. Henry II (ruled 1547–59) loved finely embossed parade armor and had his portrait painted wearing several of these. He died at the age of forty-one, after having his eye put out during a tournament.

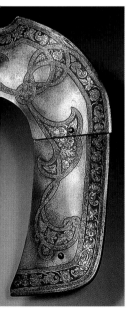

Once part of a saddle (meant to protect the rider's thighs), these plates originally came from a garniture for man and horse made for the sons of Emperor Maximilian II, archdukes Rudolf and Ernst. The armor was made for the tournaments held on the occasion of the 1571 marriage of their uncle, Archduke Charles of Styria, to Princess Maria of Bavaria. The remaining pieces of the garniture are today preserved in the Hofjagd- und Rüstkammer in Vienna (see illustration on next page).

off evil) devices: patterns of endless knots, the Gorgon's head, the "evil eye," symbols of strength and courage, as well as allegories with various shades of meaning.

As the medieval knightly class gradually transformed into courtiers, their armor (usually at the expense of its original function) evolved into spectacular male body jewelry. An essential part of this panoply was the trimmings of colorful plumes and fabrics attached to armor used in parades and pageants. The elaborate

This garniture and the pommel plates now in Cleveland, with their interlaced etched decoration, must rank among the most beautiful examples of the armorer's art dating to the second half of the sixteenth century. The pattern, in the imperial colors of black and gold, forms elegant knots, with distinctive foliage and hop sprigs filling the loops. Anton Peffenhauser was one of the richest armorers of his time. Many of the nobles of Spain, Bavaria, Saxony, and Austria ordered their splendidly decorated suits from this renowned Augsburg master.

armor crafted during the second half of the sixteenth century, with its plates lavishly embossed in relief, no longer presented a smooth glancing surface capable of deflecting a lance or sword. For the art historian, however, this extravagant decoration of arms and armor, in all its diversity of forms, styles, and modes, provides an aesthetic point of reference that can assist in establishing an approximate date and place of manufacture.

Warfare in the Seventeenth Century

By 1600 there had occurred a fundamental change in European infantry tactics predicated by the development of firearms. Reliable wheel-lock muskets and improved gunpowder made armor less useful. As armor technology strove to produce effective protection against musket shot, metal plates became thicker and therefore heavier, and hence too impractical to wear. The seventeenth century saw a steady abandonment of field armor of all types.

THE WANING OF MILITARY ARMOR

PIKEMAN'S
HELMET,
BREASTPLATE, AND
TASSETS
ENGLAND,
GREENWICH(?),
C. 1620–30
(HELMET: PERHAPS
DUTCH OR
FLEMISH?)
CMA 1923.1063.A–D
[4]

The pikeman was named after his principal weapon, the pike, a staff weapon that could measure sixteen to eighteen feet in length. With its chevron decoration, this pikeman's armor is slightly more decorative than most, perhaps suggesting that it belonged to an officer.

During the first half of the seventeenth century the English infantry, for example, was deployed in two distinct forms: companies of pikemen combined with companies of musketeers. The musketeers were generally the more numerous arm of infantry by about two to one, and were normally deployed in six ranks to provide a continuous hail of fire. Unlike the pikeman, the musketeer wore no armor at all, a point verified by numerous engravings and paintings of the period. Yet the pikeman and musketeer combination provided a deadly infantry wall for any cavalry charge.

Because the rate of fire of the musketeers was too slow for defense against cavalry charges during the reloading process, companies of pikemen were deployed in defensive formations called "squares" to protect the unarmored musketeers. An illustration in Josiah Sprigge's *Anglia Rediviva,* published in London in 1647, provides a bird's-eye view of English Civil War infantry in battle formation. The pikemen, each wearing a corselet and pot helmet for protection against slashing sword cuts, stood in massed squares with pikes held vertically. The musketeers, who were normally deployed on the flanks, retreated behind the pikemen when the cavalry attacked. The Earl of Clarendon, a contemporary historian, observed of the Royalist Cavalry at Newbury that they "endured their storm of small shot," but "could make no impression on their stand of pikes." The eventual adoption of the bayonet in the second half of the seventeenth century made the pikeman obsolete, since the musketeer could now serve both functions.

The pikeman was an infantryman so named after his principal weapon—the pike, a staff weapon measuring some sixteen feet in length. An engraving from Jacob Jacques de Gheyn's *The Excercise of Armes for Calivres, Muskettes and Pikes,* published at The Hague in 1607 and intended as an educational drill book for soldiers, shows the manner in which contemporary pikemen were outfitted. It is also worth noting that the pikeman carried a sword as a sideweapon. De Gheyn's drill book proved immensely popular throughout the seventeenth century, with many editions printed. The dissemination of these illustrations throughout Europe resulted in a certain standardization of drills among European infantries.

The pikeman was equipped with a corselet (a half-armor) consisting of a breastplate and backplate, hinged tassets (plates of steel that were suspended from

"ORDER YOUR PIKE, THE SECOND MOTION" (DETAIL FROM DE GHEYN'S *THE EXCERCISE OF ARMES FOR CALIVRES, MUSKETTES AND PIKES*) JACOB JACQUES DE GHEYN (DUTCH, 1565–1629) METROPOLITAN MUSEUM OF ART, NEW YORK

De Gheyn's book (first published in 1607) was intended as a drill book to educate inexperienced soldiers. Its copperplate illustrations show a series of maneuvers for the pikeman and also demonstrate that Continental soldiers and their English counterparts were outfitted identically.

THE PIKEMAN'S ARMOR (FROM J. BINGHAM'S TACTICS OF AELIAN) FIRST PUBLISHED IN LONDON, 1616 THE BRITISH LIBRARY, LONDON INV. 718118

Illustrated are the elements of a pikeman's armor, their means of attachment, and a pike.

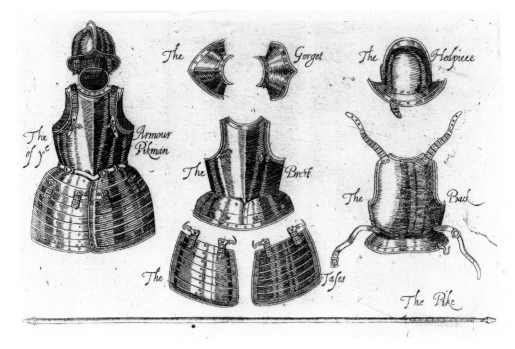

the breastplate by means of hinges or straps to protect the hips and upper thighs), and sometimes a neckpiece called a gorget. A contemporary illustration of the pikeman's armor from J. Bingham's *Tactics of Aelian* (1616) shows how the various pieces were attached. The backplate was attached to the breastplate, for example, by means of shoulder straps with round holes. These were fastened over round studs on the breastplate and held in place with swivel hooks that passed through a hole in the studs. The elements of pikeman's armor in Cleveland's col-

THE BATTLE OF NASEBY (1645) (FROM JOSIAH SPRIGGE'S *ANGLIA REDIVIVA*) PUBLISHED IN LONDON, 1647 THE BRITISH LIBRARY, LONDON INV. 9512F7

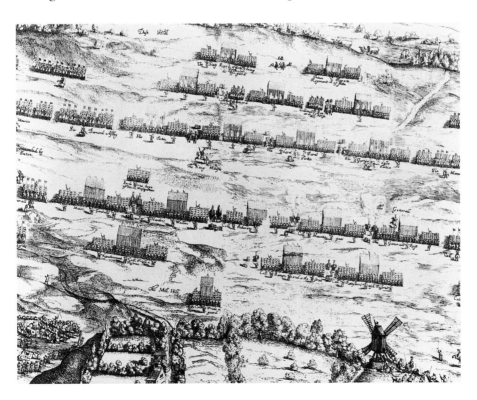

This bird's-eye view clearly shows companies of pikemen flanked by musketeers. The battle, fought between the royalist forces of King Charles I (at the top of the scene) and those of Parliament (at the bottom, just outside the town of Naseby), was one of the most climactic of the English Civil War. Both forces were similarly equipped, though the royalists were defeated.

lection (illustrated on page 101) is missing its backplate and gorget, though its swivel hooks can be clearly seen on the breastplate. This type of armor was relatively light and included no protection for the legs or arms, since swiftness and mobility were preferred for defense.

On his head, the pikeman wore a simple open-faced helmet called a "pot," characterized by its high comb and brim. These helmets usually included earpieces that extended down the side of the face and tied under the chin with a piece of ribbon. The design of the pikeman's pot, though not new in the development of European armor, was shaped for strength and deflection of musket shot and downward glancing blows to the head from the cavalry's slashing swords. As early as the fifteenth century similar open-faced designs with swooping brims could be seen on the kettle hat and, later, the morion. While most surviving pikemen's pots are simple and undecorated helmets of polished steel, some examples are embellished with embossed designs and decorative patterns of brass rivets. All generally include a brass plume holder riveted to the back of the helmet. Colorful plumes added sartorial splendor and distinguished individual companies of pikemen.

The armor worn by the pikeman was generally a readymade, unfitted, and relatively cheap form of munitions armor. It was normally mass-produced for the rank-and-file soldier as functional armor. There were, however, varying levels of

OFFICER'S PLUG
BAYONET
ENGLAND, C. 1690
CMA 1916.1659 [172]

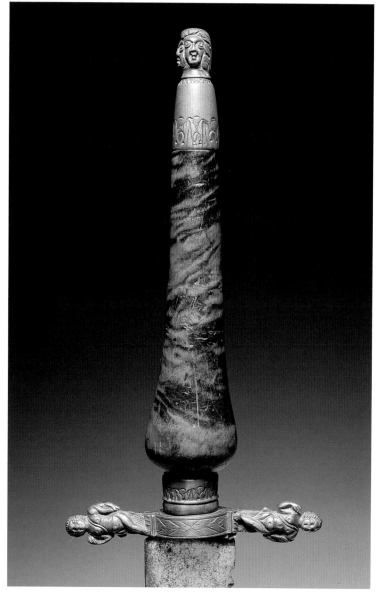

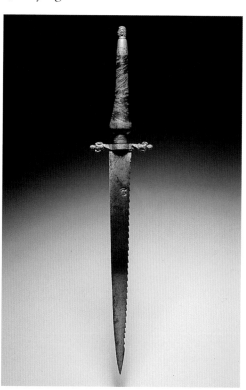

Used increasingly in warfare during the seventeenth century, the plug bayonet was inserted into the muzzle of a gun to make a weapon with a long shaft. The eventual adoption of the bayonet in the second half of the century made pikemen obsolete.

BASKET-HILT
BROADSWORD
(MORTUARY
SWORD)
HILT: ENGLAND,
C. 1640–50
BLADE: GERMANY,
SOLINGEN(?), EARLY
18TH CENTURY
CMA 1916.696 [128]

The ornate hilt of this broadsword is chiseled with foliate scrollwork, leafy grotesque masks, and what is popularly believed to be the face of King Charles I of England (beheaded in 1649). Because of the resemblance of this image to the death mask of the king, a group of English swords bearing this likeness are commonly referred to as "mortuary swords." They appear to have been made for important individuals during the English Civil War or the Protectorate of Oliver Cromwell. The present sword is traditionally said to have belonged to Sir Thomas Fairfax, a prominent general of the Parliamentary cavalry. Broadswords with large double-edged blades, such as this, were designed for heavy cavalry use and were common from the seventeenth through nineteenth centuries.

design and execution, as exemplified by a number of surviving pikemen's armors. Of superior construction, they may have formed the equipment of the royal body-guard—the Yeomen of the Guard. Some are brown in color, a technique known as russeting (or controlled rusting to prevent further corrosion). It is known that in 1631 a common pike armor cost £1,2s; if lined with red leather, £1,4s. The additional treatment of russeting cost four shillings.

The pike itself was tapered for balance and surmounted with a small leaf-shaped head. Though not always fully armored, pikemen formed the backbone of infantry tactics through the end of the English Civil War (1642–51). Pikemen probably began to abandon certain elements of pike armor for comfort and mo-

bility. Perhaps the gorget and tassets were abandoned first, leaving just the helmet, breastplate, and backplate. The Earl of Clarendon observed of the king's infantry at the Battle of Edgehill in 1642 that ". . . in the whole body there was not one pikeman had a corslet. . . ." It is also known that Cromwell's New Model Army, formed in 1645 with its regular pay and discipline, was issued no pikeman's armor.

Like the infantry, English cavalry in the years up to the Civil War tended to be deployed in two forms. The counterparts to the pikeman and the musketeer were the cuirassier and the more common harquebusier. The term "harquebusier" was applied to light cavalry in half-armor and open helmets, armed with a harquebus—a short-barreled firearm. The "cuirassier," by contrast, was the heavy cavalryman, clad in full armor save for the lower legs (which were instead covered by heavy riding boots). Shortly after the beginning of the English Civil War, the heavy cavalry armor of the cuirassier disappeared.

A number of seventeenth-century portraits of kings and statesmen portray the sitter wearing a cuirassier's armor, perhaps meant to symbolize generalship and military prowess. One such portrait of King Charles II of England (ruled 1660-85) is now in the Cleveland Museum of Art. This portrait (illustrated on page 90) was painted in 1653 by Philippe de Champaigne (1602–1674) during the king's exile in France. Charles had fled England in 1651 after his grievous defeat at the Battle of Worcester. The 1649 execution of his father, Charles I, had marked the start of the Interregnum and Protectorate of the despot Oliver Cromwell. At the time of this portrait, Charles was residing at Saint-Germain, near Paris, awaiting the restoration of his throne. The envisioned landing, indicated by Charles's gesture, is

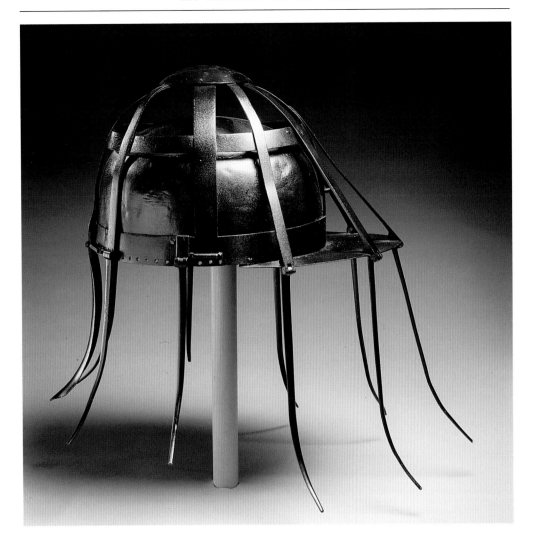

The spider-like legs of this helmet protected the mounted soldier's face and head from slashing sword blows. As shown on the facing page, the legs could be raised and locked out of the way when not required. This is a strictly utilitarian armor of a very specialized sort.

painted in the lower left-hand corner of the portrait to reveal his fleet standing off the white cliffs of Dover. Charles would indeed land at Dover in due course to reclaim his throne, not by force of arms but at the invitation of the English parliament. He would enter London in triumph on May 29, 1660. However, by 1653, the date of the Champaigne portrait of Charles, military practice had effectively abandoned the cuirassier armor.

With the advancing sophistication of firearms, armor gradually fell into disuse. However, it continued to be worn in pageants and parades, and the fashion for having one's portrait painted in full armor, even after its abandonment, was difficult to dispel. In some cases it is possible to recognize historic armors as the suits used by sitters for portraits. Records exist from the seventeenth century of suits of armor issued to painters out of the Armouries at the Tower for this very purpose. The production of custom-made and lavishly decorated princely armors, popular in the preceding century, was drawing to a close, though handsome cavalry armor, the mark of a commander, was still being sought by important nobles and heads of state. As functional equipment for the warrior, however, field armor was steadily being discarded. By the end of the English Civil War in 1651, armor had largely disappeared from the battlefield.

Weapons as Technology and Art

By his side hung Joyeuse, and there was never a sword to match it:
its color changed thirty times a day. We know well the fate of the lance with which
Our Lord was transfixed upon the cross. By the grace of God, Charles possesses the tip,
and has had it set in the golden pommel of his sword. Because of this great
honor the sword is called Joyeuse.
—*CHANSON DE ROLAND, C. 1100*

The history of arms and armor fundamentally involves competition between two rival technologies: that of the armorer (defensive) and that of the weaponsmith (offensive). Each craftsman sought to achieve the technical superiority that in turn would provide his client with a distinct advantage. The history of weapons down through the age of firearms, in all of their varied forms, follows a parallel course to that of armor: that is to say, weapons for battle, weapons for sporting purposes (especially hunting), and finally weapons for dress and embellishment—the ultimate male accessory. The application of new technologies and materials to these weapons often resulted in objects of exquisite beauty and consummate craftsmanship.

The Sword

The medieval sword was an object of simple beauty, cruciform in shape, with an austere perfection of line and proportion. These knightly swords are distinguished by their plain quillons (or cross guards) for stopping an opponent's weapon and by a heavy pommel that functioned as a counterweight to balance the blade. Countless medieval miniatures and funerary effigies depict such swords. Just as the sword had been the principal weapon of the ancient world, so it remained for the medieval warrior, the knight.

The sword, one of a variety of edged weapons, was designed for delivering cutting blows or thrusts, or both. Its lineage harks back to the simple stone daggers of prehistory. Once the working of copper and its alloy, bronze, had been mastered, the dagger was fitted with increasingly longer blades until it effectively became a short sword. The eventual supremacy of iron for the making of harder and more durable sword blades relegated bronze to use for accessory parts such as grips and sheaths.

By immediate descent, however, the European sword of the later Middle Ages derived from the ninth-century Viking sword, with tang and blade cast as one

The sword at left is one from a series carried by the state guard of Duke Julius of Brunswick and Lüneburg. These swords are distinguished by quillons filed in the shape of fish and by pierced crutch-shaped pommels. Each sword in this series is dated and numbered. On the ricasso—that portion of the blade between the hilt and the beginning of the edge—is the etched crowned monogram of Duke Julius with the date 1574 and N59, the number of this particular sword. By the late 1600s these enormous swords had assumed a largely ceremonial or bodyguard function, as was the case here. This sword weighs only eight and a half pounds and is well balanced for ease of use.

piece. Its blade was straight and double-edged and thus suitable for slashing or thrusting. It would seem, however, that the swords of the eleventh and twelfth centuries were used primarily for delivering cutting blows to an adversary. The *Bayeux Tapestry,* for example, shows Duke William's knights busily slashing with their swords; none uses the sword in a thrusting maneuver. In the Gothic period (about 1200–1500), the sword became a more specialized weapon depending on whether it was intended to be used on horseback or on foot, and a knight probably owned several swords according to his needs and preferences. There developed a number of local types. Generally, in southern and western Europe the preference was for thrusting swords; elsewhere in Europe cutting swords seem to have been preferred. Long-bladed swords with grips of increased length continued in popularity into the fifteenth century. These were designed either to deliver a heavy cutting blow or specifically for the thrust, to deal with the ever-increasing weight and strength of the knight's armor.

Until the thirteenth century, the knight had worn his sword scabbard hung on the left hip, suspended from a thick belt worn at the waist over his surcoat. Toward the 1350s the knight began to wear a heavy belt at hip level, usually decorated with enameled or jeweled clasps hinged together, from which he could suspend his sword. The belt must have been laced to the coat armor or mail to prevent it from slipping down under the weight of the sword and dagger, the latter being worn on the right hip. In the 1420s the hip belt was replaced by a diagonal sword belt. Both sword and dagger were worn inserted into respective scabbards or sheaths made of wood covered in leather, sometimes stained a bright color, and decorated with gilded appliqués and mounts. The scabbard not only provided a convenient way for a knight to carry his sword, but also prevented rain from reaching and rusting the blade when not in use.

THREE SWORDS
EUROPEAN,
15TH CENTURY
CMA 1916.1600 [163];
1919.69 [192];
1921.1252 [195]

To the medieval mind, which imparted deep spiritual meaning to everyday objects, the knight's sword was perceived as the noblest of weapons since its shape symbolized the cross on which Christ died.

By the middle of the fourteenth century, knights are routinely depicted wearing daggers as accompaniments to their swords. In order to pierce mail and protective leather garments, it was important that the dagger be constructed with a solid blade and a strong point. Initially, the dagger was made to resemble a diminutive sword with quillons, grip, and discs or roundels. The dagger's hilt was normally fashioned and decorated *en suite* with the client's sword as a matching pair. By the sixteenth century various forms of the dagger had become standardized. Such structural details of the blade, however, like its form and the proportion of the heel or the presence of ribbing or fullers, were usually determined by local tradition, as was the "furniture"—grip, quillons, and pommel.

Medieval European swordsmiths developed different ways of fashioning swords, and the relative scarcity of expensive metal and the skill necessary for casting it gave rise to many jealously guarded secrets. Indeed, iron and steel derived much of their mystery from the fact that early smiths could not always produce a uniform product. Sometimes the iron was soft and malleable, and other times hard and steel-like. The smiths knew how to extract iron from ore, then forge it at red heat into bars. Steel must have frequently been produced when the iron was exposed to the carbonizing action of the charcoal fire, thus resulting in a harder and more resilient blade. The bladesmiths of Duke William's day had no knowledge of the metallurgical principles at play, but must have attempted to re-create the conditions that resulted in desirable variations. The swordsmith who could produce a superior blade was perhaps considered as much an alchemist as a craftsman.

The fifteenth century saw the development of long, tapered thrusting swords designed to counteract the heavy armor and sophisticated plates now more or less fully enclosing the knight. One of these swords was the tuck or estoc (from a French expression meaning thrust). The tuck was hung from the saddle as an aux-

ESTOC (THRUSTING
SWORD)
GERMANY, EARLY
16TH CENTURY
CMA 1916.686 [125]

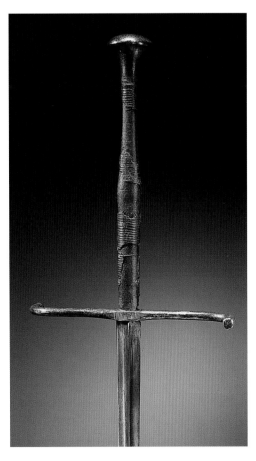

The estoc is characterized by a fairly long grip and simple cross-shaped hilt; its rigid blade, designed for thrusting at armored opponents, is three-sided for strength. This sword was sometimes carried from the saddle and was in use from the early 1300s as an auxiliary side arm, to be used when the cavalryman had dismounted.

iliary side arm, and occasionally might be used by the knight after he dismounted. It was particularly useful for piercing adversaries' mail. A somewhat larger sword was the bastard—or, as it is called today, "hand-and-a half" sword—meant for the man fighting on foot. Featuring an elongated pommel and grip (long enough so that it could be wielded with one or both hands for increased power) and rigid "diamond"-section blades that would not easily break under pressure, the hand-and-a-half sword was intended to thrust between the gaps of an opponent's plate armor. Such swords were especially favored in the Germanic territories. Until the middle of the sixteenth century their hilts remained essentially cruciform, but began to assume curving quillons, ring guards, and, on some later types, a more developed guard with knuckle bows connected by a loop, anticipating the rapier.

The hand-and-a-half sword was somewhat larger than a tuck but much smaller than the enormous two-handed swords that emerged late in the fifteenth century and remained in use through much of the sixteenth. Approaching six feet in length, the two-handed sword was strictly an infantry weapon requiring special training and great strength to wield it. The sword featured a long double-edged blade counterbalanced by a heavy pommel (triangular, faceted, or pear-shaped). It remained a favorite weapon of the German *Landesknecht,* a mercenary infantry that during the early sixteenth century established a reputation for fearless fighting. The Landesknecht wore little armor, usually just an iron skullcap and a mail collar. They did, however, affect an outlandish, multicolored, "puffed and slashed" mode of dress. Most of the two-handed swords that survive today were not made for field use, but for parade and ceremonial use by corps of princely bodyguards (see the illustration on page 108). Their blades often incorporated flamboyant wavy edges, the grips decorated with fringes and trimmings.

EXECUTIONER'S
SWORD
GERMANY,
LATE 1600s
CMA 1916.1620 [165]

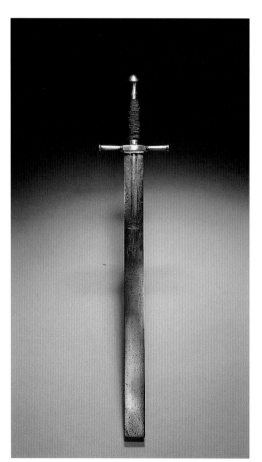

In the Middle Ages and Renaissance, execution by decapitation was generally reserved for the nobility. While the axe was favored in England, swords were widely used throughout central Europe for beheadings. The blades of executioner's swords were often etched with designs representing Justice (like this example), the gallows, the rack, or the Crucifixion, and sometimes with moralistic inscriptions. The inscription on this blade, translated from the Old German, reads: When I raise this sword, so I wish that this poor sinner will receive eternal life. *The use of swords for executions had ceased in Europe by the early eighteenth century, but they still were occasionally used in ceremonies and processions as symbols of power. This sword was probably ceremonial.*

The Rapier and the Dress Sword

THREE RAPIERS
(LEFT TO RIGHT):
SPAIN, C. 1650
CMA 1916.1811 [186];
ITALY, MILAN,
C. 1610–30
CMA 1916.706 [137];
ITALY, BELLUNO(?),
C. 1580–1610 (WITH
SPANISH BLADE)
CMA 1974.59 [201]

The late fifteenth century saw the beginning of a long evolution in the design of sword guards away from the traditional cruciform shape. Quillons began to assume a simple S-shaped configuration, thus providing rudimentary knuckle bows and guards. Eventually additional guards were added to the sword hilt, and by the mid-1500s the almost fully developed "swept" hilt was in existence. As the Middle Ages drew to a close and the classical influences of the Renaissance became more pervasive throughout Europe, there appeared an ever-increasing diversity of sword types with more emphasis on decoration and style.

Many of these changes in the form of the European sword also can be attributed to the increasing importance of infantry in European warfare and the various new modes of fighting on foot. Perhaps more significant was the need to protect the unarmored hand as infantries began to divest themselves of armor plate in favor of speed and agility. Civilians, many of whom wore swords with civilian dress in accordance with contemporary taste and fashion, also increasingly wore them for self-defense and for settling disputes by dueling.

These were the beginnings of the sword known as the rapier, essentially a southern European innovation. The term "rapier," though of uncertain origin,

Swordplay brought about a complicated structure of the rapier's guard to protect the duelist's sword hand. As shown above, these elaborate guards were frequently decorated by various techniques—chiseling, bluing, russeting, and damascening.

may derive from the Spanish *espada ropera,* meaning "robe sword" or dress sword. The rapier was a light weapon with a straight, double-edged, and pointed blade, which, with the development of the art of fencing in the sixteenth and seventeenth centuries, progressively became narrower and lighter, and thus suitable for thrusts only. The blade also became longer, based on a belief at the time that a longer blade made it possible to hit one's adversary more easily and, at the same time, to stay beyond the reach of his weapon.

The Englishman Sir John Smythe complained in his *Certain Discourses Militarie* (1590) that the slender blade of the rapier was easily broken and that its great length made it difficult to draw. Nevertheless, the new technique of swordplay, with its emphasis on the point of the blade, brought about a complicated structure of the sword's guard to protect the duelist's hand. During the sixteenth century fencing

The rapier was worn with civilian dress and used for dueling. The elaborate guard of the sword depicted in this Italian portrait of an unknown man was decorated by damascening. On the basis of style, this rapier belongs to a distinctive group of sword hilts decorated in this way between about 1570 and 1600 and is of North Italian manufacture.

academies were already in existence in cities like Milan, Venice, Verona, and Madrid, and rules of fencing evolved. Two styles of fencing emerged, the Spanish and the Italian, both of which called for the use of a "parrying dagger" to be held in the hand opposite the sword hand. The dagger was intended to block or entrap the opponent's rapier thrusts, a technique known as parrying. Parrying daggers were often made with rapiers as a matched set, or garniture, during the

CUP-HILTED RAPIER
AND LEFT-HANDED
("MAIN GAUCHE")
DAGGER
SPAIN, C. 1650
CMA 1916.1810 [185];
1916.699 [131]

Rapiers were often made with accompanying daggers as a matched set for parrying. Daggers like the one shown here have been misleadingly called "left-handed" daggers. However, only a right-handed swordsman would brandish the dagger with his left hand; a left-handed swordsman would parry with the right hand. The guard is richly decorated with chiseled and pierced arabesques.

seventeenth century. Italian and Spanish schools of fencing with two armed hands dominated Europe from about 1500 to 1650, when the French style of fencing with a small sword alone gained prominence.

The rapier evolved a bewildering array of hilt forms—ranging from the simple cup hilts popularized in Spain to complex swept hilts with various knuckle guards and up- or downturned quillons often impeccably decorated. The aristocracy's

The schiavona-type broadsword features a complex barred guard that slopes forward. Its name derives from the Italian word for "Slavonic" and refers to the Slavonian corps who served as bodyguards to the Doge of Venice until the end of the Venetian Republic in 1797. It tended to be popular mainly with the Venetians.

taste for rich and intricate styles of decoration led to extravagant gilding, chiseling, piercing, enameling, and silvering. The more costly or unusual these weapons appeared, the more they were desired by the gentlemanly clientele who commissioned them, not only for dueling but also as the ultimate accessory.

Thus, with the development of the rapier and its later descendants, the sword was no longer the prerogative of the knight alone, but of anyone who could afford to have one made. Indeed, such was the demand for personalized side arms that some of the foremost artists of the day provided fashionable designs to the swordmakers, goldsmiths, and jewelers who collaborated on these extravagant weapons. During the sixteenth century, for example, artists like Benvenuto Cellini and Hans Holbein the Younger are known to have made such designs.

Since not every swordmaker could make a good rapier blade, there emerged during the seventeenth century a tremendous export market. These blades were produced in a number of highly specialized workshops in Brescia and Milan in

The "Pappenheimer"-style hilt of the sword at right is beautifully blued. The blade is inscribed NEC TEMERE NEC TIMIDE/INTER ARMA SILENT LEGE/ VERITATEM DILIGE ET PUGNA PRO PATRIA and includes the unicorn-head mark of the bladesmith Clemens Horn.

RAPIER
HILT, C. 1620–30
BLADE BY
CLEMENS HORN
(GERMAN,
SOLINGEN,
1586–1617)
CMA 1916.697 [129]

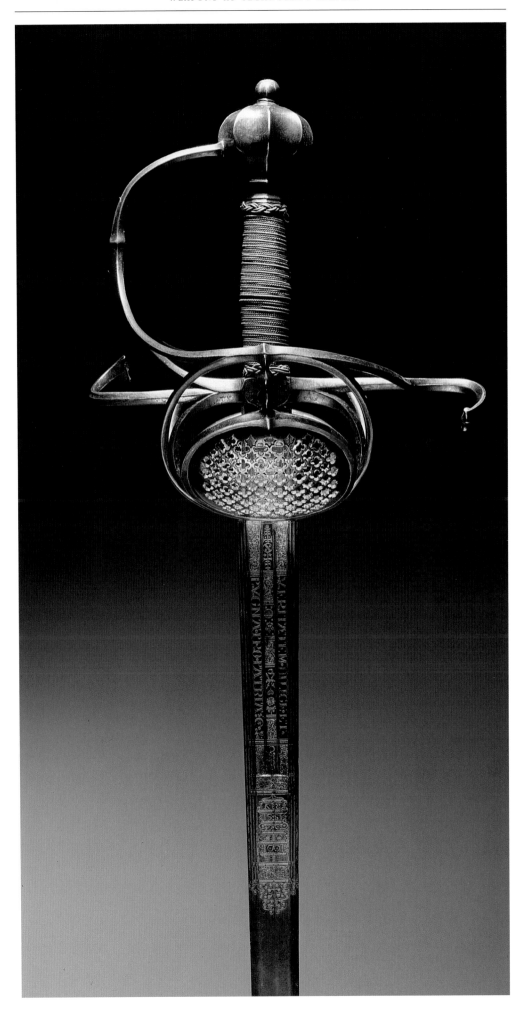

SMALLSWORD WITH
BLUED AND GOLD-
ENCRUSTED
DECORATION
FRANCE, PARIS,
C. 1730
CMA 1916.1097 [142]

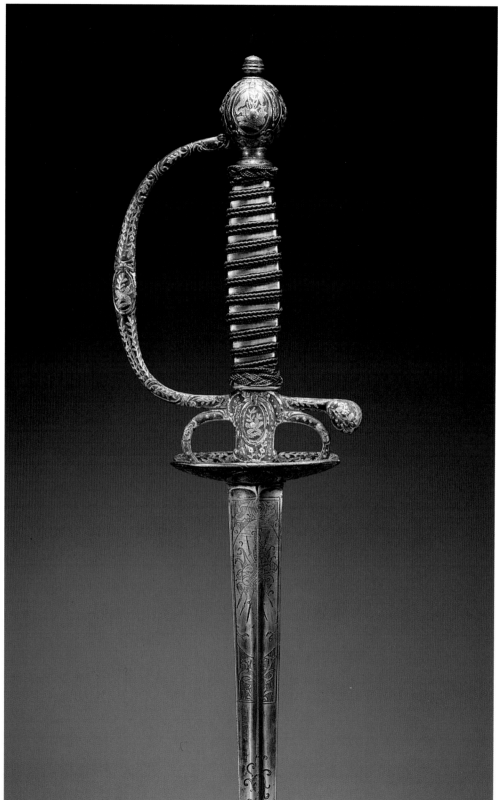

In the eighteenth century, the smallsword was designed to be a light, quick weapon. Like the rapier, it was carried by unarmored noblemen. The smallsword, however, was as decorative as it was functional. Its hilt, visible even when the blade was sheathed, became the ground for elaborate displays of taste and artistic talent. Jewelers used silver and gold, etching, chasing and inlay, precious stones, porcelain, and even enamel to decorate hilts. The decorative design was often carried down onto the blade, which could be chased or etched with designs, and gilded or blued. As decorative works, smallswords represent the final stage in the evolution of the sword.

SHEETS OF
DESIGNS FOR
SMALLSWORD
HILTS (FROM THE
BOULTON AND
FOTHERGILL
PATTERN BOOK)
ENGLAND,
BIRMINGHAM,
1775–80
BIRMINGHAM CITY
ARCHIVES (U.K.)

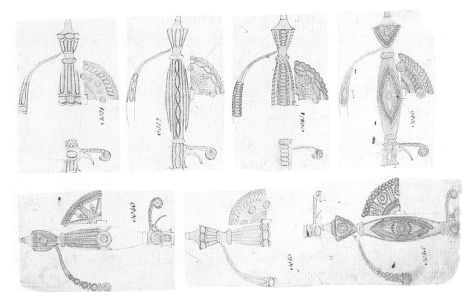

The series of drawings above was produced by the Birmingham firm of Boulton and Fothergill and formed part of a pattern book assembled over the years 1760–81. Prospective clients would choose a combination of elements according to their taste.

The hilt and shell guard of the sword below are chiseled and stamped in relief with figures of animals inspired by designs of the French artist J.-B. Oudry. Oudry's drawings in chalk and paintings often favored themes of the chase or animals in their natural environment.

SMALLSWORD
FRANCE, PARIS,
C. 1750–60
CMA 1916.1094 [139]

Italy, Toledo and Valencia in Spain, and Solingen and Passau in Germany. From there, they were exported throughout Europe and then outfitted with a locally made hilt in accordance with local taste. The demand for these reputable blades inevitably led to the forging of names and markings on inferior products, often misspelled.

The rapier gradually fell from favor among northern and central Europeans during the final decades of the seventeenth century and was replaced by the smallsword, a much lighter and more slender relative with a simple hilt and a fairly short stiff blade that offered greater control. Like its larger cousin, the smallsword was a civilian thrusting weapon customarily worn by well-to-do gentlemen in civilian dress during the weapon's heyday in the eighteenth century. Smallswords continued to be worn for brief periods afterward on formal or court occasions.

The hilt of the smallsword featured a small guard of one or two shells. Some versions were equipped with a small knuckle guard, while others omitted this feature. In virtually all cases the hilt assembly (or furniture) provided a surface for the virtuoso hiltmaker, often a jeweler or goldsmith, to cover with elegant baroque and rococo decoration. In Italian smallswords manufactured in Brescia, this could take the form of delicately pierced and chiseled scrollwork, while in German swords the hilt might comprise gilt-bronze furniture with grips made of Meissen porcelain.

Smallsword hilts with porcelain grips, as in this example, became fashionable in some circles during the second half of the eighteenth century. They added a colorful splash to male attire.

SMALLSWORD WITH PORCELAIN GRIP
GERMANY, C. 1770
CMA 1916.1501 [158]

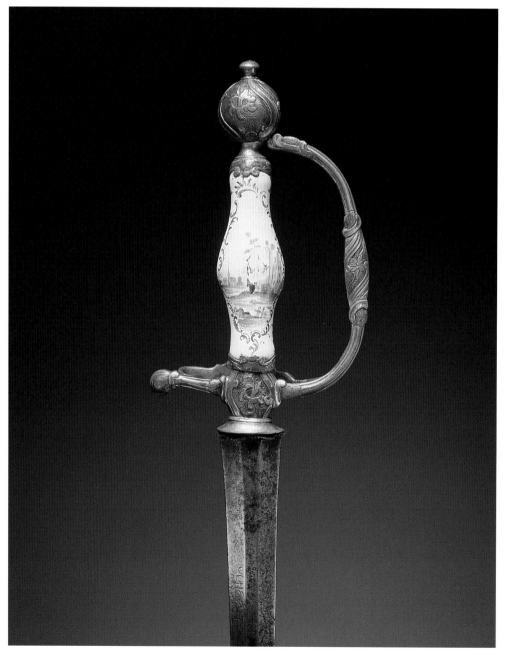

SMALLSWORD
FRANCE, PARIS(?),
C. 1780
CMA 1974.57 [199]

SMALLSWORD
FRANCE,
18TH CENTURY
CMA 1916.1096 [141]

COURT SWORD
WITH SILVER HILT
ENGLAND, LONDON
OR BIRMINGHAM,
C. 1790
CMA 1916.1095 [140]

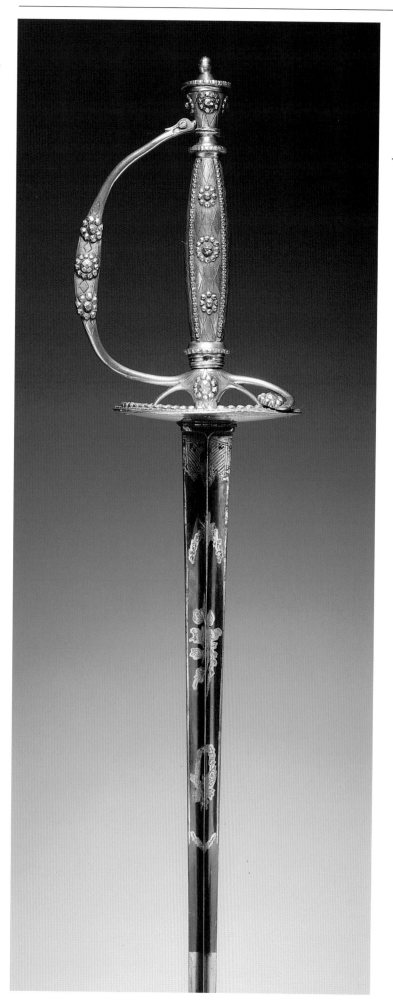

The hilt of this sword is finely finished in cut silver, burnished to resemble faceted gemstones. The neoclassical urn-shape of the pommel was particularly fashionable in England after 1780. The upper portion of the blade is blued and gilded to provide a feel of great luxury.

This hilt is made of polished steel, pierced and inset with faceted steel beads to resemble silver. By the end of the eighteenth century, civilians no longer regularly wore swords or used them as weapons. The court sword had become a piece of costume jewelry to be worn only with court dress or by military officers in dress uniform. The hilt and often the upper part of the blade were therefore lavishly decorated for ostentation.

The outward form of smallswords had become international by the early eighteenth century, with their place of manufacture being discernible only by their decoration. Numerous drawings and printed pattern books survive with designs for the decoration of smallsword hilts and shell guards. For example, between 1760 and 1781 the firm of Boulton and Fothergill of Birmingham, England, produced a book of numbered patterns for smallsword hilts. These were shown to customers

In his portrait, Lord Rivers wears an officer's dress sword, an emblem of rank in late-eighteenth-century society.

in the shop, who would then select the combination of decorative elements best suited to their tastes.

The fashion among gentlemen for wearing smallswords with everyday attire began to wane by the turn of the eighteenth century. However, the military dress sword, a counterpart of the civilian smallsword, survived and essentially preserved the outward forms of the weapon.

The Hafted Weapon

From earliest times one of man's most widespread weapons was the spear, a wooden haft or pole to which an edged point had been attached. The spear was a thrusting weapon ideally suited to both war and hunting. In antiquity it had evolved into a number of different forms, some specialized for use by horsemen, others intended for use by foot soldiers. By the High Renaissance the number and range of forms, styles, and sizes had multiplied, some elaborated chiefly by their decorative heads.

"Hafted weapons" is essentially a generic term that, along with "staff weapons" and "pole arms," refers to a family of edged weapons attached to a wooden haft by means of socketing, riveting, or nailing. With the exception of the lance, which remained the weapon of the mounted knight, by 1600 all other staff weapons were intended to be wielded by men on foot. No longer were war and hunting the only applications; sporting combats and ceremonial use now accounted for some of the finest staff weapons made.

THE BATTLE OF
PAVIA, 1525
FLEMISH MASTER,
SHORTLY AFTER
1525
THE BIRMINGHAM
MUSEUM OF ART
(ALABAMA) 61.125

One of the most important military engagements of the era, the Battle of Pavia pitted the forces of Holy Roman Emperor Charles V, ruler of much of Europe, against the French king Francis I, who sought to displace the Spanish Hapsburgs from northern Italy and reconquer the Italian duchy of Milan. The battle was a disaster for the French. Francis was captured and held prisoner in Madrid. This painting, probably made after written accounts of the battle, provides a wealth of information about the relative positions of the two forces as well as their composition and equipment. While the use of artillery and fully armored knights charging with lances played an important role, the use of massed infantries with pole arms—pikes and halberds—was fundamental to military thinking of the time. Also evident is the use of battle flags and standards to provide visual cues and rallying points for troops during the chaos of battle.

BILL
ITALY, C. 1480
CMA 1916.1835 [117]

The bill was developed from an agricultural tool. Used throughout western Europe, it was particularly popular in Italy and England where it served as an equivalent to the central European halberd.

LINSTOCK
FRANCE, C. 1600–25
CMA 1916.1786 [108]

This specialized staff weapon was used primarily for igniting the charge in pieces of artillery. The two lateral projections terminating in eagles' heads are actually clips designed to hold the smoldering matches that allowed the firer to stand a little farther from the cannon. The short, leaf-shaped blade allowed the linstock to be used as a weapon if necessary.

TWO CORSÈQUES
ITALY, C. 1520–30
CMA 1916.1802 [113];
1916.1535 [98]

The corsèque is a pole arm with a symmetrical three-pronged head consisting of a central double-edged blade and two sharp, upturned wings. The side blades served several functions: as a guard to protect the soldier's hand when a thrust was delivered with the central blade; as a hook for unseating a mounted opponent; and for

tripping the opponent's horse. The version on the left is sometimes called a chauve-souris after the French word for "bat," since the side blades are thought to resemble a bat's wings. The corsèque was used mostly in Italy and France from the fifteenth to the early seventeenth centuries.

One of the first such staff weapons to be used by medieval infantries was the bill, documented as early as the thirteenth century. The bill derived originally from an agricultural tool used to prune vines and trees, and was probably pressed into service by levied troops. Its long shaft proved useful for reaching mounted men, and a military version soon emerged. The bill was fitted with a pronounced hook whose inside and outside curves were cutting edges and was topped by a long spike. Its use was widespread in Europe during the fifteenth century, but it was especially favored by Italian foot soldiers through the middle of the sixteenth century. An English version of the weapon with a shorter blade emerged during the early sixteenth century. In 1551 the Venetian ambassador to England wrote:

> English bills have a short thick shaft with an iron like a peasant's hedging bill, but much thicker and heavier than what is used in the Venetian territories, with this they strike so heavily as to unhorse cavalry and it is made short because they like close quarters.

PARADE HALBERD WITH THE ARMS OF ELECTOR CHRISTIAN I OF SAXONY
GERMANY, SAXONY, 1586–91
CMA 1916.1819 [115]

With its elegant S-shaped axe blade and etched scrollwork decoration, this halberd is typical of the parade weapons used by the more than one hundred palace guards of the Prince Elector of Saxony, Christian I. One side of the axe blade bears the arms of the Duchy of Saxony; the other, the crossed swords of the Archmarshalship of the Holy Roman Empire.

PARADE SPEAR
GERMANY,
AUGSBURG(?),
C. 1570–1600
CMA 1916.1789 [109]

This weapon is etched with the imperial Hapsburg arms on one face and the Burgundian Stave Cross of St. Andrew on the other. In the sixteenth century, parade spears of this type became part of the insignia of infantry and light cavalry officers in the Imperial Army. In 1548 Titian painted an equestrian portrait of Emperor Charles V holding such a spear. At his abdication in 1556, Charles split the Hapsburg inheritance between his son, Philip II of Spain, to whom was awarded control of Burgundy, and his brother Frederick, to whom went the imperial title and the family's central European lands. This spear probably belongs to this later period and was likely intended for ceremonial use.

THREE HALBERDS
GERMANY AND
SWITZERLAND,
16TH AND 17TH
CENTURIES
CMA 1916.1562 [105];
1916.1559 [103];
1916.1554 [101]

The halberd—the most efficient infantry pole arm of the fifteenth and sixteenth centuries—was favored by shock troops and Swiss and German mercenaries of the period.

The most efficient arms for infantry during the fifteenth and sixteenth centuries were the staff weapons chiefly known as the long pike and the halberd. The
twelve-foot pike, called the "Queen of the Battlefield," could be used against cavalry but only in the mass formation known as the pikeman's square. The halberd,
on the other hand, was a weapon of great versatility. The word "halberd" comes
from the German words *halm* (staff) and *barte* (axe). The halberd is, in fact, an axe
with a very particular shape and function: The axe blade was used for hacking, the
spike for thrusting, and the beak either for piercing or grappling plate armor, or
for pulling a knight from his saddle.

Used by shock troops, the halberd was the weapon of choice for Swiss and
German mercenaries. In fact, the first halberds are believed to have been made for
the warriors of medieval Switzerland, and most early examples have been attributed with some certainty to Swiss and German armorers. The earliest known

*The partisan, a staff weapon with a
symmetrically shaped head, was carried by
infantry officers and members of princely
bodyguards during the 1600s and 1700s.
This one is inscribed with the coat of arms
and letters F.L.C.V.M for Franz Ludwig
Kurfurst von Mainz.*

mention of the weapon is by the Swiss poet Konrad von Würzburg (d. 1287), who writes in his *History of the Trojan War:*

Six thousand men ready on foot,
Armed with halberds
So finely honed,
That any who was struck,
Met certain death.

From the mid-sixteenth century the halberd changed significantly in appearance. Its distinctive outline invited exaggeration of its functional elements into purely ornamental shapes, while its large blade provided space for armorial devices.

Numerous forms of staff weapons followed during the sixteenth and seventeenth centuries—the corsèque, the glaive, the partisan—all defined by the shape

Glaives—pole arms with long knife-like blades—were normally carried by palace guards and were a favorite ceremonial weapon for noble Italian houses. Judging from the large number decorated with the arms of Venetian families, they were particularly favored in the city of Venice.

of their steel heads, some being symmetrical, some asymmetrical. The large flat surfaces of the heads lent themselves to engraving, etching, or other forms of decoration and provided a perfect arena for the coats of arms of noble or princely families. For this very reason, the partisan and the glaive—further embellished with colorful velvet tassels—were the favored staff weapons of palace guards and splendidly outfitted special regiments of princely bodyguards. The ceremonial use of staff weapons continues to this day by the Swiss Guards at the Vatican, and by Britain's Yeomen of the Royal Guard and the Yeomen Warders of the Tower of London.

The Crossbow

The crossbow was one of the most dangerous weapons to evolve in European warfare, particularly when used against cavalry. Though known in some form since late antiquity, it was not used widely in Europe until about 1050. By the twelfth century the crossbow's range and power had made it the most feared infantry weapon. Indeed, the Fourth Lateran Council of 1139 prohibited its use against Christians (although unbelievers were still exposed to the weapon's wrath). Crossbows fired high-velocity bolts, or "quarrels," with iron heads and wooden or leather flights. By the fourteenth century they could pierce plate armor.

The earliest crossbows used a bow made from a block of hardwood, typically ash or yew, fastened to a tiller (or stock). Initially, the bows could be "spanned" by hand. Later versions were so stiff that the archer's feet were required to bend them. The crossbowman simply held the bow firmly against the ground with his feet while he manually pulled the bowstring back until it locked against a nut. The front of the crossbow was usually fitted with a metal foot stirrup—large enough to accommodate one or both feet—to prevent the bindings of the bow from contacting the ground.

It is believed that the crossbow was introduced into England by the Normans after the conquest of 1066. The English king Richard I (ruled 1189–99) used crossbows extensively in his infantry, as did his brother King John (ruled 1199–1216). However, because of its slow rate of shooting, the crossbow soon became some-

*SIEGE OF A TOWN
(FROM LES
CHRONIQUE
D'ANGLETERRE)
FRANCE, C. 1480
THE BRITISH
LIBRARY, LONDON
ROYAL MS. 14 E. IV,
FOL. 210*

The crossbow's slow rate of fire was better suited to siege warfare. This scene, taken from a fifteenth-century miniature, shows crossbowmen firing at the defenders of a walled town. The two crossbowmen in the foreground use a windlass, a kind of pulley, to draw or "span" their crossbows while anchoring their weapons with their feet.

thing of an elite weapon, better suited to siege warfare than to the battlefield. In every army in Europe crossbowmen were considered an elite corps, and as such they occupied the central position in battle formations. Membership in this corps was regarded so highly that in Spain the crossbowman was ranked on par with the cavalryman. The rank of commanding officer of a crossbowman corps was one of the loftiest positions in the military.

CROSSBOW AND
CRANEQUIN

CROSSBOW:

GERMANY, C. 1460–70

CMA 1916.1725 [204]

CRANEQUIN:

FRANCE(?),

C. 1480–1500

CMA 1916.2082 [205]

Bows made of composite materials were developed during the fifteenth century. They were immensely powerful and could be spanned only with the aid of a winder called a cranequin. Composite bows were later replaced with steel ones.

Until the sixteenth century, the best units of crossbowmen tended to be mercenaries hired from time to time by princes and rulers for expediency. The Gascons and the Genoese were considered the cream of the crop. By the time of his Welsh campaign (1277–82), England's Edward I had but 250 native-born crossbowmen in his army. In 1282 he was able to supplement these with 585 Gascon crossbowmen, most on horseback.

Although the crossbow continued to be used in European wars until the end of the fifteenth century, the longbow gained popularity in England. English longbowmen acquitted themselves respectably at the battles of Crécy (1346) and Agincourt (1415). The crossbow was more powerful than the longbow, its quarrel was heavier, and it could be used in cramped positions. The longbow, on the other hand, could shoot a larger number of arrows more quickly—producing an overwhelming psychological impact upon the enemy.

The main shortcoming of the crossbow's hardwood bow was that, with use, it became deformed, fragile, and thus unusable. During the twelfth century, Europeans became acquainted with a new form of composite bow stave (developed in the Islamic world), which they eventually duplicated. Composite bows were made from crosscut pieces of horn, wood, and sinew glued together and tightly bound with animal tendons. The bow was then covered with parchment and often painted or decorated in some way. Despite its size, it was extremely light and powerful. In the fourteenth century, an even more powerful and longer-lasting steel version of the bow gradually began to replace the composite bow and survived it into the sixteenth century.

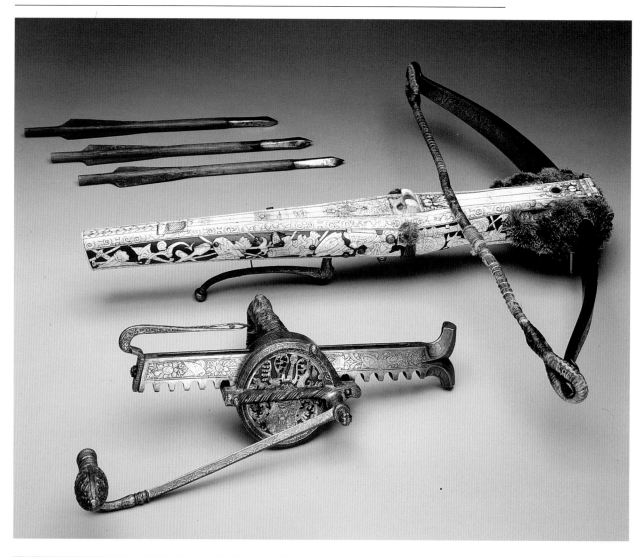

This crossbow and its cranequin, made for the Prince Elector of Saxony, August I (ruled 1553–86), is a masterpiece of Renaissance decorative arts (see detail illustrations on pages 136–37). The walnut stock of the crossbow is inlaid with engraved bone representations of trophies, arms, and musical instruments. The cranequin is also enriched with a variety of engraved designs: flowers, leaves, masks, and trophies. Even the cranking handle is minutely decorated. Not unexpectedly, the winder bears the elector's coat of arms. August I was well known for his taste in elaborate objects, including rare and costly weapons.

A man's strength was sufficient to bend and draw the early wooden bows. Eventually, however, with the adoption of the more powerful composite and steel bows (fifteenth-century steel crossbows had draw weights of 1,000 pounds), hooks and ratchet devices became necessary. These included the claw and belt, goat's-foot lever, windlass, and cranequin.

The windlass featured a winding drum and a pair of pulleys to draw the cord, whereas the cranequin consisted of a ratchet ending in a pair of claws that gripped the cord when wound. It was fixed to the tiller or stock by means of a loop. The

Hunting in Renaissance Europe was not only a sport, but essential as a source of food. The Prince Electors of Saxony were passionate practitioners of par force hunting with dogs—elaborate, highly rehearsed occasions, coordinated by the use of signals from hunting horns. The scene above reveals in remarkable detail a variety of deluxe hunting weapons: crossbows, hangers (hunting swords), and boar spears. Elector Johann Friedrich can be seen with a crossbow in the lower left. As shown in the detail at left, his weapon is very similar to that made for Elector August I of Saxony, illustrated on the opposite page.

CRANEQUIN
DETAIL SHOWING
THE ARMS OF
AUGUSTUS I OF
SAXONY
CMA 1916.1723.B
[203]

CROSSBOW
DETAIL SHOWING
ENGRAVED
DECORATION AND
WOOLEN POMPOM
CMA 1916.1723.A
[202]

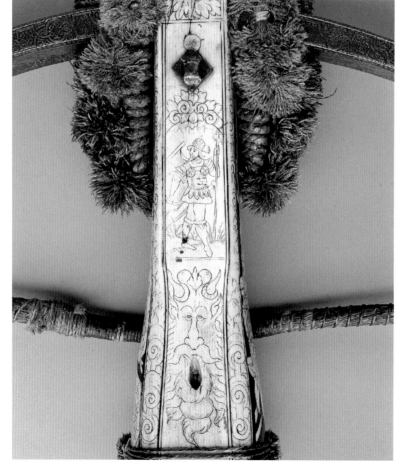

cranequin was more expensive than a simple windlass but was easier to handle, especially on horseback. It has been theorized that mounted troops and huntsmen would have used the cranequin whenever possible, while the windlass remained the common winding tool of the infantry. Once spanned, the crossbow could be kept "loaded" by means of a nut, or catch, that held the cord in place. A crossbow could shoot its bolts farther and with greater force than a longbow could shoot arrows, but reloading and discharging one took much more time.

During the fifteenth century, as crossbows became heavier and more powerful, it took so long to load them that the shooter needed an assistant to carry a large shield known as a pavise. These enormous, lively painted shields could be propped on the ground in front of the crossbowman during the reloading process. Without this portable shelter, crossbowmen were vulnerable to a rain of arrows from the faster-shooting archers.

In the first half of the sixteenth century, wartime use of the crossbow waned as firearms gradually rose to dominance. Nevertheless, the weapon became increasingly popular for hunting large and dangerous animals such as wolves, bears, stags, and wild boars. Crossbows (now equipped almost universally with steel bows) could be held or aimed ready to shoot for long periods without strain and, unlike guns, they discharged silently—a desirable feature for hunting.

By the middle of the sixteenth century, sporting crossbows were becoming very ornate, decorated with bone and mother-of-pearl inlay. Some crossbows included richly carved stocks enlivened with the owner's coat of arms. They also often were outfitted with complex lock mechanisms incorporating hair triggers and other refinements. The use of the crossbow as a sporting weapon was widespread on the Continent, particularly among the noble classes.

CROSSBOW
DETAIL SHOWING
INLAID
ORNAMENTATION
OF TROPHIES AND
ARMS
CMA 1916.1723.A
[202]

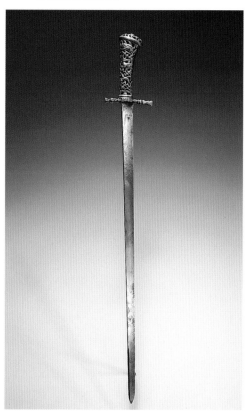

No gentleman's hunting costume was complete without a hunting sword. These special sidearms, designed primarily as defense against dangerous game in the field, were also used to dispatch game at the end of the chase. It was a point of honor among aristocratic hunters to carve and section the game in the field, a further function to which these swords were well suited. They were often made as a set, or garniture, and included smaller knives, forks, and other implements for carving the carcass.

Besides being viewed as a recreation for European nobility, and an ancient and hereditary right, par force hunting with dogs, crossbows, spears, and swords was recognized as a necessary and pragmatic skill: It supplied an additional source of food. Game provided meat, which was an important asset, and many of the wild animals then common in northern Europe—such as the wild boar and the black bear—were considered a menace. Prowess at dispatching a dangerous animal was much admired among Europe's noble classes and was viewed as a class privilege, carrying with it fine points of dress, vocabulary, and protocol. It was incumbent upon the gentleman of standing to be accomplished in the use of the crossbow, the preferred weapon for stalking deer. Its accuracy and silent discharge ensured a favored place among hunting weapons long after the introduction of firearms.

Gentleman hunters were expected to carry special hunting swords, which, in theory, would be used to administer the *coup de grâce* to the downed stag or to defend the hunter from a wounded animal. These short-bladed swords were usually highly decorative, featuring grips of carved staghorn or chiseled steel with gilding and appropriate hunting decoration. By the eighteenth century, however, hunting swords were worn as an accessory to male costume, sometimes incorporating fragile materials such as agate, porcelain, or ivory, as in court swords, and little suited to practical utility.

A unique form of sporting crossbow, known as a stonebow or prodd, was developed in Italy during the sixteenth century for hunting wildfowl, rabbits, and other small animals, and became popular in the Germanic lands during the following century. This weapon featured a steel bow fitted with a double string, at the center of which was a pouch or cradle for the projectile—a pebble, bullet, or baked-clay pellet. Also known as a "pellet" crossbow, its bow was lightweight and thus entirely spannable by hand. Unlike conventional quarrel-firing crossbows, stonebows were meant to stun the game or to kill it without damaging the pelt. They were fashionable through the nineteenth century for target shooting.

Pellet crossbows, which shot small stones or clay pellets rather than steel-tipped bolts, were used solely for hunting fowl and small animals such as squirrels, rabbits, or ermine. They lacked the power and range of conventional crossbows, but could be spanned by hand. They were used throughout Europe from about 1550 to 1700 and, like their counterparts, were often beautifully decorated.

PELLET CROSSBOW
SOUTH
GERMANY(?),
17TH CENTURY
CMA 1916.1726 [206]

DETAIL SHOWING
ENGRAVED
ORNAMENT OF
HUNTER WITH
DOGS

The Gunmaker's Art

Handfire weapons made their first appearance almost simultaneously with the artillery piece around 1300. At no time did the gun suddenly replace bows, crossbows, and armor. Instead, over the following three centuries personal firearms gradually gained ascendancy on the European battlefield until, by the middle of the seventeenth century, their increasing sophistication had rendered plate armor relatively ineffective.

The medieval handfire weapon of around 1400 was a primitive bronze or iron tube about sixteen inches long fastened to a straight stock or tiller made of wood. Instead of being held up to the gunner's eye for aim, these simple devices probably were rested on a stand or wall by means of a hook-like protrusion for both safety and absorption of recoil. Since these guns were ignited by poking a hot wire or taper through a touch-hole, resting them also simplified firing. The earliest of these handfire weapons required two men for operation: one to aim the gun, the other to ignite the gunpowder.

THE SIEGE OF ARRAS
(FROM THE
CHRONIQUES D'E DE
MONSTRELET)
FRANCE,
15TH CENTURY
BIBLIOTHÈQUE
NATIONALE DE
FRANCE, PARIS
MS. FR. 2680, FOL. 184

In this miniature, attackers of the moated and fortified town of Arras use bows and rudimentary firearms against its defenders.

These earliest guns—little more than iron tubes—were both inaccurate and dangerous to those wielding them.

With the appearance of the gun, gunsmithery became a recognized profession of considerable repute. Personal firearms, like high-quality swords and crossbows, eventually became male accessories enlivened with their owners' personal arms and mottoes. The conspicuous display of wealth and power that ownership of firearms constituted was in many ways of greater importance than the destructive capabilities of the weapons themselves.

De Gheyn's book (first published in 1607)
served as a manual for the inexperienced
soldier. Here, a musketeer fires a matchlock
gun. The forked rest helped support the
firearm's weight. Across his shoulder the
musketeer wears a bandoleer from which
are suspended waterproofed bottles, each
containing a premeasured charge of powder.

The walnut stock of this pistol is inlaid
with engraved staghorn in the form of
interlacing foliage and arabesques
interspersed with putti, birds, and
animals—an elegant weapon befitting a
noble patron. Since pistols of this type
could deliver only one shot and had to be
reloaded to fire the next round, they were
commonly made in pairs to be worn in
leather holsters. The large ball-shaped
pommel on the grip made it easier to
withdraw the pistol from its holster, and
served as a counterweight to the heavy steel
barrel. The pommel also became a useful
weapon when the firing mechanism failed
or when close quarters dictated its use. Such
pistols normally were purchased in elegant
presentation boxes that featured tools and
other accessories necessary to clean,
maintain, and use the firearms.

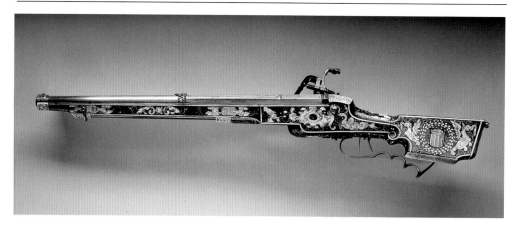

It was at the beginning of the sixteenth century that the handfire weapon began to change the face of European warfare. Most of these firearms were of the muzzleloading variety; that is, the powder and ball were loaded down the muzzle of the gun and tamped with a ramrod. The most common examples were the musket, a heavy long-barreled gun, and the arquebus, a smaller and lighter hand weapon. By the end of the century they had been adopted by the majority of European armies. With an effective range of about 250 feet, compared to the crossbow's maximum range of 130 feet, these weapons offered a distinct advantage. The gunsight was developed in the early fifteenth century, and recoil, which had been a significant problem for the new technology, was overcome by the wooden shaft and butt. Though breechloading guns had been developed by the early decades of the century, they remained rare and expensive prestige pieces. For the next three centuries, firearms would be distinguished primarily by their respective ignition systems.

Simple matchlock guns were the most common through the mid-seventeenth century. Matchlock firearms employed a smoldering cord called a "match" to ignite the weapon's charge. Made of twisted flax or hemp, the match was held in position through the jaws of an arm known as a cock. Just before firing, the gunner

Made originally as a petronel pistol (a weapon fired with its butt resting against the chest), this firearm seems to have been refitted with a new stock later in the seventeenth century to convert it into a rifle, most likely for a child's use.

would blow on the match to produce a healthy glow. As the trigger was pressed, the burning end of the cord was forced to touch the priming powder, which in turn ignited the main charge, thus firing the weapon. The matchlock firing mechanism meant that the gunner no longer had to apply the match by hand, allowing him to concentrate entirely on aiming the weapon, usually with the help of a fork-shaped rest. To prevent accidents and to keep the smoldering match dry, gunners sometimes carried the cord in a hollow iron tube with ventilation holes at one end.

At the beginning of the sixteenth century a new type of ignition system was invented: the wheel-lock, the first self-igniting mechanism for guns. There is

WHEEL-LOCK

HUNTING RIFLE

(TSCHINKE)

POLAND, SILESIA,

C. 1630–50

CMA 1916.1782 [221]

This small-caliber fowling piece owes its name to the town of Teschen in Silesia (now southern Poland), which as early as 1580 was associated with a particular type of gun. The precise date of the invention of the Tschinke is unknown, though a dated example of 1610 survives in the Imperial Armouries in Vienna. The stocks of many Tschinke, like this example, were elaborately inlaid with bone and mother-of-pearl.

some evidence that wheel-lock guns were already in use in Germany and select areas of Italy by the first decade of the century. From there, the new technology spread throughout the rest of Europe. This type of ignition involved a piece of iron pyrites held in the jaws of a cock. When the trigger was pulled, the pyrites pressed against the serrated edge of a prewound revolving wheel, creating a shower of sparks that ignited priming powder in a pan on top of the lock. This action sent a flash of flame through the vent hole to explode the main charge in the breech of the barrel.

Short wheel-lock pistols were in use by light cavalry as early as the 1530s.

WHEEL-LOCK FROM
A HUNTING RIFLE
SOUTH GERMANY
OR AUSTRIA,
C. 1660–1720
CMA 1916.1546 [236]

Originally part of a deluxe weapon, the lock plate's entire surface is inlaid with an exquisite floral pattern in gold. Carefully chiseled, the fanciful hammer is shaped as an animal head crowned by a mass of foliage. The double eagle on the wheel plate suggests that the weapon was made for a member of the Hapsburg family.

They were normally made in pairs and carried in holsters slung over either side of the saddle. However, due to the infancy of the ignition mechanism and the poor quality of the era's gunpowder, short wheel-lock firearms were often unreliable and generally effective only at point-blank range. Longer barreled wheel-lock muskets provided greater range. In war, the matchlock gun predominated through the middle of the seventeenth century by virtue of its simplicity, low cost, and rugged dependability.

WHEEL-LOCK
HUNTING RIFLE
STOCKMAKER:
HANS SCHMIDT
(D. 1669)
AUSTRIA, FERLACH,
MID-17TH
CENTURY
CMA 1959.127 [228]

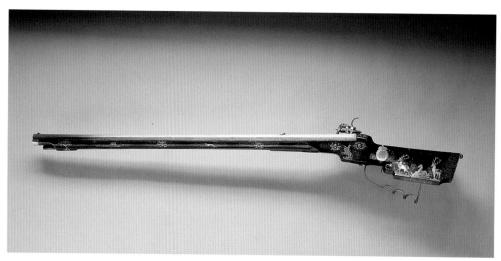

The barrel of this hunting piece is marked with the letters GS within a shield—the likely initials of the owner who, as indicated by the escutcheon on the stock, was probably a member of the Order of the Golden Fleece. A similar rifle made for another member of this order, Graf Sigmund von Dietrichstein, is preserved in Vienna.

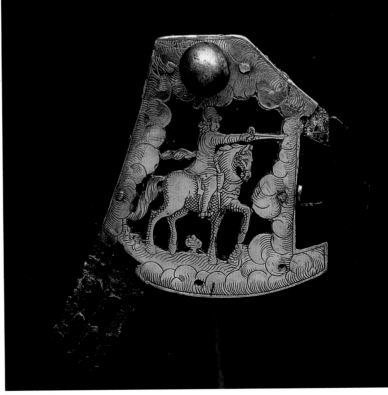

Whatever its limitations, the fact that the new wheel-lock gun did not require its owner to carry a tell-tale smoldering match caused trepidation among princes and municipal councils, who viewed it as an ideal assassin's weapon. Local ordinances against the carrying of wheel-lock pistols in city streets or into public or government buildings began to appear as early as the 1520s. In 1532 such a ban was enforced in the city of Venice by the Council of Ten: ". . . a kind of gun has been invented recently that makes fire by itself, and because these are small they are carried under the clothes so that nobody sees them."

Powder flasks are small, readily portable containers specifically designed to hold gunpowder. From the fifteenth to the nineteenth centuries, they were used to charge and prime firearms, cannon, and tinderlighters (the mechanical precursor of the modern match). Though they generally followed certain forms during specific periods, there were no rigidly set conventions. Likewise, their materials of construction varied greatly.

POWDER FLASK
GERMANY,
C. 1620–50
CMA 1916.60 [246]

The complicated and delicate wheel-lock mechanism did, however, attract the interest of rich noblemen who commissioned such guns for use in hunting. Gunmakers lavished all form of embellishment on these firearms: chiseling, engraving, and gilding of the metal parts, as well as the use of rare woods such as ebony for the stock, enlivened with inlays of horn, bone, and ivory. The winding key or spanner needed for tensioning the wheel-lock's spring was often made *en suite* along with primer and powder flasks to form a garniture with the weapon itself. These accessories were also highly decorated.

Thousands of powder flasks made from the fifteenth to nineteenth centuries have survived, presumably because of their allure as fine decorative arts objects. The variety of materials and forms of ornament used in the manufacture of luxury powder flasks for the aristocracy was virtually limitless. The bodies and mounts

Luxury powder flasks served as visible badges of rank. Many highly decorated *flasks, like this example, embody all the allure and characteristics of works of art.*

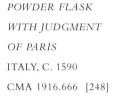

POWDER FLASK
WITH JUDGMENT
OF PARIS
ITALY, C. 1590
CMA 1916.666 [248]

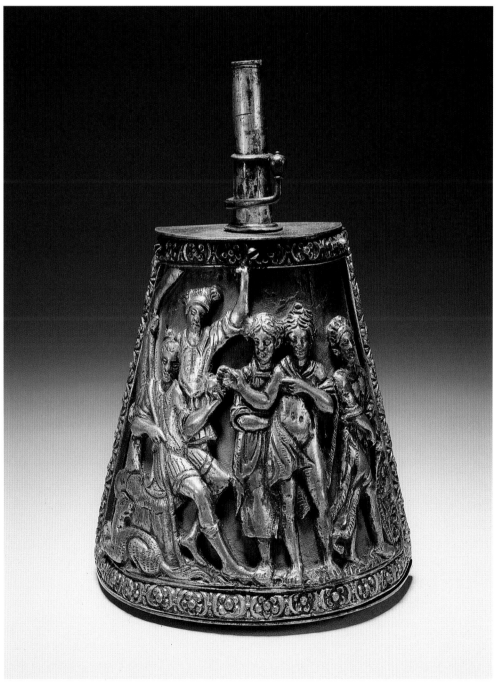

were at various times made of bronze, copper, gold, iron, silver, *cuir bouilli* (leather), ivory, staghorn, and wood. Their decoration might include religious or allegorical themes. In 1586 Londoner John Calthorpe offered one as a lottery prize:

> The elleaventh pryce conteyneth a most rich harquebouse of Millan with a most sumptuous flaske and touchboxe covered with Crimsin velvett artificially wrought with goldsmythes worke curiously graven and gilded with riche golde the stringe of crimsin silke and gold moste pleasant. . .

The metal parts of firearms, especially in France, were often decorated with chiseling and engraving. The flat lock plates in particular offered an ideal surface for engraver's tools. Until the publication of books of ornament specifically designed for the gunmaker, decorators of firearms had to choose suitable details from books intended for goldsmiths or other artisans. In the seventeenth century, however, a steady stream of pattern books was issued by Paris gunmakers or the engravers who worked for them—offering new ideas for artistic decoration and allowing prospective clients to shop for the latest fashions in firearms. Collections of designs have survived that contain not only motifs for engravings, but in some cases actual proofs taken from such engravings. Among these illustrations are wheel-lock guns with sculptured stocks and finely chiseled and engraved lock plates.

Two such collections published in Paris at the end of the seventeenth century and the beginning of the eighteenth would have a profound influence on European gunmakers: *Diverse Pièces d'arquebuserie,* with engravings by Nicolas

POWDER FLASK
ITALY, C. 1560–70
CMA 1918.65 [263]

The manner of a powder flask's decoration reflected the fashion of its day. This is an exceptionally fine example of Italian Renaissance tooled leatherwork known as cuir boulli (molded and hardened leather).

PLATE FROM
*NOUVEAUX
DESSEINS
D'ARQUEBUSERIES*
PUBLISHED IN
PARIS, 1730
VICTORIA AND
ALBERT MUSEUM,
LONDON
INV. E212/1927

Both gunmakers and customers were fashion-conscious with respect to the embellishment of their firearms. Pattern books like this provided fresh and imaginative sources of ornament. From about 1670 to 1770 the predominant influence on European firearms was French.

The barrels of these pistols are signed G. MASSIN, a gunsmith working in eastern France or French-speaking Flanders, possibly in the city of Liège. The exquisite ornament along the breech of the barrels is chiseled and engraved. The gilded lock plates and mounts can be compared to the finest contemporary work in other media, such as furniture with ormolu mounts.

Guérard, and *Nouveaux Desseins d'arquebuseries,* with engravings by Lacollombe. The dominance of France in the technical and artistic development of firearms is to some degree attributable to the influence of King Louis XIII (ruled 1610–43), who became interested in firearms as a child and eventually amassed a very fine collection. The king based his collection not only on artistic value but also on interesting technical features. Louis's impressive collection was dispersed after the French Revolution and Napoleonic Wars.

*PAIR OF FLINTLOCK
PISTOLS*
ITALY, BRESCIA,
C. 1670
CMA 1916.52.1–2
[217]

*While the barrels are signed P. MORETTA,
the lock plates of these pistols are signed
CARLO LERME, who also chiseled the
mounts. The chiseling of gun ornament is a
task comparable to sculpture on a miniature
scale, carried out in an extremely hard
material. Since this was usually beyond the
skill of most gunsmiths, it was not
uncommon for such work to be contracted
out.*

DOUBLE-BARRELED
FLINTLOCK
SPORTING GUN OF
NAPOLEON I
BONAPARTE,
DATED 1809
JEAN LE PAGE
(FRENCH, PARIS,
ACTIVE
C. 1779–1822)
SIGNED ON
BARREL (INLAID IN
GOLD): LE PAGE À
PARIS / ARQ[UEBUSIER]
DE L'EMPEREUR
SIGNED ON LOCKS:
LE PAGE / À PARIS
CMA 1966.433 [229]

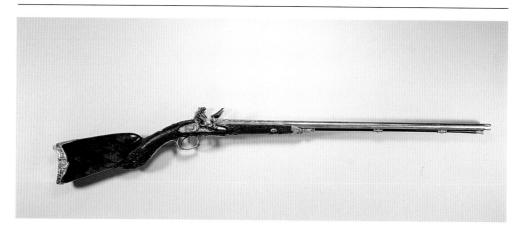

The Le Page family of Paris, father and sons, emerged as the most outstanding makers of deluxe firearms for the French nobility during the late eighteenth and early nineteenth centuries. Jean Le Page, the maker of this gun, held an appointment as royal gunmaker to the French king Louis XVI, and after the revolution to the emperor, Napoleon Bonaparte, who commissioned this weapon. The gun bears the imperial monogram N in two locations. It was apparently presented as a gift by Napoleon to the Polish count Vincent Corvin Graf von Krasine-Krasinski.

Whereas the early sixteenth century saw the development of the wheel-lock ignition mechanism, the seventeenth century is notable for the next technical advance in firearm ignition: the flintlock. The flintlock, which would remain the dominant system until the introduction of the percussion lock at the beginning of the nineteenth century, was the last and the best of the spark-striking ignition systems. Unlike the wheel-lock mechanism, it required no winding key to span an internal spring. Relatively simple in design, the flintlock mechanism was nevertheless a masterpiece of engineering, requiring high precision of its working elements. It was also stronger and less susceptible to damage through mishandling or mechanical failure.

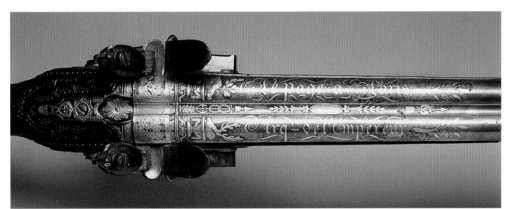

Flint and steel were used domestically to light fires, and the flintlock was based on the same principle. A piece of flint was clamped between the jaws of a cock. Once the cock was engaged, pressure on the gun's trigger caused the cock to snap forward, striking a combined pan cover and steel. Hitting the vertical face of the steel, the flint produced a shower of sparks while at the same time pushing away the pan cover and steel. The priming powder, now exposed to the sparks, was ignited. This action in turn exploded the main charge of the weapon. The French and English quickly adopted this system. The Germans, perhaps lacking good quality flint, remained faithful to the older wheel-lock. Because of its dependability, the flintlock firearm did not become obsolete until the nineteenth century.

PORTRAIT OF KING
GEORGE III (1760–
1820) OF ENGLAND,
C. 1783
BENJAMIN WEST
(AMERICAN,
1738–1820)
GIFT OF MR. AND
MRS. LAWRENCE S.
ROBBINS
CMA 1952.17

Long after armor on the battlefield had been abandoned, the English king who lost the American colonies wears full armor in his portrait. Among his accouterments are a sword with an elaborate pommel (an estoc?) and a commander's baton. On his breastplate is a star, the insignia of the Order of the Knights of the Garter. Even at the end of the eighteenth century, monarchs and nobles continued to be portrayed with the full panoply of war and leadership. This potent symbolism of rank and entitlement extended back to classical times.

Whatever its form, the handfire weapon required the knowledge, skill, and experience of several specialist craftsmen: barrelmaker, locksmith, stockmaker, and perhaps mountmaker. Surviving firearms from centuries past are often superbly crafted works of art that, typical of the age, invited decoration of every part, just like a clock or piece of fine furniture. The finest firearms brought together the talents of steel-chiselers, engravers, goldsmiths, woodcarvers, and inlayers, many of whom signed their work. Such consummate craftsmanship clearly followed high fashion as well as local tradition, producing a class of object intended to be not only functional but also an exquisite collectible.

Arms and armor have long held a place in Europe's literature, art, heraldry, and politics. They have also come to serve as a visual symbol of that historical epoch we know as the Middle Ages, the vast span of time between the Fall of Rome and the cultural rebirth known as the Renaissance. Social and literary allusions to knighthood, chivalry, feudalism, tournaments, and the Crusades usually involve both actual and imaginary references to the art of the armorer, a craft of great antiquity. The association of arms and armor with mythical or historical persons has further enhanced our fascination with these objects: the shield of Achilles; King Arthur's sword "Excalibur"; the battle axe of Clovis, King of the Franks; the helm of Edward the Black Prince; the sword of Joan of Arc.

Many non-Western cultures—Japan, India, Persia, and Turkey, for example— have rich and unique traditions in the craft of arms and armor. Indeed, armor production in some countries of eastern Europe, such as Poland and Hungary, was inspired by the armors of the Islamic East. Yet the development of arms and armor in the European West provides us with an imposing artistic tradition, one unique to the vicissitudes of European history. The art of the armorer frequently reflects the highest contemporary achievements in other media and materials: metalworking, goldsmithing, jewelry, textiles, costume, and prints and drawings.

The European Middle Ages and Renaissance witnessed the birth, flowering, and decline of armor. It is in this period that we observe armor's evolving function: foremost, protection of the body; symbol of rank and authority (reflected in funerary trappings and heraldry); and by the end of this era, purely decorative aggrandizement of the wearer. Surviving armor functions as an important document, providing evidence of the physical form, tastes, and interests of historical figures. Just as importantly, however, the working of metal, an extremely hard and difficult material, into the shape of the human body—and its often supreme embellishment—places the craft of the armorer justifiably within the highest achievements of European decorative arts.

The Severance Collection of arms and armor at the Cleveland Museum of Art continues, as it has for three generations, to provide a welcome glimpse into a venerable artistic tradition rendered obsolete by the encroaching modern world.

Bibliography

Aylward, J. D. *The Small-Sword in England: Its History, Its Forms, Its Makers, and Its Masters.* London: Hutchinson and Co., 1960.

Barber, R., and J. Barker. *Tournaments: Jousts, Chivalry and Regents in the Middle Ages.* Woodbridge (U.K.): Boydell, 1989.

Barker, J. R. V. *The Tournament in England 1100–1400.* Woodbridge (U.K.): Boydell, 1986.

Batty, John, et al. *The Sword and the Sorrows*, exh. cat., Drummossie Moor Visitor Center, Scotland. Edinburgh: National Trust for Scotland, 1996.

Blackmore, David. *Arms and Armour of the English Civil Wars.* London: Royal Armouries, 1990.

Blackmore, Howard L. *Arms and Armour.* New York: Dutton, 1965.

Blair, Claude. *Arms, Armour and Base-Metalwork: The James A. de Rothschild Collection at Waddesdon Manor.* Fribourg: Office Du Livre, 1974.

———. *European Armour circa 1066 to circa 1700.* London: Batsford, 1958.

———. *Pistols of the World.* London: Batsford, 1968.

Blair, C., V. Norman, and H. R. Robinson. *Glossarium Armorium: Arma Defensiva.* Graz: Akademische Druck, 1972.

Boccia, Lionello G. *Armi difensive dal Medioevo all'età moderna.* Florence: Centro Di, 1982.

———. *Nove secoli di armi da caccia.* Florence: Editrice Edam, 1967.

Boccia, Lionello G., and E. T. Coelho. *Armi Bianche Italiane.* Milan: Bramante, 1975.

———. *L'Arte dell'Armatura in Italia.* Milan: Bramante, 1967.

Boccia, Lionello G., Francesco Rossi, and Marco Morin. *Armi e Armature Lombarde.* Milan: Electa Editrice, 1980.

Bosson, Clément, René Géroudet, and Eugène Heer. *Armes anciennes des collections suisses.* Geneva and Lausanne: Edita, 1972.

Bradbury, J. *The Medieval Archer.* Woodbridge (U.K.): Boydell, 1985.

Bull, Stephen. *A Historical Guide to Arms and Armor.* New York: Facts on File, 1991.

Caldwell, D. H., ed. *Scottish Weapons and Fortifications, 1100–1800.* Edinburgh and Atlantic Highlands, N.J.: Humanities Press, 1981.

Cripps-Day, Francis Henry. *A Record of Armour Sales 1881–1924.* London: G. Bell and Sons, 1925.

Davidson, H. R. E. *The Sword in Anglo-Saxon England.* Oxford: Clarendon, 1962.

Dean, Bashford. *Catalogue of European Daggers, Including the Ellis, Riggs, and Reubell Collections.* New York: Metropolitan Museum of Art, 1929.

Dufty, Richard. *Catalogue of European Armour in the Tower of London.* London: Her Majesty's Stationery Office, 1968.

Edge, David, and John Miles Paddock. *Arms and Armour of the Medieval Knight.* London: Defoe Publishing, 1988.

Franzoi, Umberto. *L'Armeria del Palazzo Ducale a Venezia.* Venice: Edizioni Canova, 1990.

Gaibi, Agostino. *Armi da Fuoco italiane dal medioevo al Risorgimento.* Milan: Bramante Edictrice, 1978.

Gilchrist, Helen Ives. *Catalogue of the Severance Collection of Arms and Armor in the Cleveland Museum of Art.* Cleveland: Cleveland Museum of Art, 1924.

Grancsay, Stephen V. *Master French Gunsmiths' Designs of the Mid-Seventeenth Century.* New York: Greenberg, 1950.

———. "The Mutual Influence of Costume and Armor: A Study of Specimens in the Metropolitan Museum of Art." *Metropolitan Museum Studies* 3 (1930–31): 144–208.

Hammond, Peter. *Royal Armouries: Official Guide.* London: Trustees of the Royal Armouries, 1986.

Hawtrey Gyngell, Dudley S. *Armourers Marks: Being a Compilation of Known Marks of Armourers, Swordsmiths and Gunsmiths.* London: Thorsons Publishers, 1959.

Hayward, J. F. *The Art of the Gunmaker.* 2 vols. London: Barrie and Rockliff, 1962.

———. *European Firearms.* London: Her Majesty's Stationery Office, 1955.

Hooper, Nicholas, and Matthew Bennett. *Cambridge Illustrated Atlas: Warfare in the Middle Ages, 768–1487.* Cambridge: University Press, 1996.

Karcheski, Walter J., Jr. *Arms and Armor in the Art Institute of Chicago.* Chicago: Art Institute of Chicago, 1995.

Keen, Maurice. *Chivalry.* New Haven and London: Yale University Press, 1984.

Kienbusch, Carl Otto von. *The Kretzschmar von Kienbusch Collection of Armor and Arms.* Princeton: Princeton University Library, 1963.

Kienbusch, Carl Otto von, and Stephen V. Grancsay. *The Bashford Dean Collection of Arms and Armor in the Metropolitan Museum of Art.* Portland, Maine: Southworth Press, 1933.

Koch, H. W. *Medieval Warfare.* London: Bison Books, 1978.

Krenn, Peter, and Walter J. Karcheski Jr. *Imperial Austria: Treasures of Art, Arms, and Armor from the State of Styria*, exh. cat., Museum of Fine Arts, Houston. Munich: Prestel-Verlag, 1992.

Laking, Guy Francis. *The Armoury of Windsor Castle.* London: Bradbury, Agnew and Co., 1904.

———. *A Record of European Armour and Arms through Seven Centuries.* 5 vols. London: G. Bell and Sons, 1920–22.

Lewerken, Heinz-Werner, et al. *Dresdner Rüstkammer. Meisterwerke aus vier Jahrhunderten.* Dresden: Staatliche Kunstsammlungen Dresden, 1992.

Macomber, Frank Gair. *Catalogue of an Exhibition of Arms and Armor*, exh. cat., Museum of Fine Arts, Boston. Boston: Alfred Mudge and Son, 1899.

Mann, Sir James. *Wallace Collection Catalogues: European Arms and Armour.* 2 vols. London: Trustees of the Wallace Collection, 1962.

Mazzini, Franco, ed. *L'Armeria Reale di Torino*. Milan: Bramante Editrice, 1982.

Meyer, Angelika, and Eva E. Zehnder, eds. *Blankwaffen*. Zurich: T. Gut, 1982.

Neal, W. Keith, and D. H. L. Back. *Great British Gunmakers 1540–1740*. Norwich: Historical Firearms, 1984.

Nickel, Helmut. "Arms and Armor from the Permanent Collection." *Metropolitan Museum of Art Bulletin* 49 (Summer 1991): 1–64.

Nickel, Helmut, Stuart W. Pyhrr, and Leonid Tarassuk. *The Art of Chivalry: European Arms and Armor from the Metropolitan Museum of Art,* exh. cat., Seattle Art Museum, Detroit Institute of Arts, and others. New York: American Federation of Arts, 1982.

Norman, A. V. B. *Arms and Armour*. London: G. P. Putnam's Sons, 1964.

———. *The Rapier and the Small Sword 1460–1820*. London: Arms and Armor Press, 1980.

Norman, A. V. B., and G. M. Wilson. *Treasures from the Tower of London: An Exhibition of Arms and Armour,* exh. cat., Sainsbury Centre for Visual Arts. Norwich: Lund Humphries, 1982.

Oakshott, R. Ewart. *A Knight and His Armour*. Philadelphia: Dufour, 1961.

———. *The Sword in the Age of Chivalry*. London: Lutterworth Press, 1964.

Payne-Gallwey, Sir Ralph. *The Crossbow, Medieval and Modern, Military and Sporting*. London: Longmans, Green, and Co., 1903.

Pfaffenbichler, Matthias. *Medieval Armourers*. Medieval Craftsmen series. Toronto: University of Toronto Press, 1992.

Prestwich, Michael. *Armies and Warfare in the Middle Ages: The English Experience*. New Haven and London: Yale University Press, 1996.

Rangström, Lena, et al. *Tournaments and the Dream of Chivalry,* exh. cat., Livrustkammaren. Stockholm: Livrustkammaren, 1992.

Reverseau, Jean-Pierre. *Les Armures des Rois de France au Musée de l'Armée*. Paris: Editions F. P. Lobies, 1982.

Schneider, H. *Waffen im Schweizerischen Landesmuseum; Grifwaffen 1*. Zurich: Orell Fussli, 1980.

Schöbel, Johannes. *Princely Arms and Armour: A Selection from the Dresden Collection*. London: Barrie and Jenkins, 1975.

Scott, R. L. *Catalogue of the Collection of European Arms and Armour Formed at Greenock*. Glasgow: [privately printed], 1924.

Snodgrass, A. M. *Arms and Armour of the Greeks*. London: Thames and Hudson, 1967.

Snodgrass, Anthony. *Early Greek Armour and Weapons from the End of the Bronze Age to 600 B.C.* Edinburgh: University Press, 1964.

Stone, George Cameron. *A Glossary of the Construction, Decoration and Use of Arms and Armor in All Countries and in All Times, Together with Some Closely Related Subjects*. Portland, Maine: Southworth Press, 1934.

Tarassuk, Leonid. *Italian Armor for Princely Courts,* exh. cat., Art Institute of Chicago. Chicago: Art Institute of Chicago, 1986.

Tarassuk, Leonid, and Claude Blair, eds. *The Complete Encyclopedia of Arms and Weapons*. New York: Simon and Schuster, 1979.

Temesváry, Ferenc. *Arms and Armour*. Budapest: Helicon Kiadó, 1982.

Thomas, Bruno, Ortwin Gamber, and Hans Schedelmann. *Arms and Armor of the Western World*. New York: McGraw-Hill, 1964.

Trapp, Oswald. *The Armoury of the Castle of Churburg*. Translated by James G. Mann. London: Methuen and Company, 1929.

Wackernagel, Rudolf H. *Das Münchner Zeughaus*. Munich and Zurich: Schnell and Steiner, 1983.

Wallace, J. M. *Scottish Swords and Dirks: An Illustrated Reference Guide to Scottish Edged Weapons*. London: Arms and Armor Press, 1970.

anneal. To heat a metal until it is soft for working, followed by gradual cooling to strengthen or *temper* the metal.

armet. A helmet completely encasing the head, with hinged, movable cheekpieces overlapping on the chin, and a visor; replaced by the *close helmet* in the sixteenth century.

arquebus (also **harquebus**). A light form of handgun used by European infantries throughout the sixteenth and seventeenth centuries.

backplate. An armor plate for protection of the back; corresponds to the *breastplate,* to which it is attached by straps or hinges. Normally forged in one piece to fit the body, with additional plates (*lames*) attached to protect the lower back region.

barbute. A tall open helmet of Italian origin, often with a pointed apex (later rounded), cheekpieces, and a small face-opening; in use from about 1350 to the end of the fifteenth century.

bard. A comprehensive term for armor protecting the horse—made first of mail, later of plate.

basinet (also **bascinet** or **basnet**). A light helmet in use during the fourteenth and fifteenth centuries. The headpiece is generally ogival or egg-shaped, usually fitted with a pointed visor and a mail neckpiece (*camail*) for defense of the throat and neck.

"bastard" sword. See **hand-and-a-half sword.**

bevor. An element of plate for defense of the lower face and throat. Can be either a separate piece worn with a helmet such as the *sallet,* or an attached piece worn with the *close helmet.*

Gothic Plate Armor

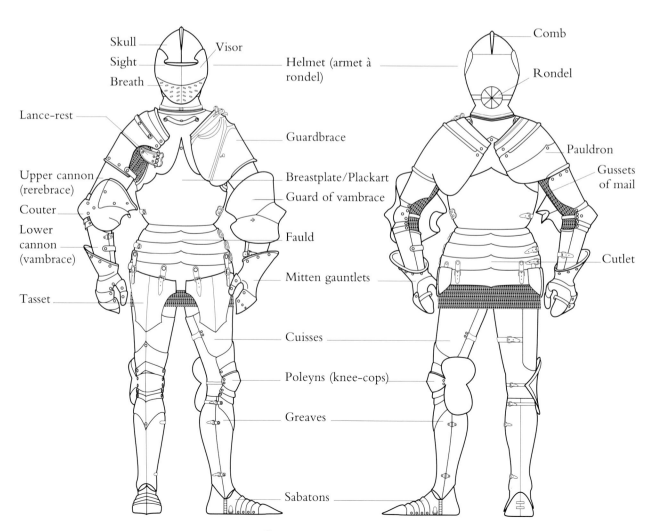

Skull
Sight
Breath
Visor
Lance-rest
Upper cannon (rerebrace)
Couter
Lower cannon (vambrace)
Tasset

Helmet (armet à rondel)
Guardbrace
Breastplate/Plackart
Guard of vambrace
Fauld
Mitten gauntlets
Cuisses
Poleyns (knee-cops)
Greaves
Sabatons

Comb
Rondel
Pauldron
Gussets of mail
Cutlet

bill. A staff weapon with an asymmetrical head usually fashioned to include a spike, a curved cutting hook in front, balanced with a short spike in back. Derived from an agricultural instrument and popular with the English and Italian infantries of the fifteenth century.

boar spear. A spear with a broad, leaf-shaped blade (often elaborately decorated) and a cross-toggle below; originally used in boar hunting.

bluing. The process of applying heat to metal to achieve a deep blue color.

breastplate. An armor plate for protection of the chest and abdomen; normally worn together with a *backplate* and fitted with flexible plates (*lames*) below to protect the lower abdomen.

brandistock. A staff weapon consisting of a tubular shaft that conceals either a single blade or a set of three blades within an aperture. By jerking the weapon forward, the blades could be released and locked with a catch, ready for action. Widely used from the sixteenth to nineteenth centuries, both in civilian and military versions.

breath. Holes or slits for ventilation in the lower visor of a helmet.

breech. The rear end of a cannon or gun barrel; usually the point of ignition.

brigandine. A type of armored sleeveless jacket, used principally by infantry throughout the fifteenth century and until the middle of the sixteenth century, consisting of numerous small overlapping plates of metal attached with rivets to the back of a cloth support. Fine examples are often faced with colorful velvet.

broadsword. A sword with a straight, wide, two-edged blade used by European heavy cavalry through the nineteenth century.

Equestrian Armor, c. 1575

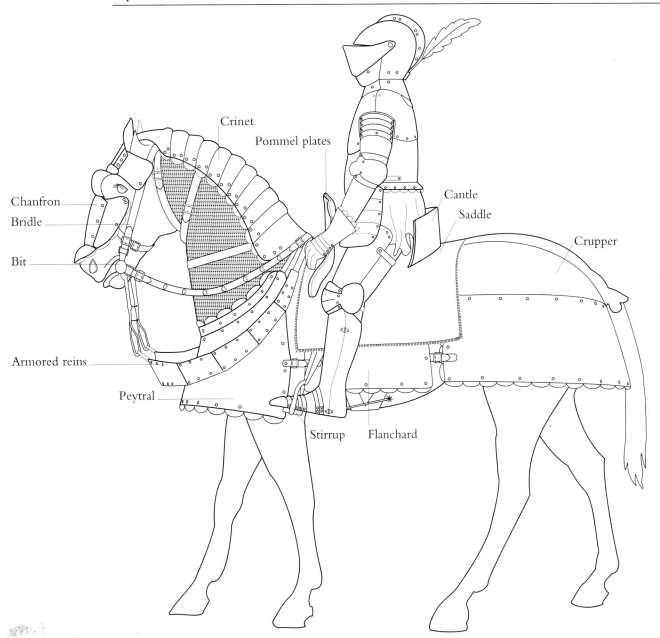

159

buffcoat. A defensive coat made of buff (*boeuf*) leather thick enough to resist a sword cut; used primarily for cavalry in the seventeenth century, when plate armor was falling into disuse.

buffe. A separate, usually detachable, element of plate armor worn with an open helmet to protect the face and throat.

burgonet. A light, open helmet characterized by a peak, a fall over the eyes, and hinged earpieces; used by cavalry in the sixteenth and seventeenth centuries. Sometimes worn with a *buffe*.

cabasset. A light, open headpiece with a conical or almond-shaped apex and a small brim; generally used by infantry.

camail. A mail defense for the throat and neck attached to a helmet like the *basinet* or *barbute*, from which it suspends to the shoulders.

chanfron. The plate headpiece for a horse, first introduced in the fourteenth century. The complete chanfron was fitted with cheekpieces and a crestpiece, and by the sixteenth century was often elaborately decorated.

chapel-de-fer. An open-faced helmet usually with a broad brim resembling a hat; used from the thirteenth to fifteenth centuries.

close helmet. A helmet fitted with a *visor* and *bevor* completely encasing the head. It has no cheekpieces and all elements function from a common set of pivots at the temples.

collar. See **gorget**.

corsèque. A staff weapon, the head of which forms two fork-like blades resembling a trident.

comb. The ridge running fore and aft along the skullpiece of a helmet.

corselet. A term usually applied to the armor of the pikeman; his body armor or *cuirass*.

cranequin. A crossbow winder consisting of a ratchet, a claw to grasp the cord, and a handle; used to span or wind the crossbow in order to fire its bolt.

cuirass. The armor for the body as opposed to the head and limbs; a combination of breast and backplates.

damascening. The technique of inlaying gold and silver into grooves gouged out of a metal surface, often favored for the decoration of sword hilts. Originated with Muslim artists of the Near East and was later adapted by North Italian and Spanish craftsmen in the fifteenth century, from whom it spread into the rest of Europe.

embossing. The decoration of metal plate by hammering it up in relief from the inside.

engraving. The application of ornament to metal by cutting the pattern directly into the surface with special tools such as the burin and graver.

estoc. A thrusting sword with a stiff, usually three-sided blade designed to penetrate armor; name derives from the French word meaning "to thrust."

etching. The decorative technique most commonly used on arms and armor. The process consists of tracing a design into the metal with an etching needle through a previously applied acid-resistant substance like varnish. The application of acid "bites" into the exposed surface, leaving a permanent pattern which can be blackened or gilded after the varnish is removed. A variation of this technique known as "raised" etching involves applying varnish with a brush to cover those areas to be decorated with a design. Subsequent application of acid leaves the decorated areas slightly elevated to achieve relief.

fauld. That part of the armor attached to the breastplate for the defense of the abdomen, usually composed of horizontal *lames*.

field armor. Armor designed for use in war, as opposed to "tournament" and "parade" armors.

flanchard. An oblong plate of armor attached to the base of the saddle, protecting the flanks of the horse. It closed the gap between the crupper (protecting the rump) and the peytral (protecting the horse's chest).

fuller. A groove that reduces the weight of the blade of a sword or dagger without weakening it.

gardbrace. A reinforcing plate closely fitted to the *pauldron*, providing additional protection to the combatant's left shoulder (the principal point of impact) during a *joust*.

garniture. A complete armor with related or exchange pieces, especially double pieces for converting the basic unit to sporting and various field uses.

glaive. A staff weapon with a long cleaver-like or scythe-shaped blade.

German joust (*Deutsch Gestech*). A form of *joust* fought with blunted lances in an open field without a tilt, requiring special equipment for both rider and horse. Popular in the German-speaking lands. See also *Stechhelm*.

gorget. Also called a "collar." An armor element providing defense for the neck, throat, and upper part of the chest; normally consists of two parts, front and back, joined by a hinge on the left shoulder and fastened with a stud on the right.

greave. An element of plate armor to protect the lower leg from the knee to the ankle.

halberd. A staff weapon combining an axe head balanced with a spike and a hook-like fluke; carried by infantry.

hand-and-a-half sword. Also known as a "bastard" sword. A large sword with a double-edged blade and a long grip which, when necessary, could accommodate both hands to wield it.

The Hilt of a Rapier

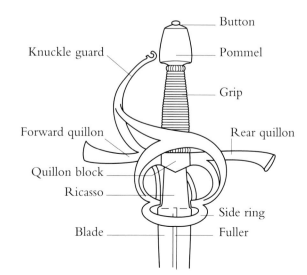

- Button
- Pommel
- Grip
- Knuckle guard
- Forward quillon
- Rear quillon
- Quillon block
- Ricasso
- Side ring
- Blade
- Fuller

harness. A term referring to the whole armor for the man.

hauberk. A shirt of mail generally extending between the hip and the knee.

joust. A sporting combat between mounted knights. The combatants charged each other with "couched" lances, and often required special armor and equipment. Jousts frequently took place within a *tournament*.

knee-cop. A protective plate for defense of the knee.

lames. Overlapping plates of metal forming a flexible defense. Mobility was achieved by riveting the plates to straps at the back or by means of sliding rivets.

lance-rest. A support for the lance when couched under the right arm, consisting of a bracket riveted to the breastplate and sometimes hinged so that it could be folded away when not in use.

linstock. A staff for holding the lighted match used for firing a cannon; sometimes combined with a spearhead at center for self-defense and often very decorative.

lists. An enclosed area, usually fenced off, where tournaments were held.

lock. The ignition mechanism for a gun.

mail. Flexible armor fashioned from interlocking rings. Commonly used throughout Europe until its replacement by plate armor in the fourteenth century.

morion. An open helmet with a tall comb and a curved brim peaking before and behind.

munitions armor. Armor mass-produced for the common soldier, usually cheaply.

partisan. A staff weapon with a symmetrical double-edged central blade, often highly decorated. Carried as a ceremonial arm by officers and bodyguards in the sixteenth and seventeenth centuries.

pauldron. A plate defense for the shoulder and upper arm.

pike. A specialized infantry staff weapon with a small leaf-shaped head, often averaging fourteen to twenty-two feet in length; used as a hedge against cavalry charges.

pole arms. A generic term for hafted weapons, nearly always carried by infantry and requiring the use of both hands, with a steel head (in a variety of shapes and configurations) attached to a long wooden pole. Ceremonial versions were often embellished with colorful woolen pompoms or velvet tassels.

pommel. The spherical knob, often highly ornate, serving as a counterweight at the opposite end of a sword to the point.

pommel plates. Steel plates attached to the upper curl of the saddle bow, designed to protect the upper thighs of the rider.

quarrel. The missile, shorter than the arrow of the longbow, shot from the crossbow. Also called a bolt.

quench. To plunge heated steel into a medium such as water to cool it. The more rapid the quenching, the harder the steel becomes.

quillons. The crossbar on the hilt of a sword.

rapier. A sword originally worn with civilian dress, distinguished by its long straight blade and complex guard. With the development of fencing techniques, the rapier became a fashionable thrusting weapon.

Rennen. A German term for a form of *joust* in which sharpened or pointed lances were used to unhorse one's opponent. Points could also be scored for the splintering of lances.

rerebrace. Armor for protection of the upper arm.

ricasso. The rectangular part of a sword blade nearest the hilt but above the edge, usually thickened and blunted to permit the fingers to grip it securely.

sabaton. Armor plates for the foot.

saber. A curved, single-edged cutting sword used exclusively by cavalry.

sallet. A light, semi-open helmet that succeeded the *basinet* in the fifteenth century. Sometimes fitted with a visor, sometimes open-faced, and sometimes with a vision slit cut in its front, it features a rounded skullpiece with a long, drawn-out tail.

sight. The vision slit in a helmet or visor.

smallsword. A light thrusting sword worn with civilian dress from about 1640; later worn with court uniform.

Stechhelm. A great helm that was bolted to the rider's breast-plate and used with blunted lances in a specifically German form of the joust. See also *German joust*.

tassets. Plates suspended from a breastplate by rivets or straps for defense of the hips and upper thighs.

temper. To soften hard, brittle steel by heating it to high temperatures.

tilt. A wall or fence, often of cloth-covered wood, intended to separate mounted participants in a *joust*. Introduced during the fifteenth century to prevent head-on collisions between riders.

tournament. A generic term for mock combat held between teams of contestants either mounted or on foot. Introduced as a useful form of practice for real combat, as well as for entertainment, becoming a formal event during the twelfth century.

two-handed sword. An extremely large (up to six feet long) infantry sword requiring both hands and special training for effective use. Eventually became a ceremonial weapon for bodyguards.

vambrace. Armor defense for the lower arm.

visor. The movable plate or plates attached to a helmet for protection of the face.

Checklist of the Severance Collection

Dimensions are in centimeters (height x width x depth), generally followed by weight in kilograms (kg). Occasionally, length or diameter is listed. PL, proper left; PR, proper right. In captions throughout this book, bracketed numbers refer to the object numbers given here.

ARMOR (COMPLETE OR PARTIAL SUITS)

1. Tilting Suit (composed)
South Germany, c. 1560–80
Steel, brass rivets, leather straps
Close helmet, 34.5 x 32 x 22 (5.12 kg); breastplate, 42.3 x 32 x 14.2 (1.54 kg); PL tasset, 28 x 22.6 (0.86 kg); PR tasset, 28.2 x 22.3 (1.16 kg); PL pauldron, 28.5 x 27.5 (with grandguard, 29 x 29.2) (1.92 kg); PR pauldron and gardbrace, 29 x 25.5 (1.16 kg); PL vambrace, l. 47 (1.20 kg); PR vambrace, l. 44.2 (1.32 kg); pasguard, 17 x 17.5 (0.30 kg); gauntlet, 21.6 x 13 (0.28 kg); PL greave, l. 33.5; PR greave, l. 31; PL cuisse, l. 43.7; PR cuisse, l. 44.8; sabatons lacking

Gift of Mr. and Mrs. John L. Severance 1916.1502 (helmet), 1916.1511.a–m
Gilchrist A11 (helmet) and A12
Collections: Saxon Electoral Armory, Dresden (helmet only); Frank Gair Macomber, Boston (cat. 319)

2. Partial Suit of Armor in Maximilian Style
Germany, Nuremberg, c. 1525
Steel, steel and brass rivets, leather straps
Close helmet, 28.7 x 30.4 x 21.7 (2.72 kg); gorget, 32.5 x 26 x 15.8 (1.02 kg); breastplate and tassets, 45.2 x 37.2 x 17.8 (2.78 kg); backplate, 42.8 x 35 x 17.5 (2.14 kg); PR arm (vambrace, rerebrace, couter), 58.5 x 15.8 (1.32 kg); PL arm (vambrace, rerebrace, couter), 62.5 x 16 (1.56 kg); PR leg (cuisse and knee-cop), 45 x 16.6 (1.30 kg); PL leg (cuisse and knee-cop), 45.2 x 17.9 (1.06 kg); PR tasset (modern), 26.6 x 22.1 (0.50 kg); PL tasset (modern), 25.1 x 22.6 (0.68 kg). Mail hauberk (6.16 kg); greaves, sabatons, and gauntlets lacking
Marks: KXR stamped on edge of helmet bevor

Gift of Mr. and Mrs. John L. Severance 1916.1714.a–j
Gilchrist A2
Collections: Christoph I Radziwill (1543–1603), Nieswiez Castle, Poland; Baron de Cosson

3. Half-Suit of Armor for the Field
North Italy, Brescia(?), c. 1575
Steel, with etched decorative bands and roundels
Close helmet, 29.5 x 28.5 x 23 (2.62 kg); gorget, 26.5 x 24.8 (0.74 kg); breastplate, 46 x 36 x 15.3 (3.42 kg); backplate, 37 x 35 x 16.7 (1.98 kg); PR pauldron, 30 x 28.3; PR arm (vambrace, rerebrace, couter), 47 x 19 (2.20 kg, combined pauldron and arm); PL pauldron, 30.5 x 23; PL arm (vambrace, rerebrace, couter), 46 x 18.3 (2.06 kg, combined pauldron and arm); PR tasset, 28.6 x 26.6 (0.88 kg); PL tasset, 28.6 x 28.2 (0.90 kg); PR gauntlet, 32.7 x 15 (0.44 kg); PL gauntlet, 33 x 13.7 (0.50 kg). Total weight: 15.30 kg

Gift of Mr. and Mrs. John L. Severance 1916.1816.a–l
Gilchrist A9
Collections: Duc d'Osuna; Frank Gair Macomber, Boston (cat. 155)

4. Pikeman's Helmet, Breastplate, and Tassets
England, Greenwich(?), c. 1620–30 (Helmet: perhaps Dutch or Flemish?)
Steel, brass rivets, black paint
Helmet, 38.5 x 26 x 23.5 (1.16 kg); breastplate, 38.7 x 35.6 (2.14 kg); tassets, 33 x 32.4 (PL, 1.08 kg; PR, 0.80 kg)

Gift of Mr. and Mrs. John L. Severance 1923.1063.a–d
Gilchrist A17
Collections: Bashford Dean, New York; American Art Galleries, New York (sale, 23–24 November 1923, lots 227c, 227i)

5. Partial Suit of Armor (Close Helmet, Breastplate and Fauld, Backplate)
Germany, c. 1510–30
Steel, leather straps
Helmet, 33.1 x 27.3 x 21 (2.64 kg); breastplate (with lance-rest and fauld), 44 x 36.3 (3.10 kg); backplate, 38 x 35.5 (1.57 kg)

Gift of Mr. and Mrs. John L. Severance 1923.1067.a–c
Gilchrist A4
Collections: Bashford Dean, New York

6. Field Armor for Man and Horse with Völs-Colonna Arms
North Italy, c. 1575
Etched steel with some gilding, brass rivets, red velvet pickadils
Man's Armor: Close helmet, 38 x 31.2 x 27 (3.50 kg); gorget, 26.5 x 23.7 x 14.5 (0.74 kg); breastplate, 46.2 x 35.5 x 15.8 (2.76 kg); backplate, 40.5 x 35.6 x 18.2 (1.60 kg); PR pauldron, 28.5 x 26.7 (1.24 kg); PL pauldron, 28 x 26.4 (1.22 kg); PR arm (vambrace, rerebrace, couter), 44.5 x 17.9 (1.10 kg); PL arm (vambrace, rerebrace, couter), 42.5 x 17.6 (1.04 kg); PR tasset, 27.5 x 21.7 (0.72 kg); PL tasset, 28.5 x 21.5 (0.74 kg); PR gauntlet, 30 x 11.7 (0.84 kg); PL gauntlet, 27 x 13 (0.74 kg); PR cuisse, 40.5 x 19.1 (1.06 kg); PL cuisse, 42 x 19 (0.90 kg); PR greave and sabaton, 43 x 31.4 (1.44 kg); PL greave and sabaton, 43.1 x 31 (1.46 kg)

Horse's Armor: Crinet, 70.2 x 27.5 x 27 (2.72 kg); curb bit and nose straps, 44 x 17 (1.32 kg); peytral, 75.2 x 58.5 (5.00 kg); crupper, 80.5 x 79 (10.38 kg); PR flanchard, 52 x 31 (1.44 kg); PL flanchard, 51.8 x 31.6 (1.40 kg); upper rein, 81.6 x 13 (max.) (1.72 kg); PR lower rein, 99.3 x 3 (0.22 kg); PL lower rein, 96.5 x 3 (0.20 kg); girth, 104 x 11 (0.40 kg); chanfron, 62.5 x 25.5 x 19.4 (2.06 kg); PR stirrup, 15.4 x 13 x 7.5 (0.56 kg, with strap); PL stirrup, 15.7 x 13 x 7.5 (0.56 kg, with strap); chain mail for neck, 68.5 x 105 (2.86 kg); saddle, 52 x 40.5 x 57 (9.08 kg)

The John L. Severance Fund 1964.88.a–z
Collections: Schloss Prösels; Town Hall in Bolzano; Prince Soltykoff; William H. Riggs; Metropolitan Museum of Art, New York (1913–64)

7. Half-Armor for the Foot Tournament
c. 1590
Pompeo della Cesa (Italian, Milan, active 1572–93)
Etched and gilded steel, brass rivets, leather and velvet fittings
Close helmet, 31.7 x 27.7 x 21.6 (5.26 kg); gorget, 16.7 x 30 x 27 (0.92 kg); breastplate, 46.5 x 33.8 (2.42 kg); backplate, 34.3 x 34.5 (1.26 kg); PR pauldron, couter, and vambrace: l. 67.5 overall (2.18 kg); PL pauldron, couter, and vambrace: l. 66.9 overall (2.10 kg); PR tasset, 21.3 x 28.7 (0.60 kg); PL tasset, 21.4 x 29.7 (0.58 kg); PR gauntlet, l. 22.9 (0.42 kg); PL gauntlet, l. 23.2 (0.34 kg). Total weight: 16.08 kg

The John L. Severance Fund 1996.299.a–l
Collections: Durlacher, London; Edward Hubbard Litchfield; Leopold Blumka, New York; Eric Vaule, Bridgewater, Connecticut; Peter Finer, Warwickshire, England

ARMOR ELEMENTS

8. Gothic Breastplate
South Germany or Austria, c. 1485
Steel
50.5 x 35.8 x 15.8 (3.14 kg)

Gift of Mr. and Mrs. John L. Severance 1916.29
Gilchrist C4
Collections: Seymour Lucas; Frank Gair Macomber, Boston (cat. 449)

9. Breastplate
Germany, c. 1540
Steel, with roped edges
32.4 x 31.4 (1.38 kg)

Gift of Mr. and Mrs. John L. Severance 1916.684
Gilchrist C5
Collections: Marquis de Belleval et de Liques; Frank Gair Macomber, Boston (cat. 343)

10. Left Arm Elements from a Boy's Armor (Vambrace, Couter, Rerebrace)
Germany, Augsburg, mostly 1560 (some modern)
Etched and lightly embossed steel with traces of gilding, leather
L. 43.5, w. 17 (0.76 kg)

Gift of Mr. and Mrs. John L. Severance 1916.708
Gilchrist C29
Collections: Frank Gair Macomber, Boston (cat. 418)

11. Right Arm Elements from a Boy's Armor (Rerebrace with Couter)

Germany, Augsburg, c. 1560 (some modern)

Etched and lightly embossed steel with traces of gilding, leather

L. 25.3, w. 16.5 (0.46 kg)

Gift of Mr. and Mrs. John L. Severance 1916.709

Gilchrist C29

Collections: Frank Gair Macomber, Boston (cat. 418)

12. Black and White Elbow Gauntlet for the Right Hand

North Germany, c. 1570

Blackened steel, leather

43.2 x 12.7 (0.78 kg)

Gift of Mr. and Mrs. John L. Severance 1916.1082

Gilchrist C40

Collections: Frank Gair Macomber, Boston (cat. 287)

13. Lower Arm Cannon

Germany, Augsburg, c. 1560

Etched and lightly embossed steel, with strapwork bands

17.7 x 10.4 (0.35 kg)

Gift of Mr. and Mrs. John L. Severance 1916.1083

Gilchrist C28

Collections: Frank Gair Macomber, Boston (cat. 563)

14. Breastplate

Germany, Landshut, mid-16th century

Steel

39.3 x 35.7 x 17.5 (2.35 kg)

Marks: *Landshut* (upper left); SB (upper right)

Gift of Mr. and Mrs. John L. Severance 1916.1091.a

Gilchrist A6

Collections: Richard Zschille; Frank Gair Macomber, Boston (cat. 158)

15. Backplate

Germany, Landshut, mid-16th century

Steel, leather straps

41.8 x 35.8 x 17.4 (1.96 kg)

Gift of Mr. and Mrs. John L. Severance 1916.1091.b

Gilchrist A6

Collections: Richard Zschille; Frank Gair Macomber, Boston (cat. 159)

16. Jousting Gauntlet (Main-de-Fer)

South Germany, c. 1530–60

Steel

33.0 x 16.8 (1.56 kg)

Gift of Mr. and Mrs. John L. Severance 1916.1511.1

Gilchrist A12

Collections: Frank Gair Macomber, Boston (cat. 378)

17. Pair of Upper Arm Cannons

Italy (Milanese style of c. 1550), probably 19th century

Steel, chiseled border with floral motif

Each 14.0 x 14.0 (0.28 kg)

Gift of Mr. and Mrs. John L. Severance 1916.1517.1–2

Gilchrist C31

Collections: Frank Gair Macomber, Boston (cat. 452)

18. Greave (Leg Defense)

Germany, 16th century

Steel, with roped edge and scroll design

L. 43.2, w. 12.4 (0.46 kg)

Gift of Mr. and Mrs. John L. Severance 1916.1519

Gilchrist C41

Collections: Frank Gair Macomber, Boston (cat. 501)

19. Breastplate from Hussar's Cuirass

Germany (Augsburg) or Hungary, c. 1580

Blued (now russet) steel, with etched and gilded strapwork bands; lower breast constructed of three lames; vertical rows of holes formerly contained settings for stones

42.2 x 35 (2.48 kg)

Marks (on PR): TAMGA mark of Constantinople Armory

Gift of Mr. and Mrs. John L. Severance 1916.1521

Gilchrist C8

Collections: Constantinople Armory; Kevorkian; Frank Gair Macomber, Boston (cat. 398)

20. Pauldron for Right Shoulder (Exchange Piece for Foot Combat)

Italy, c. 1600

Blued steel, with gilt borders

28.2 x 24 (1.28 kg)

Gift of Mr. and Mrs. John L. Severance 1916.1524

Gilchrist C30

Collections: Frank Gair Macomber, Boston (cat. 502)

21. Pauldron for Right Shoulder

Italy, c. 1560–70

Blued and gilded steel

26.4 x 28 (1.32 kg)

Gift of Mr. and Mrs. John L. Severance 1916.1528

Gilchrist C32

Collections: Duc d'Osuna; Frank Gair Macomber, Boston (cat. 503)

22. Gothic Breastplate

Perhaps Domenico dei Barini, detto Negroli

Italy, Milan, c. 1490–1500

Steel, with lance-rest mount

45 x 35.2 (3.24 kg)

Marks: Crossed keys beneath a crown

Gift of Mr. and Mrs. John L. Severance 1916.1566

Gilchrist C3

Collections: Baron de Cosson; Richard Zschille; Frank Gair Macomber, Boston (cat. 27)

23. Gothic Backplate

Germany, late 15th century

Steel, modern leather straps

44.5 x 34.5 x 16.5 (2.90 kg)

Gift of Mr. and Mrs. John L. Severance 1916.1613

Gilchrist A1

Collections: Franz Thill, Vienna; Frank Gair Macomber, Boston (cat. 466)

24. Pair of Gothic Fan-Shaped Pauldrons

Italy, Milan, c. 1485–1500

Steel

Each 21.5 x 25.2 x 14.8 (PR, 0.81 kg; PL, 0.84 kg)

Marks (on each): GAN(?) beneath a crown and YA beneath a split cross (twice repeated)

Gift of Mr. and Mrs. John L. Severance 1916.2080.1–2

Gilchrist A1

Collections: Franz Thill, Vienna; Frank Gair Macomber, Boston (cat. 466)

25. Gothic Mitten Gauntlet for the Right Hand

South Germany or Austria (Innsbruck), c. 1490

Steel

32 x 9.5 (0.30 kg)

Gift of Mr. and Mrs. John L. Severance 1916.2081

Gilchrist A1

Collections: Franz Thill, Vienna; Frank Gair Macomber, Boston (cat. 466)

26. Gorget

Germany, Nuremberg, c. 1560

Steel

31.6 x 25.2 x 17.2 (0.94 kg)

Mark: Nuremberg guild mark

Gift of Mr. and Mrs. John L. Severance 1916.1639

Gilchrist C22

Collections: Frank Gair Macomber, Boston (cat. 298)

27. Breastplate in Maximilian Style

Germany, c. 1500–10

Steel

48.3 x 40.3 x 16 (2.94 kg)

Gift of Mr. and Mrs. John L. Severance 1916.1640.a

Gilchrist C6

Collections: Spiller; Frank Gair Macomber, Boston (cat. 297)

28. Backplate in Maximilian Style

Germany, c. 1500–10

Steel, leather straps

42 x 33.9 x 15.5 (1.76 kg)

Gift of Mr. and Mrs. John L. Severance 1916.1640.b

Gilchrist C6

Collections: Spiller; Frank Gair Macomber, Boston (cat. 297)

29. Gothic Mitten Gauntlet

Italy, c. 1450

Steel

30.2 x 10.8 (0.28 kg)

Gift of Mr. and Mrs. John L. Severance 1916.1645

Gilchrist C34

Collections: Frank Gair Macomber, Boston (cat. 467)

30. Breastplate with Etched Figure Kneeling before Crucifixion

Germany, Nuremberg, c. 1550

Etched steel

31.3 x 35 x 20 (1.84 kg)

Marks: Nuremberg town mark

Gift of Mr. and Mrs. John L. Severance 1916.1647

Gilchrist C7

Collections: Director of the Porte de Hals of Brussels; Frank Gair Macomber, Boston (cat. 160)

31. Breastplate

North Italy, c. 1550–1600

Etched steel, with bands of trophies and medallions

46 x 34.7 x 15.9 (2.82 kg)

Gift of Mr. and Mrs. John L. Severance 1916.1654

Gilchrist C10

Collections: Edwin Brett; Frank Gair Macomber, Boston (cat. 157)

32. Gothic Breastplate (lower plate surmounted with fleur-de-lys)
South Germany or Austria (Innsbruck?), late 15th century
Steel
53.2 x 35.2 x 16.3 (4.48 kg)
Marks: Crescent face, struck twice
Gift of Mr. and Mrs. John L. Severance 1916.1720
Gilchrist C2
Collections: Franz Thill, Vienna; Frank Gair Macomber, Boston (cat. 481)

33. "Waistcoat" Cuirass
North Italy, c. 1580
Steel, brass rivets simulating buttons
47.6 x 29.5 x 25.7 (4.90 kg)
Gift of Mr. and Mrs. John L. Severance 1916.1721
Gilchrist C12
Collections: Marquis de Rossi; Frank Gair Macomber, Boston (cat. 397)

34. Breastplate
Germany, c. 1540
Steel, with lance-rest and roped edges; fauld of three lames
43.8 x 36.9 (2.82 kg)
Gift of Mr. and Mrs. John L. Severance 1916.1804.b
Gilchrist A7
Collections: Spiller; Frank Gair Macomber, Boston (cat. 306)

35. Gorget and Pauldrons
Germany, Brunswick(?), c. 1540–50
Steel, with roped edges; leather straps
Gorget, 31 x 26.2 x 16.8; PL pauldron, 31.5 x 18.9; PR pauldron, 30.3 x 19 (2.42 kg total)
Gift of Mr. and Mrs. John L. Severance 1916.1804.c
Gilchrist A7
Collections: Frank Gair Macomber, Boston (cat. 301)

36. Gothic Bevor
Spain (Hispano-Flemish?), c. 1480
Steel
27.4 x 16.3 (0.54 kg)
Marks (interior): Square with dot at center
Gift of Mr. and Mrs. John L. Severance 1916.1920
Gilchrist C19
Collections: Frank Gair Macomber, Boston (cat. 579)

37. Buffe
North Italy, c. 1550–1600
Etched steel, with bands of trophies
25.5 x 17.5 x 13.8 (0.88 kg)
Gift of Mr. and Mrs. John L. Severance 1916.1930
Gilchrist B44
Collections: Frank Gair Macomber, Boston (cat. 150)

38. Gothic Breastplate and Taces (from the Garrison of the Knights of St. John at Rhodes)
North Italy, late 15th century
Steel, brass rosette rivets
41.0 x 31.7 x 14.0 (1.98 kg)
Gift of John L. Severance 1919.63
Gilchrist C1
Collections: Garrison of the Knights of St. John, Rhodes; American Art Association, New York (Theodore Offerman sale, 7–8 February 1919, lot 321)

39. Brigandine (front panel)
Italy(?), c. 1500–25
Linen, gold velvet, tinned steel plates, brass rivets
56.5 x 47.6 (2.5 kg)
Gift of Mr. and Mrs. John L. Severance 1921.1250
Gilchrist C14
Collections: American Art Association, New York (sale, 18–19 November 1921, lot 236)

HELMETS
40. Pear-Stalk Cabasset
Italy, c. 1580–90
Steel
40.8 x 25.7 x 30.5 (1.70 kg)
Gift of Mr. and Mrs. John L. Severance 1916.26
Gilchrist B5
Collections: Frank Gair Macomber, Boston (cat. 359)

41. Black and White Burgonet (of Civic Guard of Bologna)
Italy, late 16th century
Steel, black paint
31.8 x 35.6 x 19.0 (1.56 kg)
Gift of Mr. and Mrs. John L. Severance 1916.891
Gilchrist B33
Collections: Frank Gair Macomber, Boston (cat. 151)

42. Black and White Morion
Germany, c. 1600
Embossed steel, black paint
36.3 x 28.6 x 24.4 (1.08 kg)
Gift of Mr. and Mrs. John L. Severance 1916.1080
Gilchrist B34
Collections: Frank Gair Macomber, Boston (cat. 144)

43. Helmet with Barred Visor
England(?), 16th century (modern visor and neck lames by S. J. Whawell)
Steel
31.1 x 31.4 x 25.1 (3.32 kg)
Gift of Mr. and Mrs. John L. Severance 1916.1084
Gilchrist B6
Collections: Bowden Church, Cheshire, England; James Drew, Manchester, England; Christian Hammer; Bateman; Bilson; S. J. Whawell; Frank Gair Macomber, Boston (cat. 137)

44. Peaked Morion
North Italy, Milan(?), c. 1580–90
Etched russet steel with traces of gilding, roped brim, brass plume holder
35.4 x 23.7 x 26.7 (1.42 kg)
Gift of Mr. and Mrs. John L. Severance 1916.1085
Gilchrist B7
Collections: Frank Gair Macomber, Boston (cat. 421)

45. Burgonet with Hinged Cheekpieces
North Italy, c. 1560–70
Steel with brass rivets, roped edges terminating in decorative spiral, fragments of leather liner
37 x 31.2 x 19.2 (2.16 kg)
Gift of Mr. and Mrs. John L. Severance 1916.1086
Gilchrist B8
Collections: Frank Gair Macomber, Boston (cat. 570)

46. Burgonet with Hinged Cheekpieces
Germany, Nuremberg, c. 1540
Steel, leather chin strap
Marks: Nuremberg town mark on visor/interior neck lame
33 x 28.5 x 26.2 (1.50 kg)
Gift of Mr. and Mrs. John L. Severance 1916.1088
Gilchrist A6
Collections: Richard Zschille; Frank Gair Macomber, Boston (cat. 569)

47. Morion of the State Guard of Elector Christian I of Saxony
Germany, Nuremberg, c. 1580–91
Etched and gilded russet steel
33.3 x 27.0 x 23.5 (1.44 kg)
Marks: Nuremberg town mark and conjoined HP on brim
Gift of Mr. and Mrs. John L. Severance 1916.1516
Gilchrist B30
Collections: Saxon Electoral Armouries, Dresden; Frank Gair Macomber, Boston (cat. 146)

48. Close Helmet from a Small Garniture, Perhaps for Siegmund Friedrich, Freiherr von Herbertstein (d. 1621)
Germany, Augsburg, c. 1580
Etched and gilded steel, brass rivets; lacking upper visor
40 x 35.5 x 23 (4.36 kg)
Gift of Mr. and Mrs. John L. Severance 1916.1531
Gilchrist B19
Collections: Richard Zschille; Frank Gair Macomber, Boston (cat. 142)

49. Armet à Rondel
Italy, Milan, c. 1460–75
Steel
28.6 x 32.4 x 20.3 (3.10 kg)
Gift of Mr. and Mrs. John L. Severance 1916.1551
Gilchrist B3
Collections: Frank Gair Macomber, Boston (cat. 552)

50. War Hat (or Kettle Hat)
Italy, Milan, perhaps 1475–1500
Missaglia Workshop
Steel
36 x 22 x 26.6 (1.78 kg)
Marks (twice repeated): MY beneath a crown and M beneath a split cross
Gift of Mr. and Mrs. John L. Severance 1916.1565
Gilchrist B2
Collections: Frank Gair Macomber, Boston (cat. 385)

51. Burgonet ("Casquetele" Type)
Italy, Milan(?), c. 1510–40
Steel, radiate flutings
25.3 x 26 x 25.3 (1.0 kg)
Gift of Mr. and Mrs. John L. Severance 1916.1642
Gilchrist B11
Collections: Frank Gair Macomber, Boston (cat. 568)

52. Closed Sallet with Grotesque Face (Shembartlaufen Visor)
Germany, Nuremberg, c. 1500
Painted steel
27.3 x 25.7 x 22.2 (2.40 kg)
Gift of Mr. and Mrs. John L.
Severance 1916.1646
Gilchrist B12
Collections: Franz Thill, Vienna;
Frank Gair Macomber, Boston
(cat. 518)

53. Closed Burgonet
Italy, Milan(?), early 16th century
Steel
34.3 x 25.7 x 22.2 (2.88 kg)
Gift of Mr. and Mrs. John L.
Severance 1916.1649
Gilchrist B13
Collections: Frank Gair Macomber,
Boston (cat. 469)

54. Burgonet
Italy, c. 1540
Steel
23.8 x 29.2 x 24.2 (1.8 kg)
Gift of Mr. and Mrs. John L.
Severance 1916.1650
Gilchrist B14
Collections: Frank Gair Macomber,
Boston (cat. 24)

55. Close Helmet in Maximilian Style
Germany, Nuremberg(?), c. 1530
Steel
29.2 x 34.9 x 23.5 (2.82 kg)
Gift of Mr. and Mrs. John L.
Severance 1916.1651
Gilchrist B15
Collections: Frank Gair Macomber,
Boston (cat. 139)

56. Burgonet
North Italy, c. 1550–1600
Etched steel, with trophies and
griffins
31.5 x 35.4 x 21.3 (1.88 kg)
Gift of Mr. and Mrs. John L.
Severance 1916.1653
Gilchrist B16
Collections: Duc d'Osuna; Edwin
Brett; Frank Gair Macomber,
Boston (cat. 150)

57. Close Helmet and Gorget (from a Funerary Achievement?)
Holland(?), c. 1590–1625
Gilded steel (invaded with rust), red
velvet lining, plume holder
Helmet, 33.0 x 34.0 x 21.3 (3.82 kg);
gorget, 32.4 x 24.8 x 19.1 (1.18 kg)
Gift of Mr. and Mrs. John L.
Severance 1916.1787, 1916.1806
Gilchrist B21, C24
Collections: Frank Gair Macomber,
Boston (cat. 289)

58. Triple-Crested Burgonet
Germany, Augsburg(?), c. 1560–70
Steel, leather bands
28 x 30.2 x 18.4 (1.9 kg)
Gift of Mr. and Mrs. John L.
Severance 1916.1804a
Gilchrist A7
Collections: Frank Gair Macomber,
Boston (cat. 306)

59. Pear-Stalk Cabasset
North Italy, Brescia(?), c. 1580–1600
Etched steel, with roped edge and
brass rivets
30.5 x 36.8 x 22 (1.26 kg)
Gift of Mr. and Mrs. John L.
Severance 1916.1805
Gilchrist B17
Collections: Edwin Brett; Seymour
Lucas; Frank Gair Macomber,
Boston (cat. 147)

60. Morion
North Italy, c. 1575–1600
Etched steel, with floral motif; me-
dallion on comb with boar under
oak tree
39 x 23.5 x 33 (1.84 kg)
Gift of Mr. and Mrs. John L.
Severance 1916.1808
Gilchrist B29
Collections: Edwin Brett; Spiller;
Frank Gair Macomber, Boston
(cat. 281)

61. Close Helmet in Maximilian Style
Germany, c. 1520
Steel, brass
30.5 x 21.8 x 32 (3.50 kg)
Marks: Stamped KXR
Gift of Mr. and Mrs. John L.
Severance 1916.1855
Gilchrist B9
Collections: Christoph I Radziwill
(1543–1603), Nieswiez Castle,
Poland; Drummond; Frank Gair
Macomber, Boston (cat. 138)

62. "Secrete" or Skull Cap (Hat Lining)
England(?), c. 1630–50
Steel
20.3 x 16.5 x 10.2 (0.56 kg)
Gift of Mr. and Mrs. John L.
Severance 1916.1895
Gilchrist B40
Collections: Frank Gair Macomber,
Boston (cat. 533)

63. War Hat (Kettle Hat)
Italy, c. 1460
Steel
30.3 x 25.9 x 17.5 (5.52 kg)
Gift of Mr. and Mrs. John L.
Severance 1916.1919
Gilchrist B4
Collections: S. J. Whawell; Frank
Gair Macomber, Boston (cat. 22)

64. Close Helmet for the Field
Germany, c. 1550–70
Iron, steel, leather, brass rivets
34.5 x 20 x 31.2 (2.96 kg)
Gift of Mr. and Mrs. John L.
Severance 1916.1946.l
Gilchrist A8
Collections: Bashford Dean,
New York

65. Cabasset
Italy, c. 1570
Steel, black paint, brass rosette rivets
18.4 x 25.7 x 21.6 (1.18 kg)
Marks: Shield with three stars and
crown(?)
Gift of Mr. and Mrs. John L.
Severance 1919.56
Gilchrist B26
Collections: American Art Associa-
tion, New York (Theodore
Offerman sale, 7–8 February 1919,
lot 254)

66. Black and White Morion (of Munich Town Guard)
Germany, c. 1575–1600
Steel, with roped edge; decorative
brass rivet washers as rosettes; black
paint
25.4 x 36.2 x 23.2 (1.08 kg)
Gift of Mr. and Mrs. John L.
Severance 1919.57
Gilchrist B27
Collections: American Art Associa-
tion, New York (Theodore
Offerman sale, 7–8 February 1919,
lot 255)

67. Cavalry Spider Helmet
France, 17th century
Iron with black paint
30.2 x 21.3 x 17.7; legs (longest),
l. 22 (1.52 kg)
Gift of Mr. and Mrs. John L.
Severance 1921.1258
Gilchrist B41
Collections: Pierre Lorillard
Ronalds; Frank Gair Macomber,
Boston (unrecorded); American Art
Association, New York (sale, 18–19
November 1921, lot 294)

68. Barbute (from the Venetian Garrison at Chalcis)
North Italy, c. 1350–1420
Iron
29 x 21 x 25 (1.58 kg)
Gift of Mr. and Mrs. John L.
Severance 1923.1065
Gilchrist D1
Collections: Bashford Dean, New
York; American Art Association,
New York (sale, 23–24 November
1923, lot 246)

EQUESTRIAN ARMOR

69. Demi-Chanfron
Germany, Augsburg, c. 1550
Etched and gilded steel, leather
6.8 x 24.5 (0.80 kg)
Gift of Mr. and Mrs. John L.
Severance 1916.1526
Gilchrist J4
Collections: Philip II of Spain [pur-
portedly]; Frederic Spitzer, Paris;
Frank Gair Macomber, Boston
(cat. 135)

70. Rowel Spur
Spain, c. 1700
Steel
L. 20.3, w. 9.5, rowel diam. 7.2
(0.34 kg)
Gift of Mr. and Mrs. John L.
Severance 1916.1568
Gilchrist J29
Collections: Franz Thill, Vienna;
Frank Gair Macomber, Boston
(cat. 527)

71. Curb Bit
Italy, late 16th century
Iron, gilt-bronze bosses
25.4 x 15.6 (1.04 kg)
Gift of Mr. and Mrs. John L.
Severance 1916.1581
Gilchrist J37
[Unprovenanced]

72. Pricked Spur
Spain(?), 13th century
Steel
14.9 x 7.9 (0.06 kg)
Gift of Mr. and Mrs. John L.
Severance 1916.1604
Gilchrist J6
Collections: Franz Thill, Vienna;
Frank Gair Macomber, Boston
(cat. 527)

73. Pricked Spur

Spain(?), 13th century

Steel

11.1 x 7.7 (0.04 kg)

Gift of Mr. and Mrs. John L.
Severance 1916.1611

Gilchrist J5

Collections: Frank Gair Macomber,
Boston (cat. 527)

74. Pricked Spur

Spain(?), 13th century

Steel

19 x 8.4 (0.06 kg)

Gift of Mr. and Mrs. John L.
Severance 1916.1953

Gilchrist J7

Collections: Franz Thill, Vienna;
Frank Gair Macomber, Boston
(cat. 527)

**75. Chanfron in Maximilian
Style**

Germany, Nuremberg(?), c. 1510

Steel

59.2 x 33.2 x 10.1 (1.54 kg)

Gift of Mr. and Mrs. John L.
Severance 1916.1845

Gilchrist J2

Collections: Edwin Brett; Frank
Gair Macomber, Boston (cat. 316)

**76. Child's Saddle with Lion
Pommel**

France, 17th century

Tooled leather, wood, canvas, steel;
gilt brass mounts with lion pommel,
chiseled and chased

35.6 x 31.8 x 27.3 (4.46 kg)

Gift of Mr. and Mrs. John L.
Severance 1916.1846

Gilchrist J19

Collections: Frank Gair Macomber,
Boston (cat. 267)

**77. Pommel Plate of a Saddle
(from the Garniture of Rudolf II
and Archduke Ernst)**

Germany, Augsburg, 1571

Anton Peffenhauser (1525–1603)

Blued, etched, and gilded steel

33 x 17.8 (0.46 kg)

Gift of Mr. and Mrs. John L.
Severance 1916.1888.1

Gilchrist J43

Collections: Imperial Armouries,
Vienna; Hastings; Richard Zschille;
Frank Gair Macomber, Boston
(cat. 171)

**78. Pommel Plate of a Saddle
(from the Garniture of Rudolf II
and Archduke Ernst)**

Germany, Augsburg, 1571

Anton Peffenhauser (1525–1603)

Etched and gilded steel

31.3 x 17 (0.44 kg)

Gift of Mr. and Mrs. John L.
Severance 1916.1888.2

Gilchrist J43

Collections: Imperial Armouries,
Vienna; Hastings; Richard Zschille;
Frank Gair Macomber, Boston
(cat. 171)

79. Curb Bit

Germany, 16th century

Steel, traces of gilding

Mouthpiece, w. 14.0; branches,
l. 28.0 (0.80 kg)

Gift of Mr. and Mrs. John L.
Severance 1916.2083

[Not in Gilchrist]

[Unprovenanced]

80. Pair of Stirrups

England(?), 17th century

Brass

Larger stirrup (1919.49.2): 17.2 x
12.1 (0.60 kg)

Gift of Mr. and Mrs. John L.
Severance 1919.49.1–2

Gilchrist J36

[Unprovenanced]

81. Pair of Stirrups (unmatched)

Germany(?), second half of 16th
century

Steel with modern black paint

1923.1122: 10.8 x 13.2 (0.38 kg)

1923.1123: 7.6 x 14.0 (0.38 kg)

Gift of Mr. and Mrs. John L.
Severance
1923.1122–1123

Gilchrist A4

[Unprovenanced]

CHAIN MAIL

82. Hauberk

European, 15th century

Riveted steel rings, short sleeves

Across sleeves, 121.3; l. 85.7
(9.58 kg)

Gift of Mr. and Mrs. John L.
Severance 1916.1543

Gilchrist D5

Collections: Frank Gair Macomber,
Boston (cat. 433)

83. Hauberk

European, 15th century

Riveted steel rings, close woven,
reinforced collar

Across sleeves, 110.5; l. 86.3 (10 kg)

Gift of Mr. and Mrs. John L.
Severance 1916.1552

Gilchrist D6

Collections: Frank Gair Macomber,
Boston (cat. 434)

84. Hauberk

European, 15th century

Fine steel rings, leather collar

Across sleeves, 124.5; l. 127 (10 kg)

Gift of Mr. and Mrs. John L.
Severance 1916.1567

Gilchrist D11

Collections: Frank Gair Macomber,
Boston (cat. 178)

85. Brayette

European, 15th century

Riveted steel rings, strongly
reinforced

Diam. of each ring, about 1.0;
l. 31.8; w. 47.7 (1.08 kg)

Gift of Mr. and Mrs. John L.
Severance 1916.1574

Gilchrist D10

Collections: Franz Thill, Vienna;
Frank Gair Macomber, Boston
(cat. 458)

86. Collar

European, 15th century

Riveted steel rings, neck strongly
reinforced

Diam. of each ring, about 0.5;
l. 25.7; w. 61.5 (0.92 kg)

Gift of Mr. and Mrs. John L.
Severance 1916.1584

Gilchrist D12

Collections: Franz Thill, Vienna;
Frank Gair Macomber, Boston
(cat. 457)

87. Hauberk

European, 15th century

Riveted steel rings, half-length
sleeves

Diam. of each ring, about 1.1; across
sleeves, 128.3; l. 91.4 (9.29 kg)

Gift of Mr. and Mrs. John L.
Severance 1916.1817

Gilchrist D8

Collections: Frank Gair Macomber,
Boston (cat. 572)

88. Hauberk

Turkey(?), 15th century

Riveted steel rings

Diam. of each ring, about 1.1; l. 91.5
(9.45 kg)

Gift of Mr. and Mrs. John L.
Severance 1916.1890

Gilchrist D3

Collections: Frank Gair Macomber,
Boston (cat. 435)

89. Hauberk

European, 16th century

Very fine steel rings, border of brass
rings at bottom edge

Diam. of each ring, from 0.2 to 0.3;
across sleeves, 145.5; l. 74.3 (7.01 kg)

Gift of Mr. and Mrs. John L.
Severance 1916.1897

Gilchrist D4

Collections: Frank Gair Macomber,
Boston (cat. 431)

90. Hauberk

European, 16th century

Steel and brass rings, sleeveless

Diam. of each ring, from 0.4 to 0.7;
w. 52.1; l. 78.2 (about 9 kg)

Gift of Mr. and Mrs. John L.
Severance 1916.1918

Gilchrist D2

Collections: Frank Gair Macomber,
Boston, (cat. 370)

91. "Bishop's Mantle" (Cape)

European (German or Swiss?), early
16th century

Riveted steel (some brass) rings,
reinforced collar

Diam. of each ring, about 1.0;
w. 95.8; l. 57.2 (4.08 kg)

Gift of Mr. and Mrs. John L.
Severance 1921.1256

Gilchrist D15

Collections: Clemens, Munich;
American Art Association, New
York (sale, 18–19 November 1921,
lot 268)

92. Hauberk

Germany(?), c. 1400–50

Riveted steel and brass rings,
modern buckles and straps

L. 76.2; each sleeve, l. 43.2
(10.47 kg)

Gift of Mr. and Mrs. John L.
Severance 1923.1120

Gilchrist D1

Collections: Bashford Dean, New
York; American Art Association,
New York (sale, 23–24 November
1923, lot 246)

SHIELDS

93. Round Shield (Rondache)

Italy, Milan, c. 1570
Etched and gilded steel, brass rivets
Diam. 57.8 (4.10 kg)
Gift of Mr. and Mrs. John L.
Severance 1916.1504
Gilchrist L5
Collections: Yerkes; Frank Gair
Macomber, Boston (cat. 553)

94. Round Shield (Rondache)

North Italy, c. 1550–1600
Steel, with etched panels and roped
border
Diam. 56.5 (4.34 kg)
Gift of Mr. and Mrs. John L.
Severance 1916.1615
Gilchrist L6
Collections: Frank Gair Macomber,
Boston (cat. 410)

POLE ARMS

95. Partisan

France, c. 1650
Etched steel, round wooden haft
Overall, l. 200 (1.50 kg); blade, l. 33
Gift of Mr. and Mrs. John L.
Severance 1916.31
Gilchrist H74
Collections: Frank Gair Macomber,
Boston (cat. 366)

96. Partisan

France, 17th century
Gilded, etched, and chiseled steel
(silvered medallions with relief
heads), green tassel, round wooden
haft
Overall, l. 209.5 (1.14 kg); blade,
l. 32.4
Gift of Mr. and Mrs. John L.
Severance 1916.33
Gilchrist H67
Collections: Frank Gair Macomber,
Boston (cat. 193)

97. Glaive (with Arms of Giustiniani Family)

Italy, Venice, c. 1600–20
Etched steel, wooden haft
Overall, l. 184.5 (2.30 kg); blade,
l. 76.5, w. 15.2
Gift of Mr. and Mrs. John L.
Severance 1916.1532
Gilchrist H45
Collections: Frank Gair Macomber,
Boston (cat. 362)

98. Corsèque

Italy, c. 1520
Steel, round wooden haft, tassel
Overall, l. 269.2 (2.38 kg); blade,
l. 61, w. 36.5
Marks (on each face): Star?
Gift of Mr. and Mrs. John L.
Severance 1916.1535
Gilchrist H26
Collections: Richard Zschille; Frank
Gair Macomber, Boston (cat. 45)

99. Glaive

Italy, Venice, c. 1600–20
Etched steel, with masks, figures,
arms, and lion of St. Mark; octago-
nal wooden haft
Overall, l. 179 (2.60 kg); blade,
l. 71.7, w. 22.2
Gift of Mr. and Mrs. John L.
Severance 1916.1536
Gilchrist H27
Collections: Frank Gair Macomber,
Boston (cat. 363)

100. Halberd

Germany, c. 1550
Steel, pierced trefoils; rectangular
wooden haft with planed corners
Overall, l. 200.7 (1.86 kg); blade,
l. 51, w. 25.4
Gift of Mr. and Mrs. John L.
Severance 1916.1542
Gilchrist H31
Collections: Frank Gair Macomber,
Boston (cat. 66)

101. Halberd

Switzerland, 17th century
Steel, rectangular wooden haft with
planed corners
Overall, l. 160 (2.12 kg); blade,
l. 39.3, w. 19.3
Gift of Mr. and Mrs. John L.
Severance 1916.1554
Gilchrist H18
Collections: Frank Gair Macomber,
Boston (cat. 3)

102. Halberd

Switzerland, c. 1480–1500
Steel, rectangular wooden haft (in
sections) with planed corners
Overall, l. 205.7 (2.34 kg); blade,
l. 41.9, w. 20.3
Marks: Three incised marks grouped
on one side
Gift of Mr. and Mrs. John L.
Severance 1916.1556
Gilchrist H21
Collections: Frank Gair Macomber,
Boston (cat. 4)

103. Halberd

Germany, c. 1500
Steel, pierced circular holes; wooden
haft (oval section)
Overall, l. 230.7 (2.44 kg); blade,
l. 48.8, w. 21.9
Marks: A crown?
Gift of Mr. and Mrs. John L.
Severance 1916.1559
Gilchrist H4
Collections: Frank Gair Macomber,
Boston (cat. 377)

104. Halberd

Germany, c. 1500–25
Steel, pierced quatrefoil; rectangular
wooden haft with planed corners
Overall, l. 217.4 (2.38 kg); blade,
l. 30.5, w. 24.2
Gift of Mr. and Mrs. John L.
Severance 1916.1561
Gilchrist H37
Collections: Frank Gair Macomber,
Boston (cat. 64)

105. Halberd

Switzerland, 17th century
Steel, new rectangular wooden haft
with planed corners
Overall, l. 159.7 (2.10 kg); blade,
l. 38.3, w. 18.5
Marks: IP
Gift of Mr. and Mrs. John L.
Severance 1916.1562
Gilchrist H12
Collections: Zurich Arsenal; Frank
Gair Macomber, Boston (cat. 2)

106. Bardiche (Pole Axe)

Germany or Russia, 16th century
Steel, leather, brass, wooden haft
Overall, l. 178.5 (1.66 kg); blade,
l. 60.2, w. 14.2
Gift of Mr. and Mrs. John L.
Severance 1916.1563
Gilchrist H15
Collections: Baron de Cosson; Frank
Gair Macomber, Boston (cat. 442)

107. Halberd

Germany, c. 1520
Steel, pierced quatrefoil; round
wooden haft
Overall, l. 182.3 (1.84 kg); blade,
l. 45.7, w. 24.2
Gift of Mr. and Mrs. John L.
Severance 1916.1564
Gilchrist H38
Collections: Frank Gair Macomber,
Boston (cat. 65)

108. Linstock

France, c. 1600–25
Steel (match holders fashioned as
eagles' heads), octagonal wooden
haft covered with green velvet, brass
studs
Overall, l. 201.9 (2.38 kg); blade,
l. 37.7, w. 25.2
Gift of Mr. and Mrs. John L.
Severance 1916.1786
Gilchrist H64
Collections: Frank Gair Macomber,
Boston (cat. 403)

109. Parade Spear

Germany, Augsburg(?), c. 1570–1600
Etched steel with traces of gilding;
Imperial Hapsburg arms on one face
and the Burgundian Stave Cross on
the other; brass lugs; hexagonal
wooden haft with leather straps;
woolen tassel
Overall, l. 208.2 (1.40 kg); blade,
l. 29.5
Gift of Mr. and Mrs. John L.
Severance 1916.1789
Gilchrist H39
Collections: Richard Zschille; Frank
Gair Macomber, Boston (cat. 307)

110. Partisan

France, c. 1600–50
Etched and chased steel, with scrolls,
masks, and animals; octagonal
wooden haft with studs and leather;
remnants of velvet tassel
Overall, l. 217.2 (2.04 kg); blade,
l. 57.2
Gift of Mr. and Mrs. John L.
Severance 1916.1795
Gilchrist H43
Collections: Frank Gair Macomber,
Boston (cat. 364)

111. Halberd

France, early 17th century
Pierced steel, appliqué masks in
brass, octagonal wooden haft with
studs and leather straps
Overall, l. 239 (2.36 kg); blade, l. 48
Gift of Mr. and Mrs. John L.
Severance 1916.1797
Gilchrist H63
Collections: Spiller; Frank Gair
Macomber, Boston (cat. 341)

112. Corsèque (Chauve-Souris)
North Italy, c. 1530
Steel, square (in section) wooden haft with planed corners, brass collars on socket
Overall, l. 254 (2.66 kg); blade, l. 57.2, w. 26
Marks: [Unidentified]
Gift of Mr. and Mrs. John L. Severance 1916.1801
Gilchrist H5
Collections: Richard Zschille; Frank Gair Macomber, Boston (cat. 368)

113. Corsèque (Chauve-Souris)
North Italy, c. 1530
Steel, round wooden haft with leather straps
Overall, l. 183.5 (2.60 kg); blade, l. 58.4, w. 22.2
Gift of Mr. and Mrs. John L. Severance 1916.1802
Gilchrist H20
Collections: Richard Zschille; Frank Gair Macomber, Boston (cat. 367)

114. Partisan
Italy, c. 1550–1600
Chiseled steel, oval wooden haft
Overall, l. 236.2 (2.24 kg); blade, l. 92.7, w. 17.1
Gift of Mr. and Mrs. John L. Severance 1916.1818
Gilchrist H51
Collections: Frank Gair Macomber, Boston (cat. 401)

115. Parade Halberd with Arms of Elector Christian I of Saxony
Germany, Saxony, 1586–91
Gilded and etched steel, round wooden haft
Overall, l. 238.2 (3.54 kg); blade, l. 62.2, w. 30.5
Gift of Mr. and Mrs. John L. Severance 1916.1819
Gilchrist H52
Collections: Saxon Electoral Armouries, Dresden; Richard Zschille; Frank Gair Macomber, Boston (cat. 57)

116. Parade Halberd
Italy, c. 1600–50
Engraved steel with masks, rectangular wooden haft with planed corners, wool tassel
Overall, l. 252 (2.46 kg); blade, l. 65.6
Gift of Mr. and Mrs. John L. Severance 1916.1826
Gilchrist H50
Collections: Richard Zschille; Frank Gair Macomber, Boston (cat. 53)

117. Bill
Italy, c. 1480
Steel, wooden haft
Overall, l. 184.8 (2.24 kg); blade, l. 77.5, w. 11.4
Gift of Mr. and Mrs. John L. Severance 1916.1835
Gilchrist H3
Collections: Frank Gair Macomber, Boston (cat. 373)

118. Partisan
Italy, c. 1600–20
Steel, rectangular wooden haft with planed corners
Overall, l. 229.2 (2.46 kg); blade, l. 76.7, w. 7.6
Marks: Blade incised LUCCA; XIIII on socket
Gift of Mr. and Mrs. John L. Severance 1916.1923
Gilchrist H24
Collections: Frank Gair Macomber, Boston (cat. 44)

119. Halberd
Germany, c. 1580
Steel leaf-shaped head, octagonal wooden haft, woolen pompom
Overall, l. 197.5 (2.46 kg); blade, l. 41.9, w. 22.8
Gift of John L. Severance 1919.58
Gilchrist H72
Collections: Austin (cat. 393); American Art Association, New York (Theodore Offerman sale, 7–8 February 1919, lot 248)

120. Brandistock
Italy, early 17th century
Steel, with retractable blades; round wooden haft
Overall, l. 162.2 (closed), 207 (open) (2.48 kg); blade, l. 44.7
Gift of Mr. and Mrs. John L. Severance 1921.1257
Gilchrist H36
Collections: American Art Association, New York (sale, 18–19 November 1921, lot 288)

121. Partisan
Germany, 1729–32
Etched steel, haft broken
Blade, l. 48.7, w. 29.1 (1.60 kg)
Inscribed: Coat of arms and F.L.C.V.M [Franz Ludwig Kurfurst von Mainz]
Gift of Mr. and Mrs. William F. Wieman 1951.352
Collections: Franz Ludwig Kurfurst von Mainz

PERCUSSION WEAPONS

122. Seven-Flanged Mace
Italy(?), c. 1540–50
Gilded russet steel, with chiseled foliate decoration
Overall, l. 64.5 (1.60 kg); head, l. 16.2, w. 11.4
Gift of Mr. and Mrs. John L. Severance 1916.1589
Gilchrist K9
Collections: Frank Gair Macomber, Boston (cat. 35)

123. Battle Axe
Italy, late 16th century
Steel inset with copper rosette; haft missing
Across head, 27.3 (0.40 kg); blade, w. 8.3
Gift of Mr. and Mrs. John L. Severance 1916.1599
Gilchrist H60
Collections: Sir Samuel Meyrick; Raoul Richards, Rome; Frank Gair Macomber, Boston (cat. 535)

124. Battle Axe
Scandinavia(?), 15th century
Steel, wood
Overall, l. 93.3 (1.22 kg); across blade, 18.7
Gift of Mr. and Mrs. John L. Severance 1916.1601
Gilchrist H14
Collections: Stadtrat Rich; Raoul Richards, Rome; Richard Zschille; Frank Gair Macomber, Boston (cat. 12)

EDGED WEAPONS

125. Estoc
Germany, early 16th century
Steel, wood, leather
Overall, l. 156.6 (1.60 kg); blade, l. 125.3; grip, l. 30; quillons, w. 26.2
Marks: [Unidentified; inlaid copper on blade]
Gift of Mr. and Mrs. John L. Severance 1916.686
Gilchrist E5
Collections: Sauran; Richard Zschille; Frank Gair Macomber, Boston (cat. 31)

126. Schiavona Broadsword
Italy, Venice, early 18th century
Steel, leather, wood, brass
Overall, l. 109.9 (1.32 kg); blade, l. 94.0; guard, l. 13.3; grip, l. 9.2
Inscribed (on blade): POTZDAM
Gift of Mr. and Mrs. John L. Severance 1916.693
Gilchrist E48
Collections: Frank Gair Macomber, Boston (cat. 93)

127. Rapier
Italy, Milan(?), c. 1625–50
Federico Picinino (signed on ricasso)
Steel with russeted hilt, wire grip
Overall, l. 144.8 (1.38 kg); blade, l. 108.3; quillons, w. 22.5; grip, l. 15.5
Gift of Mr. and Mrs. John L. Severance 1916.695
Gilchrist E56
Collections: Frank Gair Macomber, Boston (cat. 83)

128. Basket-Hilt Broadsword ("Mortuary Sword")
Hilt: England, c. 1640–50
Blade: Germany, Solingen(?), early 18th century
Chiseled steel with gilt silver foil inlay, wood and wire grip
Overall, l. 101.6 (1.12 kg); blade, l. 85.2; hilt, l. 13.0
Inscribed (on blade): ANDRIA FERRARA
Marks: Orb and cross
Gift of Mr. and Mrs. John L. Severance 1916.696
Gilchrist E79
Collections: General Thomas Fairfax [purportedly]; Sir Cuthbert Sharp; Duke of Sussex; Earl of Londesborough; Edwin Brett; S. J. Whawell; Frank Gair Macomber, Boston (cat. 211)

129. Rapier
Hilt, c. 1620–30
Blade: Clemens Horn (German, Solingen, 1586–1617)
Blued and gilded steel
Overall, l. 111.1 (1.34 kg); blade, l. 89.2; quillons, w. 21.3
Inscribed (on blade): NEC TEMERE NEC TIMIDE / INTER ARMA SILENT LEGE / VERITATEM DILIGE ET PUGNA PRO PATRIA
Marks: Unicorn head
Gift of Mr. and Mrs. John L. Severance 1916.697
Gilchrist E57
Collections: Baron de Cosson; Frank Gair Macomber, Boston (cat. 440)

130. Schiavona Broadsword

Italy, Venice, 18th century
Steel, brass, leather, wood
Overall, l. 100.3 (1.28 kg); blade,
l. 84.4; grip, l. 10.5; guard, w. 14.8
Marks: [Unidentified]

Gift of Mr. and Mrs. John L.
Severance 1916.698
Gilchrist E69
Collections: Frank Gair Macomber,
Boston (cat. 360)

131. Left-Handed Dagger or "Main Gauche"

Spain(?) or Italy (Neapolitan?),
c. 1650
Pierced and chiseled steel
Overall, l. 57.2 (0.50 kg); blade,
l. 44.4; quillons, w. 25.4

Gift of Mr. and Mrs. John L.
Severance 1916.699
Gilchrist I44
Collections: Baron de Cosson; Frank
Gair Macomber, Boston (cat. 427)

132. Basket-Hilted Broadsword

Hilt: Scotland, c. 1720
Blade: Germany, Solingen, early
18th century
Steel, with liner of buff leather; grip
of wood, copper wire, and fishskin
(ray?)
Overall, l. 101.6 (1.40 kg); blade,
l. 85.7; grip, l. 11; hilt, w. 12.8
Inscribed (on blade): CLEMENS
WILLEMS ME FECIT SOLINGEN
Marks (on blade): Running wolf,
mermaid, pair of oval marks
(anchors?)

Gift of Mr. and Mrs. John L.
Severance 1916.701
Gilchrist E84
Collections: Frank Gair Macomber,
Boston (cat. 414)

133. Rapier

Germany, Solingen, c. 1600
Russeted and gilded steel, inlaid
with silver; pommel and quillon
termini chiseled in form of warriors'
heads
Overall, l. 125.4 (0.96 kg); blade,
l. 111; quillons, w. 15; grip, l. 12.7
Inscribed: PETTHERR / WIRSBERGH
Marks: Cross and orb (both blade
faces)

Gift of Mr. and Mrs. John L.
Severance 1916.702
Gilchrist E63
Collections: Frank Gair Macomber,
Boston (cat. 92)

134. Basket-Hilted Broadsword

Scotland, Stirling(?), c. 1740
Steel, pierced hilt; wood and leather
grip
Overall, l. 106.6 (1.24 kg); blade,
l. 91.3; grip, l. 11.3; hilt, w. 14.6

Gift of Mr. and Mrs. John L.
Severance 1916.703
Gilchrist E98
Collections: Frank Gair Macomber,
Boston (cat. 213)

135. Parade Sword

Italian, Ferrara, c. 1500–25
Ercole dei Fideli (blade only)
Etched and gilded steel blade, with
bands of allegorical figures, amorini,
and triumphs; modern hilt of silver,
brass, wood, and leather
Overall, l. 101.9 (1.00 kg); blade,
l. 85.4; quillons, l. 17.5; grip, l. 11.1
Marks (both faces of blade):
Candelabrum?

Gift of Mr. and Mrs. John L.
Severance 1916.704
Gilchrist E35
Collections: Frank Gair Macomber,
Boston (cat. 95)

136. Schiavona Broadsword

Italy, Venice, early 18th century
Steel, silver wire grip, silver pommel
Overall, l. 107.3 (1.28 kg); blade,
l. 92.7; guard, l. 12.7; grip, l. 9.8
Marks: Orb and cross

Gift of Mr. and Mrs. John L.
Severance 1916.705
Gilchrist E71
Collections: Frank Gair Macomber,
Boston (cat. 558)

137. Cup-Hilted Rapier

Italy, Milan(?), c. 1610–30
Steel; pierced, chased, and chiseled
cup, with scenes of the Nativity and
the Flight into Egypt; wire ferrules
on leather-covered wood grip
Overall, l. 123.2 (1.20 kg); blade,
l. 100.9; quillons, w. 25.2; grip,
l. 15.2
Inscribed: FPNDRITH (on one face),
RDFTPHNI (on other)
Marks: Sickle (on blade, near cup)

Gift of Mr. and Mrs. John L.
Severance 1916.706
Gilchrist E72
Collections: Ralph Bernal; Earl of
Londesborough; Edwin Brett; S. J.
Whawell; Frank Gair Macomber,
Boston (cat. 90)

138. Smallsword

Dutch, c. 1650–60
Steel, wood, copper wire; chiseled
hilt; engraved blade
Overall, l. 95.3 (0.58 kg); blade,
l. 78; grip, l. 11.8; shell guard, l. 8.3

Gift of Mr. and Mrs. John L.
Severance 1916.1093
Gilchrist E92
Collections: Frank Gair Macomber,
Boston (cat. 472)

139. Smallsword

France, Paris, c. 1750–60
Gilded and russeted steel, copper,
wood; hilt and shell guard chiseled
and stamped with relief figures of
animals after designs by J.-B. Oudry
Overall, l. 105.4 (0.42 kg); blade,
l. 87.9; shell guard, w. 7.9

Gift of Mr. and Mrs. John L.
Severance 1916.1094
Gilchrist E108
Collections: Frank Gair Macomber,
Boston (cat. 491)

140. Court Sword

England, London or Birmingham,
c. 1790
Steel blade, partially blued and
gilded; silver hilt (hallmarked on
knuckle guard), polished and faceted
Overall, l. 99.7 (0.42 kg); blade,
l. 82.9; shell guard, w. 8.3

Gift of Mr. and Mrs. John L.
Severance 1916.1095
Gilchrist E109
Collections: Frank Gair Macomber,
Boston (cat. 487)

141. Smallsword

France, 18th century
Steel with copper alloy inlays;
wooden grip with steel wire
Overall, l. 90.7 (0.32 kg); blade,
l. 60.2; quillons, w. 8.6

Gift of Mr. and Mrs. John L.
Severance 1916.1096
Gilchrist E82
Collections: Frank Gair Macomber,
Boston (cat. 223)

142. Smallsword

France, Paris, c. 1730
Blued steel with gold-encrusted
decoration, chased and engraved;
silver wire
Overall, l. 94.5 (0.36 kg); blade,
l. 77.2; grip, l. 13.2; shell guard, l. 8

Gift of Mr. and Mrs. John L.
Severance 1916.1097
Gilchrist E111
Collections: Frank Gair Macomber,
Boston (cat. 494)

143. Smallsword

Germany, Passau(?), 1640–60
Steel, wood, steel wire, copper; chis-
eled shell guard (cavalry skirmish)
Overall, l. 104.5 (0.60 kg); blade,
l. 86.0; shell guard, w. 7.6
Marks: Running wolf (inlaid copper)

Gift of Mr. and Mrs. John L.
Severance 1916.1099
Gilchrist E78
Collections: Frank Gair Macomber,
Boston (cat. 221)

144. Smallsword

Holland, c. 1650–60 (blade: Spanish)
Steel, wood, steel wire; chiseled shell
guard (warriors storming a city wall);
blued, gilded, pierced, and engraved
blade
Overall, l. 92.7 (0.62 kg); blade,
l. 75.9; shell guard, w. 7.9
Inscribed (on ricasso): VIVA RE DI
NAPOLI

Gift of Mr. and Mrs. John L.
Severance 1916.1100
Gilchrist E95
Collections: Frank Gair Macomber,
Boston (cat. 471)

145. Smallsword

Italy(?), c. 1700
Steel, wood, copper wire; engraved
scrolls on blade; shell guard lacking
Overall, l. 100.3 (0.28 kg); blade,
l. 83.7; guard, w. 10.5

Gift of Mr. and Mrs. John L.
Severance 1916.1101
Gilchrist E96
Collections: Frank Gair Macomber,
Boston (cat. 225)

146. Smallsword

France, c. 1770–80
Steel, with chiseled relief decoration;
blade engraved; wire grip; shell guard
decorated with scenes from
J.-B. Oudry
Overall, l. 97 (0.36 kg); blade,
l. 79.2; grip, l. 13.8; shell guard, w. 7.5

Gift of Mr. and Mrs. John L.
Severance 1916.1484
Gilchrist E104
Collections: Frank Gair Macomber,
Boston (cat. 495)

147. Smallsword

France, c. 1650–70
Steel, iron, silver inlay, wood, brass
wire
Overall, l. 90.8 (0.52 kg); blade,
l. 74.1; shell guard, w. 6.7

Gift of Mr. and Mrs. John L.
Severance 1916.1485
Gilchrist E105
Collections: Frank Gair Macomber,
Boston (cat. 493)

148. Smallsword for a Boy
Italy, c. 1650–80
Steel, wood; hilt inlaid with silver
floral designs; grip wrapped with
steel and brass wire
Overall, l. 78.1 (0.30 kg); blade,
l. 63.2; shell guard, w. 5.2
Inscribed (on blade): ANTHONIO
PICHINIO
Gift of Mr. and Mrs. John L.
Severance 1916.1486
Gilchrist E93
Collections: Frank Gair Macomber,
Boston (cat. 224)

149. Smallsword
Hilt: Dutch, c. 1660–80
Blade: Germany, Solingen, 17th
century
Steel, chiseled guard and pommel,
with masks and figures; copper wire
Overall, l. 104 (0.52 kg); blade,
l. 87.2; grip, l. 12.5; shell guard,
w. 7.6
Marks (on blade): Running wolf
Gift of Mr. and Mrs. John L.
Severance 1916.1488
Gilchrist E 90
Collections: Frank Gair Macomber,
Boston (cat. 470)

150. Smallsword
England, c. 1720–60
Steel, pierced guard, perforated
blade
Overall, l. 97 (0.44 kg); blade,
l. 80.5; grip, l. 12.6; shell guard,
w. 7.7
Gift of Mr. and Mrs. John L.
Severance 1916.1489
Gilchrist E102
Collections: Frank Gair Macomber,
Boston (cat. 218)

**151. Hunting Sword and
Scabbard**
France, c. 1780 (blade German?)
Sword: Blued, etched, and gilded
steel; silver; wood
Overall, l. 72.1 (0.54 kg); blade,
l. 56.5; grip, l. 14.0; guard, w. 7.3
Scabbard: Silver mounts, sharkskin,
steel tip
Overall, 58.1 (0.10 kg); opening,
w. 4.5
Gift of Mr. and Mrs. John L.
Severance 1916.1492.a–b
Gilchrist E107
Collections: Frank Gair Macomber,
Boston (cat. 236)

152. Smallsword
Italy, c. 1730
Steel, iron, silver, copper wire,
wood; hilt inlaid with silver scroll
designs
Overall, l. 95.2 (0.56 kg); blade,
l. 78.8; shell guard, w. 7.6
Inscribed (on blade): AMOR VINCIT
OMNIA
Gift of Mr. and Mrs. John L.
Severance 1916.1494
Gilchrist E101
Collections: Frank Gair Macomber,
Boston (cat. 492)

153. Pillow Sword
Italy, c. 1650
Pierced steel, leather, wood; copper
wire on grip
Overall, l. 93.0 (0.46 kg); blade,
l. 77.8; quillons, w. 9.5
Gift of Mr. and Mrs. John L.
Severance 1916.1495
Gilchrist E66
Collections: Frank Gair Macomber,
Boston (cat. 81)

154. Smallsword
France, Paris, c. 1750–70
Gilded steel, wood
Overall, l. 103.2 (0.46 kg); blade,
l. 86.0; shell guard, w. 7.0
Gift of Mr. and Mrs. John L.
Severance 1916.1496
Gilchrist E112
Collections: Frank Gair Macomber,
Boston (cat. 496)

155. Smallsword
England, c. 1650
Pierced, chiseled, and engraved steel
Overall, l. 93.5 (0.58 kg); blade,
l. 79.7; guard, w. 12; grip, l. 11.8
Gift of Mr. and Mrs. John L.
Severance 1916.1497
Gilchrist E81
Collections: Frank Gair Macomber,
Boston (cat. 220)

156. Rapier
Germany, c. 1630–50
Steel; blued, gilded, and perforated
blade; hilt formed as a stork grasping
a snake
Overall, l. 100.3 (0.82 kg); blade,
l. 86.5; quillons, w. 13; grip, l. 12.3
Gift of Mr. and Mrs. John L.
Severance 1916.1498
Gilchrist E88
Collections: Frank Gair Macomber,
Boston (cat. 485)

157. Smallsword
France, late 17th century
Chiseled and pierced steel, iron,
wood; wire-bound grip; double shell
guard with four royal portraits
Overall, l. 104.1 (0.36 kg); blade,
l. 87.6; shell guard, w. 7.9
Gift of Mr. and Mrs. John L.
Severance 1916.1500
Gilchrist E110
Collections: Frank Gair Macomber,
Boston (cat. 497)

158. Smallsword
Germany, c. 1770
Steel, gilt-brass; porcelain grip
Overall, l. 90.5 (0.32 kg); blade,
l. 76.9; grip, l. 11.3; hilt, w. 8.3
Gift of Mr. and Mrs. John L.
Severance 1916.1501
Gilchrist E113
Collections: Frank Gair Macomber,
Boston (cat. 490)

159. Hand-and-a-Half Sword
Germany, mid-16th century
Steel; blued pommel and quillons;
leather grip
Overall, l. 123.9 (1.68 kg); blade,
l. 92.3; grip, l. 30.5; quillons, w. 24.8
Marks: Three [undeciphered] on
fuller
Gift of Mr. and Mrs. John L.
Severance 1916.1506
Gilchrist E12
Collections: Frank Gair Macomber,
Boston (cat. 489)

160. Two-Handed Sword
Spain, Toledo(?), second half of 16th
century
Steel; wood and leather grip; urn-
shaped pommel with button
Overall, l. 167.3 (2.24 kg); blade,
l. 126.0; grip, l. 40.0; quillons,
w. 31.8; ricasso, l. 17.2
Inscribed (in groove on ricasso):
IVLIAN
Marks (both sides of blade): X
Gift of Mr. and Mrs. John L.
Severance 1916.1507
Gilchrist E13
Collections: Frank Gair Macomber,
Boston (cat. 436)

**161. Two-Handed Sword of the
State Guard of Julius of
Brunswick-Lüneburg**
Germany, Brunswick, dated 1574
Steel; leather and wire-bound grip
(No. 59 of series)
Overall, l. 186.1 (3.34 kg); blade,
l. 132.1; quillons, w. 51.4; grip,
l. 45.7; ricasso, l. 25.1
Gift of Mr. and Mrs. John L.
Severance 1916.1508
Gilchrist E29
Collections: Armory of
Wolfenbüttel; Arsenal of Vienna;
Richard Zschille; Frank Gair
Macomber, Boston (cat. 78)

162. Two-Handed Sword
Spain, Toledo, second half of 16th
century
Steel; wood and leather grip; fluted
pommel
Overall, l. 168.3 (2.20 kg); blade,
l. 126.4; grip, l. 41.3; quillons,
w. 35.2; ricasso, l. 20.3
Marks (on ricasso guard): OT within
a shield; SL within a shield
Inscribed (within fuller): TOLEDO
and IVAN LVIS
Gift of Mr. and Mrs. John L.
Severance 1916.1509
Gilchrist E11
Collections: Baron de Cosson; Frank
Gair Macomber, Boston (cat. 438)

163. Sword
Germany(?), 15th century
Steel; wood and leather grip
Overall, l. 140.2 (1.72 kg); blade,
l. 87.3; quillons, w. 20.3
Gift of Mr. and Mrs. John L.
Severance 1916.1600
Gilchrist E2
Collections: Franz Thill, Vienna;
Frank Gair Macomber, Boston
(cat. 559)

164. Executioner's Sword
Germany, blade dated 1634
Steel; modern gilt-brass hilt with
copper wire; blade etched with
Virgin and Child on one face,
Crucified Christ on other
Overall, l. 98.1 (2.04 kg); blade,
l. 75.3; grip, l. 22.5; quillons, w. 15.5
Inscribed: VIAT JUSTICIA ET
VERBUM CARO FACTUM EST, *1634*
Gift of Mr. and Mrs. John L.
Severance 1916.1616
Gilchrist E67
Collections: Frank Gair Macomber,
Boston (cat. 207)

165. Executioner's Sword
Germany, late 17th century
Steel, wood, brass, copper wire
Overall, l. 108.9 (2.30 kg); blade,
l. 85.7; quillons, w. 22.5; grip, l. 15.0
Inscribed (on blade): WAN ICH DAS
SCHWERDT THU AUFF HEBEN SO /
WUNCSCH ICH DEM ARMEN
SUNDER DAS EWEGE LEBEN

Gift of Mr. and Mrs. John L.
Severance 1916.1620
Gilchrist E97
Collections: Edwin Brett; Frank
Gair Macomber, Boston (cat. 209)

166. Falchion
Italy(?), 18th century (blade only;
hilt is modern copy, original in
Munich)
Steel, blade lightly etched with
pseudo-Kufic characters; bright steel
hilt terminating in eagle's heads at
pommel and quillons
Overall, l. 78.7 (1.00 kg); blade,
l. 64.9; quillons, w. 20.3

Gift of Mr. and Mrs. John L.
Severance 1916.1624
Gilchrist E28
Collections: Frank Gair Macomber,
Boston (cat. 99)

167. Hunting Sword
Hilt: England, c. 1630
Blade: Clemens Willems, Germany,
Solingen, 17th century
Steel, wood; scroll ornaments
Overall, l. 84.5 (0.74 kg); blade,
l. 71.2; grip, l. 12.8; hilt, w. 11.8
Inscribed (on blade): CLEMENS
WILLEMS / FECIT SOLINGEN

Gift of Mr. and Mrs. John L.
Severance 1916.1626
Gilchrist E85
Collections: Earl of Londesborough;
Frank Gair Macomber, Boston
(cat. 337)

168. Hunting Sword
Dutch, c. 1700
Steel, wood, brass
Overall, l. 81.3 (0.84 kg); blade,
l. 66.7; guard, l. 16.2
Inscribed (on blade): IOHAN VINNDT
/ NICHOLAS DORRAN

Gift of Mr. and Mrs. John L.
Severance 1916.1627
Gilchrist E91
Collections: Frank Gair Macomber,
Boston (cat. 285)

169. Hanger
Italy, dated 1553
Steel; gold, brass, and silver dama-
scened hilt
Overall, l. 73 (0.62 kg); blade,
l. 57.7; quillons, w. 17.5
Marks: Stag with crown

Gift of Mr. and Mrs. John L.
Severance 1916.1629
Gilchrist E46
Collections: Baron de Cosson;
Richards; Frank Gair Macomber,
Boston (cat. 98)

170. Rapier
Italy, c. 1600
Steel; wire grip; blued and chiseled
hilt with foliate pattern
Overall, l. 110 (1.14 kg); blade, l. 94;
quillons, w. 16.2; grip, l. 14.7
Marks (on blade): Three spade-
shaped marks (two brass-inlaid)

Gift of Mr. and Mrs. John L.
Severance 1916.1634
Gilchrist E94
Collections: Franz Thill, Vienna;
Frank Gair Macomber, Boston
(cat. 478)

171. Parrying Dagger
Italy, c. 1580–1610
Steel, copper wire
Overall, l. 26.5 (0.08 kg); blade,
l. 17.2; quillons, w. 8.4

Gift of Mr. and Mrs. John L.
Severance 1916.1657
Gilchrist I19
Collections: Frank Gair Macomber,
Boston (cat. 103)

172. Officer's Plug Bayonet
England, c. 1690
Steel serrated blade, brass, wood
Marks (on blade): Two busts and a
candelabrum (copper inlaid)
Overall, l. 46.6 (0.24 kg); blade,
l. 30.2; grip, l. 15.4; quillons, w. 8.6

Gift of Mr. and Mrs. John L.
Severance 1916.1659
Gilchrist I50
Collections: Frank Gair Macomber,
Boston (cat. 255)

173. Dagger
Germany, mid-16th century
Steel; elk horn grip
Mark: [Indecipherable]
Overall, l. 37.8 (0.22 kg); blade,
l. 27.7; quillons, w. 6.5

Gift of Mr. and Mrs. John L.
Severance 1916.1663
Gilchrist I10
Collections: Frank Gair Macomber,
Boston (cat. 550)

**174. Hunting Sword and
Scabbard**
England, London, 1797
William Kinman
Sword: Blued, etched, and gilded
steel; hilt of silver and wood
Overall, l. 74.9 (0.50 kg); blade,
l. 60.3; grip, l. 13.7; guard, w. 10.8
Marks (on knuckle guard): London
hallmarks; date mark for 1797;
and the maker's mark, initials WK,
for William Kinman
Scabbard: Leather, wood, silver
mounts, steel tip
L. 63.3, w. 4.6 (0.18 kg)
Inscribed: D. DRURY, CUTLER TO
HIS MAJESTY, STRAND

Gift of Mr. and Mrs. John L.
Severance 1916.1685.a–b
Gilchrist E117
Collections: Richard Zschille; Frank
Gair Macomber, Boston (cat. 100)

175. Hunting Sword
Dutch, c. 1760–70
Steel; pierced and chiseled cast-iron
hilt; engraved blade
Overall, l. 65 (0.3 kg); blade, l. 52.9;
grip, l. 11.6; quillons, w. 8.9

Gift of Mr. and Mrs. John L.
Severance 1916.1686
Gilchrist E100
Collections: Richard Zschille; Frank
Gair Macomber, Boston (cat. 100)

176. Dagger
Italy, c. 1550–1600
Steel; russeted and damascened
guard and pommel; wood and wire
grip
Overall, l. 50.7 (0.60 kg); blade,
l. 36.5; quillons, w. 16.5; grip, l. 13.3
Marks (on ricasso): D

Gift of Mr. and Mrs. John L.
Severance 1916.1687
Gilchrist I14
Collections: Richard Zschille; Frank
Gair Macomber, Boston (cat. 117)

177. Dagger
Dutch, c. 1620–50
Steel; wire grip; perforated blade
Overall, l. 46 (0.44 kg); blade,
l. 30.9; grip, l. 12; quillons, w. 9.8

Gift of Mr. and Mrs. John L.
Severance 1916.1688
Gilchrist I42
Collections: Edwin Brett; Frank
Gair Macomber, Boston (cat. 104)

**178. Dagger with Horn Grip
Carved as the Sacrifice of Isaac**
Italy, early 17th century
Steel, horn (associated grip and
blade)
Overall, l. 27.6 (0.06 kg); blade,
l. 19.1; quillons, w. 4

Gift of Mr. and Mrs. John L.
Severance 1916.1696
Gilchrist I33
Collections: Count Gayeski; Edwin
Brett; Frank Gair Macomber,
Boston (cat. 119)

**179. Stiletto with Grip Fash-
ioned as Two Standing Monkeys**
Italy, Brescia, c. 1650
Steel
Overall, l. 23.4 (0.06 kg); blade,
l. 14.3; quillons, w. 6

Gift of Mr. and Mrs. John L.
Severance 1916.1699
Gilchrist I27
Collections: Edwin Brett; Frank
Gair Macomber, Boston (cat. 109)

**180. Stiletto with Grip
Fashioned as Charity, Justice,
and Hope**
Italy, c. 1650
Steel, brass, ivory
Mark: A crowned W(?)
Overall, l. 34.0 (0.12 kg); blade,
l. 23.3; quillons, w. 4.6

Gift of Mr. and Mrs. John L.
Severance 1916.1709
Gilchrist I2
Collections: Frank Gair Macomber,
Boston (cat. 330)

**181. Dagger with Grip Sculpted
as Bacchantes with Grapes**
Italy, late 17th century
Steel, ivory
Overall, l. 30.2 (0.08 kg); blade,
l. 20.3; quillons, w. 6.4

Gift of Mr. and Mrs. John L.
Severance 1916.1713
Gilchrist I47
Collections: Edwin Brett; Frank
Gair Macomber, Boston (cat. 322)

182. Sword
Italy, c. 1550
Steel; russeted hilt; leather grip
Overall, l. 100 (1.00 kg); blade, l. 87;
grip, l. 11.5; quillons, w. 6.3
Marks: Inlaid mark on blade; three
on ricasso [indeterminate]

Gift of Mr. and Mrs. John L.
Severance 1916.1715
Gilchrist E24
Collections: Baron de Cosson; Frank
Gair Macomber, Boston (cat. 446)

183. Rapier

Germany, c. 1610
Steel; deeply blued steel hilt; wood
Overall, l. 125.2 (1.40 kg); blade,
l. 110; quillons, w. 25; grip, l. 13.5
Marks (on ricasso): [Unidentified]

Gift of Mr. and Mrs. John L.
Severance 1916.1719
Gilchrist E18
Collections: Frank Gair Macomber,
Boston (cat. 400)

184. Cup from a Rapier's Hilt

Italy, c. 1650–75
Etched steel, with floral, foliate, and
bird designs
H. 16.9, diam. 12.3 (0.22 kg)

Gift of Mr. and Mrs. John L.
Severance 1916.1809
Gilchrist E58
Collections: Frank Gair Macomber,
Boston (cat. 577)

185. Cup-Hilted Rapier

Spain, Toledo, c. 1650
Pierced and chiseled steel; cup deco-
rated with floral and bird motifs
Overall, l. 125.7 (0.88 kg); blade,
l. 108.3; quillons, w. 26.4; grip,
l. 10.7; cup, diam. 13.3
Inscribed (on ricasso): PEDRO DEL
MONTE / IN TOLEDO

Gift of Mr. and Mrs. John L.
Severance 1916.1810
Gilchrist E74
Collections: Sir Samuel Meyrick;
Gurney; Frank Gair Macomber,
Boston (cat. 227)

186. Rapier

Spain, c. 1650
Pierced and chiseled steel; cup decorated with bird and foliate motifs;
engraving; leather and wood grip
Overall, l. 105.6 (0.78 kg); blade,
l. 99.5; quillons, w. 29.6; grip, l. 9.5;
cup, diam. 13

Gift of Mr. and Mrs. John L.
Severance 1916.1811
Gilchrist E75
Collections: Sir Samuel Meyrick;
Gurney; Frank Gair Macomber,
Boston (cat. 228)

187. Dagger

Italy, early 17th century
Steel with perforated blade and
openwork grip; pommel
and quillons fashioned as grotesques
Overall, l. 46 (0.34 kg); blade,
l. 32.1; grip, l. 11; quillons, w. 8.8

Gift of Mr. and Mrs. John L.
Severance 1916.1865
Gilchrist I48
Collections: Frank Gair Macomber,
Boston (cat. 116)

188. Parrying Dagger

Germany, c. 1600
Steel; wire grip with arched quillons
and side ring
Overall, l. 34.6 (0.18 kg); blade,
l. 22.7; grip, l. 10.9; quillons, w. 7.6

Gift of Mr. and Mrs. John L.
Severance 1916.1891
Gilchrist I12
Collections: Frank Gair Macomber,
Boston (cat. 121)

**189. Dagger and Scabbard
(composite)**

Switzerland and/or France, 17th
century (16th-century blade)
Steel and wire; chiseled quillons and
pommel; scabbard, with mythologi-
cal scenes chiseled in high relief:
Vulcan and Venus, Orpheus,
Pyramis and Thisbe, Mars
Dagger: overall, l. 44.3 (0.46 kg);
blade, l. 27.3; quillons, w. 9.2
Scabbard: l. 28.6 (0.20 kg)

Gift of Mr. and Mrs. John L.
Severance 1916.1894.a–b
Gilchrist I23
Collections: Frédéric Spitzer, Paris;
Frank Gair Macomber, Boston
(cat. 448)

190. Cavalry Sword

Germany, Saxony, c. 1700–30
Steel, with vestiges of bluing and
gilding on hilt; wire grip
Overall, l. 105 (1.20 kg); blade,
l. 88.8; grip, l. 14.5; guard, l. 11
Marks: AR [August Rex]

Gift of Mr. and Mrs. John L.
Severance 1919.55
Gilchrist E87
Collections: American Art Associa-
tion, New York (Theodore
Offerman sale, 7–8 February 1919,
lot 234)

**191. Two-Handed Sword with
Flamboyant Blade**

Germany, second half of 16th
century
Steel; leather and wood grip, cloth-
covered middle
Overall, l. 191.5 (3.88 kg); blade,
l. 144.8; quillons, w. 41.5; grip,
l. 40.7; ricasso, l. 33.4

Gift of John L. Severance 1919.68
Gilchrist E45
Collections: American Art Associa-
tion, New York (Theodore
Offerman sale, 7–8 February 1919,
lot 423)

192. Sword

European, 15th century
Steel
Overall, l. 103.5 (1.06 kg); quillons,
w. 19.1

Gift of Mr. and Mrs. John L.
Severance 1919.69
Gilchrist E9
Collections: Frank Gair Macomber,
Boston (unrecorded); American Art
Association, New York (Theodore
Offerman sale, 7–8 February 1919,
lot 427)

193. Two-Handed Sword

Germany, second half of 16th
century
Steel; leather and wood grip; bronze
pommel
Overall, l. 170.5 (3.28 kg); blade,
l. 125.6; quillons, w. 53.7; grip,
l. 43.2; ricasso, l. 34.7

Gift of Mr. and Mrs. John L.
Severance 1919.70
Gilchrist E37
Collections: Frank Gair Macomber,
Boston (unrecorded); American Art
Association, New York (Theodore
Offerman sale, 7–8 February 1919,
lot 430)

**194. Two-Handed Sword with
Flamboyant Blade**

Germany, second half of 16th
century
Steel; leather and wood grip with
brass rivets; russeted steel pommel
Overall, l. 168.9 (2.98 kg); blade,
l. 118.7; quillons, w. 50.5; grip,
l. 49.2; ricasso, l. 26.7

Gift of Mr. and Mrs. John L.
Severance 1919.71
Gilchrist E33
Collections: Frank Gair Macomber,
Boston (unrecorded); American Art
Association, New York (Theodore
Offerman sale, 7–8 February 1919,
lot 434)

195. Sword

European, c. 1400
Steel, leather, wire (0.96 kg)
Overall, l. 85.3 (0.96 kg); blade,
l. 71.7; quillons, w. 16.7; grip, l. 12.7

Gift of Mr. and Mrs. John L.
Severance 1921.1252
Gilchrist E4
Collections: American Art Associa-
tion, New York (sale, 18–19
November 1921, lot 240)

196. Hand-and-a-Half Sword

South Germany, c. 1500
Steel, wood, leather; quillons and
spirally fluted pommel of blackened
steel
Overall, l. 117.5 (1.34 kg); blade,
l. 90.2; quillons, w. 26.4; grip,
l. 21.0

Gift of Mr. and Mrs. John L.
Severance 1921.1253
Gilchrist E20
Collections: Franz Thill, Vienna;
American Art Association, New
York (sale, 18–19 November 1921,
lot 244)

197. Hilt from a Court Sword

England, c. 1790–1800
Polished steel, pierced and inset with
faceted steel beads
H. 18.4; shell guard, w. 9.7 (0.24 kg)

Gift of Mr. and Mrs. John L.
Severance 1923.1061
Gilchrist E125
Collections: Bashford Dean, New
York; American Art Galleries, New
York (sale, 23–24 November 1923,
lot 101)

198. Sword

Germany(?), c. 1350
Iron; wood grip and brass pommel
replacements
Overall, l. 79.4 (0.90 kg); blade,
l. 62.9; quillons, w. 15.3; grip, l. 10.8

Gift of Mr. and Mrs. John L.
Severance 1923.1121
Gilchrist E3
Collections: Bashford Dean,
New York

199. Smallsword

France, Paris(?), c. 1780
Forged steel blade; partially gilded
and russeted steel hilt; steel wire,
leather bands, wood core
Overall, l. 103.5 (0.36 kg); blade,
l. 86.1; shell guard, w. 8.3

Gift from the Bascom Little Estate
1974.57
[Not in Gilchrist]
[Unprovenanced]

200. Hand-and-a-Half Sword

Germany, c. 1540–80
Steel; wood, leather, and sharkskin
grip
Overall, l. 116.8 (1.62 kg); blade,
l. 94.8; quillons, w. 31; grip, l. 21
Marks: Two on blade

Gift from the Bascom Little Estate
1974.58
[Not in Gilchrist]
[Unprovenanced]

201. Rapier
Spain, Toledo, c. 1580–1610
Hilt: Italy, Belluno(?)
Steel, ribbed guard and pommel;
wood; wire
Overall, l. 135.9 (1.48 kg); blade,
l. 111.1; quillons, w. 25.5; grip,
l. 16.5
Inscribed (on blade within fuller):
PIETRO HERNAN[D]EZ
Marks: Three on ricasso (Toledo and
half-moon)
Gift from the Bascom Little Estate
1974.59
[Not in Gilchrist]
[Unprovenanced]

CROSSBOWS AND
RELATED PARTS

202. Crossbow of Elector
Augustus I of Saxony
Germany, Saxony, c. 1553–73
Wood (walnut?), bone veneers, flax
cord, etched steel with traces of
gilding, woolen pompoms (stock
decorated with inlaid trophies of
arms)
L. 63.5; bow spread, 58.5; across
butt, 5.7 (3.82 kg)
Gift of Mr. and Mrs. John L.
Severance 1916.1723.a
Gilchrist G9
Collections: Richard Zschille; Frank
Gair Macomber, Boston (cat. 277)

203. Cranequin with Arms of
Elector Augustus I of Saxony
Germany, Saxony, c. 1553–73
Etched, chased, and gilded steel
Rack, l. 34.4; crank, l. 27; gear
housing, largest diam. 14.2 (2.46 kg)
Gift of Mr. and Mrs. John L.
Severance 1916.1723.b
Gilchrist G9
Collections: Richard Zschille; Frank
Gair Macomber, Boston (cat. 277)

204. Crossbow
Germany, c. 1460–70
Wood (walnut?), inlaid with bone;
horn; iron and steel; composite bow
(horn and parchment)
L. 87; bow spread, 74.5; across butt,
4.2 (3.74 kg)
Gift of Mr. and Mrs. John L.
Severance 1916.1725
Gilchrist G1
Collections: Franz Thill, Vienna;
Frank Gair Macomber, Boston
(cat. 509)

205. Cranequin
France(?), c. 1480–1500
Steel and brass; incised decoration;
pierced traceried Gothic windows
Rack, l. 39.4; crank, l. 30.2; gear
housing, largest diam. 12.1 (2.94 kg)
Marks: [Unidentified; inlaid copper]
Gift of Mr. and Mrs. John L.
Severance 1916.2082
Gilchrist G1
Collections: Franz Thill, Vienna;
Frank Gair Macomber, Boston
(cat. 509)

206. Pellet Crossbow
South Germany(?), 17th century
Wood, inlaid with stag horn; flax
cord; steel with traces of paint and
gilding
L. 82.6; bow spread, 59.4; across
butt, 9.5 (1.80 kg)
Gift of Mr. and Mrs. John L.
Severance 1916.1726
Gilchrist G11
Collections: Frank Gair Macomber,
Boston (cat. 240)

207. Cranequin
Germany, 17th century
Etched steel, flax cord; crank lacking
Rack, l. 36; gear housing, diam. 14.5
(2.34 kg)
Inscribed: 1612 [not original];
maker's mark [indecipherable]
Gift of Mr. and Mrs. John L.
Severance 1916.1727
Gilchrist G7
Collections: Earl of Londesborough;
Frank Gair Macomber, Boston
(cat. 555)

208. Cranequin
Germany, Nuremberg(?), c. 1580
Steel, flax cord, wood and bone
handle
Rack, l. 36.3; crank, l. 30.5; gear
housing, largest diam. 10.8 (2.76 kg)
Maker's mark: Star surmounted by
the letters HW
Inscribed (on gear case): CW SIBALL,
1665 [later owner's name]
Gift of Mr. and Mrs. John L.
Severance 1916.1728
Gilchrist G8
Collections: Frank Gair Macomber,
Boston (cat. 76)

209. Crossbow
Germany, early 17th century
Wood, stag horn, flax cord, steel;
stock decorated with bands of horn
and ebony
L. 63.5; bow spread, 60.2; across
butt, 5 (4.32 kg)
Gift of Mr. and Mrs. John L.
Severance 1916.1729
Gilchrist G8
Collections: Frank Gair Macomber,
Boston (cat. 75)

210. Crossbow Bolts (various)
Germany, 16th–17th century
Wood, leather, steel
L. 37.2 (average) (0.06–0.08 kg)
Gift of Mr. and Mrs. John L.
Severance 1916.1731–73
Gilchrist G4
Collections: Franz Thill, Vienna;
Frank Gair Macomber, Boston
(cat. 528)

211. Crossbow Bolt
Germany, 17th century
Wood (flights missing), steel
L. 38 (0.04 kg)
Gift of Mr. and Mrs. John L.
Severance 1916.1961
Collections: Frank Gair Macomber,
Boston (cat. 77)

212. Crossbow Bolt
Germany, 17th century
Wood (flights missing), steel
L. 37 (0.06 kg)
Gift of Mr. and Mrs. John L.
Severance 1916.1962
Collections: Frank Gair Macomber,
Boston (cat. 77)

213. Pellet Crossbow for a Child
Germany, c. 1600–50
Wood, bone inlay, steel
L. 44.3; bow spread, 29.2; across
butt, 5.2 (1.42 kg)
Gift of Mr. and Mrs. John L.
Severance 1928.671
[Not in Gilchrist]
[Unprovenanced]

FIREARMS

214. Flintlock Pistol
Italy, Brescia, 18th century
Steel with traces of gilding, walnut
stock
Overall, l. 24.5 (0.34 kg); barrel,
l. 12.7; bore, diam. 1.2
Lock signed: BORTOLO AGAZZI
Barrel signed: LAZARO LAZARINO
Marks: Crowned double-headed
eagle
Gift of Mr. and Mrs. John L.
Severance 1916.45
Gilchrist F20
Collections: Frank Gair Macomber,
Boston (cat. 256)

215. Flintlock Pistol
Italy, Brescia, dated 1788
Steel, walnut and bone stock
Overall, l. 49.2 (0.90 kg); barrel,
l. 31.5; bore, diam. 1.9
Lock signed: CARLO LERME BC.
Gift of Mr. and Mrs. John L.
Severance 1916.49
Gilchrist F22
Collections: Frank Gair Macomber,
Boston (cat. 260)

216. Pair of Flintlock Pistols
Franco-Flemish, Liège, early 18th
century
Steel, inlaid with gold; gilt-brass
mounts; walnut burl stock; chiseled
high-relief decoration
Each: overall, l. 49.5 (1.10 kg);
barrel, l. 32.1; bore, diam. 1.5
Barrels signed on top: G. MASSIN
(underneath marked M M with a
crowned shield)
Gift of Mr. and Mrs. John L.
Severance 1916.50.1–2
Gilchrist F16
Collections: Frank Gair Macomber,
Boston (cat. 261)

217. Pair of Flintlock Pistols
Italy, Brescia, c. 1670
Chiseled steel, walnut stock
Each: overall, 45.1 (1916.52.1, 0.96
kg; 1916.52.2, 1.00 kg); barrel,
l. 27.7; bore, diam. 1.1
Signed on barrel (1916.52.1 only):
P. MORETTA
Gift of Mr. and Mrs. John L.
Severance 1916.52.1–2
Gilchrist F14
Collections: Frank Gair Macomber,
Boston (cat. 262)

218. Wheel-lock Hunting Pistol
South Germany, dated 1578
Steel, walnut stock with engraved staghorn, ball butt
Overall, l. 54.6 (2.20 kg); barrel, l. 31.8; bore, diam. 1.4
Engraved near lock plate: HSVZ [initials] and *1578*

Gift of Mr. and Mrs. John L. Severance 1916.672
Gilchrist F3
Collections: Earl of Londesborough; Frank Gair Macomber, Boston (cat. 416)

219. Pair of Flintlock Pistols
Italy, Brescia, c. 1690–1700
Steel, chiseled steel, walnut
Each: overall, l. 49.5 (1916.679.1, 0.74 kg; 1916.679.2, 0.72 kg); barrel, l. 30.9; bore, diam. 1.3
Barrel signed: LAZARINO COMINAZZO (LAZRINO COMINAZZO on second)
Lockplates signed: GIO BORGOGNONE IN BRESIA

Gift of Mr. and Mrs. John L. Severance 1916.679.1–2
Gilchrist F15
Collections: Frank Gair Macomber, Boston (cat. 264)

220. "Rat-tailed" Miquelet-lock Pistol
Balkan, late 18th–early 19th century
Steel and silver (all metal); ramrod missing
Overall, l. 53.3 (1.02 kg); barrel, l. 34.9; bore, diam. 1.7

Gift of J. H. Wade 1916.734
[Not in Gilchrist]
Collections: J. H. Wade, Cleveland

221. Wheel-lock Hunting Rifle (Tschinke)
Poland, Silesia, c. 1630–50
Steel with traces of gilding; walnut stock, inlaid with bone, staghorn, mother-of-pearl
Overall, 122.9 (2.94 kg); barrel, l. 94.9; across butt, 9.6; bore, diam. 1.3

Gift of Mr. and Mrs. John L. Severance 1916.1782
Gilchrist F12
Collections: Hollingworth Magniac; Frank Gair Macomber, Boston (cat. 282)

222. Snaphance Pistol
Spain, Ripoll, 17th century
Steel, ebonized wood with silver inlay
Overall, l. 29.5 (0.68 kg); barrel, l. 20.0; bore, diam. 1.5

Gift of Mr. and Mrs. John L. Severance 1918.68
Gilchrist F5
Collections: Charles M. Schott, Jr.

223. Ball-butted Miquelet-lock Pistol
Caucasus, Daghestan, c. 1850
Steel, brass, silver, gold inlay
Overall, l. 53; barrel, l. 38.7; bore, diam. 1.4
Barrel signed: LAZARINO COMINAZZO; Arabic inscription on stock

Gift of Mr. and Mrs. John L. Severance 1918.69
Gilchrist F6
Collections: Charles M. Schott, Jr.

224. Ball-butted Miquelet-lock Pistol
Caucasus, Daghestan, c. 1850
Steel, silver, gold inlay, leather, ivory ball butt
Overall, l. 44.4 (0.66 kg); barrel, l. 31.2; bore, diam. 1.4

Gift of Mr. and Mrs. John L. Severance 1918.70
Gilchrist F7
Collections: Charles M. Schott, Jr.

225. Flintlock Pistol
Germany, Bavaria, Regensberg(?), c. 1750
Steel, walnut stock, brass mounts (chiseled in high relief with hunting subjects); barrel inlaid with gold, brass, and silver
Overall, l. 25.7 (0.48 kg); barrel, l. 14.5; bore, diam. 1.2
Barrel signed: IOH AND KUCHENREUTER [Johann Andreas Kuchenreuter, 1716–1795]
Marks: A mounted cavalier

Gift of Mr. and Mrs. John L. Severance 1918.76
Gilchrist F18
Collections: Charles M. Schott, Jr.

226. Wheel-lock Hunting Rifle
Sardinia, c. 1650
Steel, pierced and chiseled mounts, walnut stock
Overall, l. 122.7 (2.06 kg); barrel, l. 90.8; across butt, 12.7; bore, diam. 1.1
Inscribed (on barrel): A PATIS and PEVRVV ET FILS [partially indecipherable]
Barrelmaker's mark: AC [Angelo Cominazzo?]
Mark (inside of lock): FG

Gift of Mr. and Mrs. John L. Severance 1919.64
Gilchrist F9
Collections: American Art Association, New York (Theodore Offerman sale, 7–8 February 1919, lot 367)

227. Wheel-lock Rifle
Germany, Bavaria(?), 1618
Steel; brass; walnut stock, inlaid with bone, horn, and ivory (birds, animals, and scrolls)
Overall, l. 77.5 (2.10 kg); barrel, l. 49.8; across butt, 7.0; bore, diam. 1.5
Inscribed: *1618* and the initials S.H. [on barrel]; FF [on stock]
Marks: Star within a circle

Gift of Mr. and Mrs. John L. Severance 1919.65
Gilchrist F10
Collections: American Art Association, New York (Theodore Offerman sale, 7–8 February 1919, lot 374)

228. Wheel-lock Hunting Rifle
Austria, Ferlach, mid-17th century
Stockmaker: Hans Schmidt (d. 1669)
Steel; varnished walnut stock, inlaid with silver wire and appliqués
Overall, l. 110.2 (3.68 kg); barrel, l. 83.2; across butt, 8.6; bore, diam. 1.3
Barrelsmith's mark: GS within a shield

Gift of Mr. and Mrs. Lewis R. Schilling 1959.127
[Not in Gilchrist]
Collections: James Grogan

229. Double-Barreled Flintlock Sporting Gun of Napoleon I Bonaparte
Dated 1809
Jean Le Page
(French, Paris, active c. 1779–1822)
Blued steel with gilt decoration, carved walnut stock with ram's head, gilt silver chiseled mounts (trigger guard and butt cap with imperial monogram N); dated 1809 inside locks
Overall, l. 116.8 (3.16 kg); barrel, l. 76.3; across butt, 10.8; bore, diam. 1.6
Signed on barrel (inlaid in gold): LE PAGE À PARIS / ARQ[UEBUSIER] DE L'EMPEREUR
Signed on locks: LE PAGE / À PARIS
Marks: Numerous marks on butt cap, trigger guard, locks, and barrels, including: Paris excise mark; guaranty mark; mark of Jean Le Page; restricted warranty marks

Gift of David S. Ingalls 1966.433
Collections: Presented by Napoleon Bonaparte to Vincent Corvin Graf von Krasine-Krasinski, Poland

FIREARM PARTS

230. Wheel-lock from a Hunting Rifle
Germany, 17th century
Engraved steel, with hunting subjects
22.7 x 16.5 x 5.8 (0.88 kg)
Lock signed: GEORG BERNARDTON HAUSER
Inscribed (on plate, behind hammer): IN SCHROMN[?] HAUSER

Gift of Mr. and Mrs. John L. Severance 1916.39
Gilchrist F80
Collections: Frank Gair Macomber, Boston (cat. 241)

231. Wheel-lock from a Sporting Rifle
Germany, Munich, c. 1720–40
Engraved steel, with scenes of combating cavaliers and Turks, acanthus leaves, and trophies
29.2 x 11.7 (0.98 kg)
Lock signed: IOAN GEORG DAX IN MUNCHEN
Engraver's signature: I. C. STENGLIN SR.

Gift of Mr. and Mrs. John L. Severance 1916.40
Gilchrist F81
Collections: Frank Gair Macomber, Boston (cat. 243)

232. Snanance Gunlock
Italy, Brescia(?), c. 1660–80
Chiseled steel, with grotesques, masks, and foliage
14.0 x 7.3 (0.32 kg)
Gift of Mr. and Mrs. John L. Severance 1916.41
Gilchrist F83
Collections: Gurney; Frank Gair Macomber, Boston (cat. 244)

233. Snaphance Gunlock
Spain, 18th or early 19th century
Engraved and chased steel
14.7 x 11.4 (0.44 kg)
Signed: TANINE, and L. ANDYOLOZ
Gift of Mr. and Mrs. John L. Severance 1916.42
Gilchrist F87
Collections: Frank Gair Macomber, Boston (cat. 245)

234. Trigger Guard for a Pistol
Italy, Brescia(?), c. 1680–1700
Chiseled steel, with grotesques and scrolls
15.9 x 2.9 (0.06 kg)
Gift of Mr. and Mrs. John L. Severance 1916.55
Gilchrist F69
Collections: Frank Gair Macomber, Boston (cat. 269)

235. Mount for the Upper Stock of a Flintlock Pistol
Italy, Brescia(?), c. 1680–1700
Chiseled steel, with a grotesque and foliage
10.2 x 3.0 (0.02 kg)
Gift of Mr. and Mrs. John L. Severance 1916.56
Gilchrist F70
Collections: Frank Gair Macomber, Boston (cat. 269)

236. Wheel-lock from a Hunting Rifle
Austria, c. 1660–1720
Chiseled steel, inlaid with gold, with Hapsburg double eagle
30.8 x 17.2 (1.44 kg)
Gift of Mr. and Mrs. John L. Severance 1916.1546
Gilchrist F65
Collections: Frank Gair Macomber, Boston (cat. 242)

237. Butt-cap from a Flintlock Pistol
Italy, Brescia, c. 1650–60
Chiseled steel, with animals and foliage
H. 1.9, diam. 4.8 (0.02 kg)
Gift of Mr. and Mrs. John L. Severance 1916.1909
Gilchrist F66
Collections: Frank Gair Macomber, Boston (cat. 269)

238. Butt-cap from a Flintlock Pistol
Italy, c. 1690–1700
Chiseled steel, with masks and foliage
8.6 x 9.7 (0.06 kg)
Gift of Mr. and Mrs. John L. Severance 1916.1910
Gilchrist F67
Collections: Frank Gair Macomber, Boston (cat. 271)

239. Miquelet Lock
Spain, Eibar, c. 1790–1800
Steel
11.6 x 9.6 (0.34 kg)
Marks: DOMINGO GABIOLA
Gift of Mr. and Mrs. John L. Severance 1918.71
Gilchrist F90
Collections: Charles M. Schott, Jr.

240. Miquelet Lock
Spain, late 17th century
Steel, inlaid with gold and silver floral patterns
11.8 x 10.8 x 3.2 (0.52 kg)
Inscribed: AVS/TRIA [on plate]; EN CORDOVA [on frizzen]
Gift of Mr. and Mrs. John L. Severance 1918.72
Gilchrist F84
Collections: Charles M. Schott, Jr.

241. Wheel-lock from a Hunting Rifle
Germany, early 18th century
Engraved steel, with hunting subjects
20.8 x 13.4 x 4.8 (0.66 kg)
Gift of Mr. and Mrs. John L. Severance 1918.73
Gilchrist F71
Collections: Charles M. Schott, Jr.

FIREARM ACCESSORIES

242. Powder Flask (with Standing Figures of a Man and Woman)
Germany, dated 1570
Elk horn, steel mounts
23.4 x 11.8 (0.34 kg)
Gift of Mr. and Mrs. John L. Severance 1916.37
Gilchrist F31
Collections: Frank Gair Macomber, Boston (cat. 177)

243. Combined Priming Flask and Wheel-lock Spanner
Germany or Austria, first half of 17th century
Horn, brass and steel mounts
18.1 x 5.7 (0.12 kg)
Gift of Mr. and Mrs. John L. Severance 1916.43
Gilchrist F46
Collections: Frank Gair Macomber, Boston (cat. 247)

244. Powder Flask
Germany, c. 1620–50
Walnut, inlaid with horn in concentric circles; turned bone funnel with brass spring cap; iron suspension loops
H. 15.9, diam. 12.1 (0.20 kg)
Gift of Mr. and Mrs. John L. Severance 1916.57
Gilchrist F48
Collections: Frank Gair Macomber, Boston (cat. 275)

245. Powder Flask
Austria, Tyrol, 17th century
Horn with engraved geometric decoration; funnel missing
21.3 x 20.0 (0.38 kg)
Gift of Mr. and Mrs. John L. Severance 1916.59
Gilchrist F51
Collections: Frank Gair Macomber, Boston (cat. 311)

246. Powder Flask
Germany, c. 1620–50
Walnut, inlaid with ivory decoration (medallions and birds); turned steel funnel with spring cap
H. 17.2, diam. 12.1 (0.44 kg)
Gift of Mr. and Mrs. John L. Severance 1916.60
Gilchrist F37
Collections: Frank Gair Macomber, Boston (cat. 314)

247. Powder Flask
Germany, c. 1570
Staghorn (two branches), with carved relief decoration of Judith and Holofernes; mounts missing
15.9 x 12.1 (0.18 kg)
Gift of Mr. and Mrs. John L. Severance 1916.452
Gilchrist F25
Collections: Frank Gair Macomber, Boston (cat. 334)

248. Powder Flask (with Scene of Judgment of Paris)
Italy, c. 1590
Gilt brass over fabric-covered wood
19.4 x 12.7 (0.64 kg)
Gift of Mr. and Mrs. John L. Severance 1916.666
Gilchrist F36
Collections: Frank Gair Macomber, Boston (cat. 335)

249. Powder Flask
Transylvanian, late 17th–early 18th century
Staghorn (two branches), with incised and painted geometric decoration; mounts missing
29.9 x 21.0 (0.38 kg)
Gift of Mr. and Mrs. John L. Severance 1916.667
Gilchrist F26
Collections: Frank Gair Macomber, Boston (cat. 336)

250. Spanner for a Wheel-lock Gun
Germany, c. 1600–50
Steel with punched, engraved, and pierced decoration
L. 16.4, w. 4.5 (0.08 kg)
Gift of Mr. and Mrs. John L. Severance 1916.669
Gilchrist F39
Collections: Frank Gair Macomber, Boston (cat. 340)

251. Powder Flask
Germany, late 16th–early 17th century
Horn (two branches), with engraved allegorical scenes (unidentified); mounts missing
18.4 x 15.8 (0.18 kg)
Gift of Mr. and Mrs. John L. Severance 1916.674
Gilchrist F32
Collections: Frank Gair Macomber, Boston (cat. 537)

252. Powder Flask

Austria(?) or Germany, c. 1550–80
Staghorn (two branches), with
carved scene of Judgment of Paris;
mounts missing
17.8 x 13.4 (0.18 kg)
Gift of Mr. and Mrs. John L.
Severance 1916.676
Gilchrist F44
Collections: Don A. Gonzales,
Seville; Frank Gair Macomber,
Boston (cat. 539)

253. Powder Flask

Germany, c. 1580–1600
Staghorn, with carved relief decoration of the Resurrection; mounts
missing
14.0 x 8.9 (0.16 kg)
Gift of Mr. and Mrs. John L.
Severance 1916.678
Gilchrist F34
Collections: Frank Gair Macomber,
Boston (cat. 541)

254. Hunting Horn

Italy, late 16th or early 17th century
Embossed steel, with acanthus scrolls
L. 28.5 (0.18 kg)
Gift of Mr. and Mrs. John L.
Severance 1916.1775
Gilchrist M16
Collections: Count Gayeski; Frank
Gair Macomber, Boston (cat. 174)

255. Powder Flask

France, late 16th or early 17th
century
Carved staghorn (two branches),
with Old Testament scene in relief;
modern brass mounts
22.2 x 14.0 (0.32 kg)
Gift of Mr. and Mrs. John L.
Severance 1916.1843
Gilchrist F30
Collections: Frank Gair Macomber,
Boston (cat. 331)

256. Powder Flask

Germany, c. 1550
Carved staghorn (two branches),
with knight kneeling before the
Crucifixion; mounts missing
14.3 x 10.2 (0.22 kg)
Gift of Mr. and Mrs. John L.
Severance 1916.1856
Gilchrist F23
Collections: Frank Gair Macomber,
Boston (cat. 333)

257. Spanner for a Wheel-lock Gun

Germany, early 17th century
Steel
15.5 x 7.1 (0.06 kg)
Gift of Mr. and Mrs. John L.
Severance 1916.1866
Gilchrist F43
Collections: Earl of Londesborough;
Spiller; Frank Gair Macomber,
Boston (cat. 308)

258. Powder Flask

c. 1680
Johann Michael Maucher(?)
(German, Swabian, Gmünd,
1645–1701)
Carved boxwood, with stag and
hounds in high relief; steel funnel,
mounts, springcatch
H. 14.3, diam. 13.3 (0.18 kg)
Gift of Mr. and Mrs. John L.
Severance 1916.1887
Gilchrist F24
Collections: Frank Gair Macomber,
Boston (cat. 583)

259. Powder Horn

Germany, c. 1580
Carved staghorn (two branches),
with relief decoration of David and
Bathsheba; iron suspension loop;
mounts missing
16.9 x 11.1 (0.24 kg)
Gift of Mr. and Mrs. John L.
Severance 1916.1906
Gilchrist F28
Collections: Frank Gair Macomber,
Boston (cat. 543)

260. Combined Wheel-lock Spanner and Powder Measure

Germany, c. 1625–50
Steel, trefoil top pierced with square
holes
L. 16.2 (extendable to 23.5) (0.14 kg)
Gift of Mr. and Mrs. John L.
Severance 1916.1908
Gilchrist F42
Collections: Frank Gair Macomber,
Boston (cat. 184)

261. Patron (Cartridge Box)

Germany, c. 1600
Steel sheet, over wood, brass; leather
base; embossed decorations of
scrolls, masks, and mounted
horsemen
H. 14.0, base diam. 8.9 (0.24 kg)
Gift of Mr. and Mrs. John L.
Severance 1916.1911
Gilchrist F40
Collections: Frank Gair Macomber,
Boston (cat. 175)

262. Powder Flask

Italy, late 16th century(?) [questionable authenticity]
Leather (*cuir bouilli*), modern steel
mounts and fitting
17.2 x 13.5 (0.22 kg)
Gift of Mr. and Mrs. John L.
Severance 1916.1916
Gilchrist F27
Collections: Frank Gair Macomber,
Boston (cat. 188)

263. Powder Flask

Italy, c. 1560–70
Leather (*cuir bouilli*), with embossed
and fluted decoration; brass funnel
17.2 x 11.9 (0.24 kg)
Gift of Mr. and Mrs. John L.
Severance 1918.65
Gilchrist F29
Collections: Charles M. Schott, Jr.

264. Powder Horn

Spain, late 18th–early 19th century
Cowhorn, with incised designs of
crowned figures, coats of arms,
animals, and geometric patterns
L. 26.4, diam. 8.8 (0.28 kg)
Gift of Mr. and Mrs. John L.
Severance 1918.66
Gilchrist F52
Collections: Charles M. Schott, Jr.

ARTILLERY

265. Falconet with Arms of Alessandro Farnese, Pope Paul III (1534–49)

Italy, 1534–49
Bronze
L. 148.8; muzzle, diam. 9.7; bore,
diam. 4.7 (61 kg)
Gift of Mr. and Mrs. John L.
Severance 1916.1903
Gilchrist F63
Collections: Frank Gair Macomber,
Boston (cat. 182)

266. Falconet with Arms of Gian Pietro Carafa, Pope Paul IV (1555–59)

Italy, possibly Genoa, 1555–59
Bronze
L. 162.2; muzzle, diam. 11.2; bore,
diam. 4.7 (102 kg)
Gift of Mr. and Mrs. John L.
Severance 1916.1915
Gilchrist F62
Collections: Frank Gair Macomber,
Boston (cat. 137)

BANNERS

267. Banner Head in the Form of a Fleur-de-Lys

France, 18th century
Steel
25 x 6.7 (0.70 kg)
Gift of Mr. and Mrs. John L.
Severance 1916.1490
Gilchrist M11
Collections: Pembroke Family;
Frank Gair Macomber, Boston
(cat. 69)

268. Banner

Spain, 18th century
Crimson silk brocade; scalloped
border with fringe
124.5 x 108
Gift of Mr. and Mrs. John L.
Severance 1916.1529
Gilchrist M9
Collections: Bashford Dean,
New York

269. Banner with Royal Coat of Arms of Great Britain

Great Britain, probably England,
18th century
Green silk ground with embroidery;
crimson cords and tassels
127 x 118.1
Gift of Mr. and Mrs. John L.
Severance 1916.1548
Gilchrist M1
Collections: Bashford Dean,
New York

270. Banner

Spain, 18th century
Crimson silk brocade; scalloped
border with fringe and tassels
129.5 x 113
Gift of Mr. and Mrs. John L.
Severance 1916.1594
Gilchrist M10
Collections: Bashford Dean,
New York

271. Banner with Embroidered Crest

Spain, 18th century
Crimson silk brocade, with applied
embroidery; scalloped border with
fringe and tassels
114.2 x 107.9
Gift of Mr. and Mrs. John L.
Severance 1916.1783
Gilchrist M7
Collections: Bashford Dean,
New York

Illustration Credits

272. Banner with Medallions of Christ's Passion
Spain, 18th century
Crimson silk brocade, satin; scalloped border with fringe and tassels
119.4 x 108

Gift of Mr. and Mrs. John L. Severance 1916.1784
Gilchrist M8
Collections: Bashford Dean, New York

273. Banner with the Lion of St. Mark
Italy, Venice, late 17th–early 18th century
Brown silk with fringe
87.2 x 87.2

Gift of Mr. and Mrs. John L. Severance 1916.1807
Gilchrist M2
Collections: Bashford Dean, New York

274. Banner with Quartered Royal Arms of Spain and the Madonna and Child
Spain, 16th century
Red and dark brown velvet, with embroidery; fringe
109.2 x 138.4

Gift of Mr. and Mrs. John L. Severance 1916.1885
Gilchrist M12
Collections: Bashford Dean, New York

Index